The Luzerne County Railroad

By Larry Hohol

The Luzerne County Railroad

All rights reserved. No part of this book may be reproduced or transmitted in any form or by any means without the expressed written permission of the author. All reproduced copyrighted material in this book remains the property of the legally registered copyright holder and has been reproduced with permission and/or acknowledgment.

Copyright 2010 by Larry Hohol

Printed in the USA

www.TheLuzerneCountyRailroad.com

Published by St Johns Publishing

ISBN 978-0-615-42335-7

Table of Contents

PREFACE.....1

CHAPTER ONE-*L*ife was Good.....4

CHAPTER TWO-*T*he Journey Begins.....6

CHAPTER THREE-*T*he Winds of Change.....8

CHAPTER FOUR-*S*et for Life.....14

CHAPTER FIVE-*A* Friend Indeed.....18

CHAPTER SIX-*A* Plan for Action.....20

CHAPTER SEVEN-*I*n the Clear.....25

CHAPTER EIGHT-*D*éjà Vu, All Over Again!.....30

CHAPTER NINE-*O*ne Hell of a Coincidence.....32

CHAPTER TEN-*W*hat to do about a Rogue Judge.....37

CHAPTER ELEVEN-*T*he Merits of the Case.....41

CHAPTER TWELVE- *P*rivate Eyes.....42

CHAPTER THIRTEEN-*T*he New Sheriff Takes the Stand.....47

CHAPTER FOURTEEN-*T*estifying Turncoats.....51

CHAPTER FIFTEEN -*I* Was **NOT** the Only One.....56

CHAPTER SIXTEEN-*I*'m a "**SUPREME**" Example.....60

CHAPTER SEVENTEEN-*B*ack To My Case.....71

CHAPTER EIGHTEEN-*B*rass Tacks.....74

CHAPTER NINETEEN-*G*ame Over.....81

CHAPTER TWENTY-*T*he Horns of a Dilemma.....86

CHAPTER TWENTY-ONE-*N*ot You Again.....89

CHAPTER TWENTY-TWO-*A* Long Time to Get Here.....96

CHAPTER TWENTY-THREE-Superior Court Mystery.....101

CHAPTER TWENTY-FOUR-*A*ll In.....106

CHAPTER TWENTY-FIVE-
Judge Cappellini Doesn't Disappoint 123

CHAPTER TWENTY-SIX-*N*OW WHAT?.....133

CHAPTER TWENTY-SEVEN-Judicial Safeguards.....137

CHAPTER TWENTY EIGHT-Deep Throat.....145

CHAPTER TWENTY-NINE-
Debbie and the Judicial Conduct Board.....150

CHAPTER THIRTY- What Really Happened to the JCB INVESTIGATION?.....157

CHAPTER THIRTY-ONE-Liquidation.....161

CHAPTER THIRTY-TWO-
Time for this "Coal Cracker" to Move On.....164

CHAPTER THIRTY-THREE-
A Judge's Son in Luzerne County.....167

CHAPTER THIRTY-FOUR-
Judge Gifford Cappellini, "The Man".....180

CHAPTER THIRTY-FIVE-The Wheels of Injustice.....202

CHAPTER THIRTY-SIX-
Doing the Right Thing in Luzerne County.....217

CHAPTER THIRTY-SEVEN-
What to do about a Whistle Blower.....245

CHAPTER THIRTY-EIGHT-
Judge Toole's Kangaroo Court.....253

CHAPTER THIRTY-NINE-
The Dynamic Duo and Michael Leftchak.....291

CHAPTER FORTY-Unreported Cash.....296

CHAPTER FORTY-ONE-Corruption and the County.....301

CHAPTER FORTY-TWO-
Luzerne County: This is the Scary Part.....306

CHAPTER FORTY-THREE-
The Dynamics of Being a Judge (It's no Joke).....309

CHAPTER FORTY-FOUR-What Have We Learned?.....313

CHAPTER FORTY-FIVE- "Kids for Cash".....314

CHAPTER FORTY-SIX-I Am a Reluctant Author.....316

$\mathcal{P}$REFACE

$\mathcal{T}$his is a book that will stun your senses and batter your perceptions of what you were raised to believe in. Everything you are about to read is based on actual events. Although I am the main character in most of this book, the story is really not about me. This is a book about a corrupt judicial system that was, and still is, totally out of control. I not only write about my firsthand experience with this judiciary but also about the corrupted "checks and balances" that are supposedly in place to protect the general public should the judiciary go awry. This book is not an interpretation of my personal bias. It is a reality that I lived through. It has also been a reality for thousands of other people, including hundreds of children (Yes, I said children, and yes, I said HUNDREDS) here in Luzerne County, Pennsylvania.

Within these pages we will examine other cases as well as mine. It is a reality that you may someday be exposed to as this *could* happen anywhere. I hope not. These pages will provide documented proof of my outrage. As you read this book you will shake your head in total disbelief. Your disbelief will turn into anger. Your anger will metamorphosis into fear. You will probably feel like you are riding a roller coaster……….no, an "Express Train" of emotions that will leave you speechless. At some point you may even shout out loud, "How could this possibly happen?" By the time you reach the end of this book you will probably feel totally powerless. You are. As individuals we are powerless against this form of corruption. Only with the consolidation of good, honest citizens can the demon known as corruption be slain.

I had been prodded over the years by friends and family to write a book about what happened to me in the Luzerne County

Court System. Each and every time that someone would push the idea I simply said, "Why bother? The story is so incredible that no one would believe a word of it. Heck, I was there and I still don't believe it."

The 2009 arrests by the FBI of three sitting judges on corruption charges at the very same Luzerne County Courthouse I write about in this book, has given me hope. The question is, hope for what? I think about this hope a lot. I am still not sure what I am hoping for.

In the back of my mind, way back at the beginning of this entire fiasco, I had made a promise. I promised myself that when all was said and done, I would make sure my opponents knew they were in one "Hell of a Fight." It is over fifteen years since then, and as I write this book I am smiling because I'm still not done and the fight is still not over. Winning my litigation is a goal no longer feasible. Apparently, it never was. Whether it was a fair fight or not the facts remain, I lost. I have accepted that reality and I have moved on.

This book is all about exposure. You see, if corrupt judges and attorneys are allowed to simply continue without consequence, they, and the people who take their places, will continue similar behavior. More importantly, the honest people who know what is going on will remain silent. In a very direct way their silence validates the corrupt behavior of others. Attorneys, court employees, even honest judges then have a laundry list of reasons why they "must" remain silent.

The judicial system in Pennsylvania is broken. It is not just a little broken and it didn't just recently occur. When addressing the arrest of sitting Luzerne County Judges on bribery and corruption charges, Pennsylvania Supreme Court Chief Justice Ronald D. Castille called what has happened recently in Luzerne County an "anomaly." One of my goals in writing this book is to prove Chief Justice Castille wrong. What has happened in Luzerne County is *not* an anomaly; it is a reality and has been a reality for decades. Additionally, I will prove the powers that be in Harrisburg have consistently known about the corruption in the Luzerne County Courts all along and have *chosen* to do nothing about it. How can I

prove these outrageous claims? In the pages of this book, I promise you I will prove it far beyond any doubt in your mind. I promise.

While writing this book, I have often thought about my Uncle Joe, whom I never met. He is buried in the Luxemburg City Cemetery, along with General George S. Patton. In my eyes my Uncle Joe is a bigger hero than General Patton. General Patton is just more famous. My uncle Joe was killed in action during the "Battle of the Bulge". When called to defend our nation, he fought, died, and sacrificed all of his tomorrows so that we, as citizens of these United States, could and would live in freedom. His sacrifice, in part, allowed for all of our rights to continue on as guaranteed by our Constitution, or so it should be.

These rights are sacred and are to be defended from threat either foreign or <u>DOMESTIC</u> and must be secured not only for ourselves, but for our children's children. I will do everything in my power to assure that my Uncle Joe's ultimate sacrifice and the sacrifices of all of the other men and women who have defended our nation and our rights, not be in vain.

I am especially outraged by the corrupted who wear black robes. A Judge's power, as well as unquestionable trust, has been cautiously given to them by the voters of this democracy, on the backs of our Military Veterans. My Uncle Joe died in the trenches of Europe. If I have to die on the steps of the Luzerne County Courthouse exposing this massive corruption ....so be it.

Uncle Joe, this book is dedicated to you. May you forever "Rest in Peace."

CHAPTER ONE

ℒife was Good

𝒯he black snow that splashed up from the roadway didn't appear dirty to me on that particular day, it just seemed black, and that was okay. Everything was okay with me that day. It was a rare day indeed.

As was my usual habit, I was in a hurry to get somewhere, rushing along the west side of Public Square in downtown Wilkes-Barre, Pennsylvania. I walked briskly, slightly tilting my head against the cold December wind. Loosening my tie, I pulled my overcoat tighter against my body. As I passed the long abandoned Pomeroy's Department Store, one of its display windows caught my reflection.

There it was a crystal clear image of me, similar to what one would anticipate when trying on clothes in an expensive clothing store. There wasn't a crack in the window, not even a smudge on the glass. I stood there transfixed, looking at my reflection while people scurried by me in their own personal hurry to get to their "somewhere." It was as if I were looking at someone whom I had never seen before. This person should be familiar, but wasn't. Puzzled at first by my own reaction, I then smiled from ear to ear. I pulled my cold hand out of my coat pocket, pointed my index finger at my crystal clear image and made a noise like a pistol going off.

"Ka-pow!"

The image I was looking at was the "New" me, a person financially set for life. No debt, no employees, and no financial worries for the rest of my life! I patted the pocket in my overcoat that contained an honest-to-goodness certified check for well over a million dollars, just to make sure it was real and still there. My hurried demeanor was because of my desire to get to the bank so I could deposit my good fortune into my personal savings account.

After a year of, on-again, off-again, negotiations, I had finally sold my seven-year-old company, Penox Technologies Inc., to a privately owned "aerospace/defense contracting" firm from St. Louis called Essex Industries. They had been trying to buy my company for years before I finally gave into their offer. The best part was that there were many more millions to come. Everything was signed, sealed, and delivered. It was only then that I allowed myself to feel that forever elusive sense of calm relief and total satisfaction.

Continuing onto the bank to make my deposit, I didn't have the slightest clue as to the road, or should I say, "RAILROAD," I had just unknowingly climbed aboard. The "Luzerne County Railroad" was leaving the station and I was but the latest passenger who had fallen victim to its merciless deceit and treachery.

CHAPTER TWO

The Journey Begins

The Luzerne County Railroad is very unique. It does not have tracks or a fixed schedule, and unlike other railroads, this train selects the passengers that will ride her. If you are unlucky enough to be chosen for a ride, there is nothing you can do to avoid boarding the train. This railroad simply consists of a station and a final destination. The station that I am speaking of is the Luzerne County Courthouse. The destination differs from passenger to passenger and it is predetermined long before anyone even knows they are leaving on a trip.

Millions of dollars went into the construction of this courthouse during the turn of the 20th century. Adjusted for inflation this building would cost over seventy-six million dollars to build today if you don't take into consideration changes to building codes. It stands, in all its glory and with deep contrast to the poor immigrant coal miners who lived in the company owned shacks that surrounded this monolith. Coal miners and their families flocked here from Europe in search of their "American Dream." My grandfather was one of those coal miners who sought to better himself in this country and in this county. He raised his family on Kemp St. in the small town of Pringle, not more than five miles from this very spot.

This courthouse also stands as a permanent memorial to the "Coal Barons" who built and controlled it. Justice has a price in Luzerne County and the "Coal Barons" were very willing to pay that price. Busloads of school children on almost a daily basis come to marvel at the structure's imported marble, gold inlaid quotations and massive pillars of justice.

Although a railroad has many conductors, it usually has only one per train. The Luzerne County Railroad differs. The responsibility for each and every train that leaves this station is shared by two conductors: A willing judge, and usually, a more than willing attorney. That's all it takes to get a trip underway. The bond between the two can be as simple as friendship or as sinister as bribery. The fabric that bonds these two together is not nearly as important as the destination of the trip, and what a trip it has been.

CHAPTER THREE

The Winds of Change

As is common with many company buyouts, things change dramatically after the sale is finalized. It was at my closing, that I was advised, I would not remain in the position of "Company President". My thought was, "Who cares? A title doesn't pay the bills."

I was told that the brother of the new owners would be moving here from Texas to take over the reigns. I hadn't been aware there was a brother in Texas, but it really didn't matter to me. I was secure with my five year employment contract for $100,000 per year, plus full benefits. Add to that the $100,000 per year non-compete contract and the $30,000 per year rental being paid to me for the use of my company's headquarters building. Then there were the three or four other major income sources addressed in the buyout. Things were looking pretty peachy, and as I said earlier, everything was signed, sealed and delivered. Keep in mind that this was 1988 money. I could write an entire book about my company. It was quite a ride, but the following article does a pretty good job with the basic background information and as I said earlier, this book really isn't about me.

Wilkes-Barre, PA, Saturday, March 7, 1987

Hohol's fortune Born from frustration

By DAWN SHURMAITIS
Staff Writer

DUPONT — He may be the only executive in town who relieves tension by shooting his administrators.

"We call it 'War Games'" Larry Hohol says of the sport he and his chief officers play, harmlessly enough, with paint guns.

"Splat, you got me" is one way the owner of Penox Technologies shakes off the strain of running a multi-million dollar company on the move.

Hohol founded the company, which manufactures and distributes medical equipment, in 1982. "The company was born out of total frustration," the 30-year-old says.

Hohol took a job in the home health care field shortly after high school, delivering the products he would eventually manufacture.

He was young and full of ideas. Unfortunately, the products he was dealing with were full of holes.

"One day I said, 'That's enough'," he said. "I'm going to make the changes myself." It was 1977.

Hohol borrowed $3,000 from the bank, his folks took out a second mortgage on their home, and Pensee Medical Corp. was born. "I started out with one employee, me," Hohol said.

The company, a retail operation versus a manufacturer, sold medical equipment.

Shortly after that, Hohol's brother Danny, now his production manager, helped Hohol make a prototype of a liquid oxygen tank. Hohol took it to an Atlanta trade show in the back of his other brother David's pick-up truck.

David is now the machine shop superintendent at Penox. The rest, as they say, is history.

From that first mock-up tank, Hohol fashioned Penox, a company whose sales last year approached $6 million. Hohol sold Pensee last year, four years after creating Penox.

Penox is a manufacutring company that makes home liquid oxygen systems and lift chairs and distributes other medical products.

During the two years years Pensee grew into Penox, Hohol paid the bills working evenings as a policeman in Luzerne, his hometown.

He grew up the son of a factory worker and a waitress. His mother now lives in Florida. He still fishes in local spots with his dad.

Along the way he married his wife, Denise, and had two children, Michele, 3½ and Sara, 1½.

Pictures of his family take up a lot of space on the book shelves in his office. There are few books in the case; it is filled instead with a collection of ducks, trophies from Hohol's high school drag-racing days and one of his old police hats.

It is rare that the executive gets to join his family for supper. To compensate, Hohol turns weekends into small adventures and takes mini vacations.

The Hohol family residence sits on 130 acres in Hunlock Creek and is complete with its own ponds, stream and fields. He describes it as "a small home with a lot of property."

Hohol is trying to teach his older daughter to fish, so she can catch the kind he has stuffed and hanging on his office wall. He caught the sailfish off the Mexican coast on a vacation last year. "My guppie" he calls it.

The sportsman missed the first day of buck season this year because he was meeting with the King of Spain. "It's the first year in five I didn't get one," he said.

Hohol distributes his product to Spain so meeting and becoming friends with the king was just good business sense. It helped that King Carlos spoke fluent English and turned out to be a personable man, Hohol said.

Besides Spain, Penox distributes its products to foreign ports in France and Italy. That, in addition to distribution to all 50 states, Canada, Mexico and the Caribbean, has earned Hohol a reputation as a businessman worldwide.

Penox has patents in several countries, Hohol said. He seeks out the foreign business by attending trade shows and spending a lot of advertising dollars. "If a product has a lot of possibilities, you will be sought out," he said of his success overseas.

Hohol calls himself a habitual or compulsive businessman. "Since the beginning I've wanted to go for all the marbles," he said of his drive for success. "If I'm this size today, I want to be twice that tomorrow."

In order to accomplish all his goals Hohol gets an early start on his day. He skips breakfast, preferring to jump into his silver 450 SLC Mercedes by 8 a.m., sip from a cup of coffee on the dash, and maybe make a few calls from the car on his way to the office. "I put the sneakers on," he jokes.

Hohol has plants in Dupont and Kingston, but keeps his office at Dupont. Presently, the plant operates one shift, from 7 a.m. to 3 p.m., but may soon expand to three. Of his 120 employees, about 85 work on the production line. They get paid an average of $6-7 an hour.

The shop is not unionized, Hohol said, and he would fight any efforts toward organizing. "The day one comes I'm putting a padlock on the door and selling," he said of union organizers who might risk a trip to his shop.

Once at the plant, Hohol spends his day in meetings, on the phone and visiting with his employees and department heads.

The rock music playing in the production room can be heard in Hohol's office, mixing in with the sound of the line at work.

If he wants to kill the sound, he turns on the radio in his office, tuned to Rock 107.

Or, he loads up one of his paint guns and "shoots" it.

TIMES LEADER/CLARK VAN ORDEN
Larry Hohol, the founder and chief executive officer of Penox Technologies Inc., stands in his plant on Suscon Road, Dupont

After the sale of my company, which happened the day after Christmas in 1988, I spent the first week in January as a guest of Harvard University's School of Business in Cambridge, Massachusetts. It was nerve racking to fly there in my twin engine Beechcraft during an ice storm, but after I settled in, the week became extremely productive. I am inserting a picture of my plane

and my car simply to let you know that I really had them and to also let you know that today somebody else now owns both of them.

Every January, one hundred of the top company presidents from around the world, who are under the age of forty-five, are invited to actually "dorm" at Harvard University. They are gathered there in order to interact with the faculty as well as the other "Movers and Shakers" in the world of business. It was quite an honor to have been invited.

While I was there, I befriended a number of people, some of whom I had admired from a distance. The list included John Rehnfeld, President of Toshiba America. While visiting Toshiba's headquarters in Japan, this man single handedly identified the laptop computer in Toshiba's research and development laboratory as essential to Toshiba's future. After much strong arming, he convinced the powers-that-be to move the laptop computer's development to the company's highest priority. As they say, "the rest is history." Wow, to be in such company at my tender young age of thirty-three! John and I quickly developed a good personal friendship and he actually asked me for both business and personal advice. I am still humbled by the experience.

The day my pilot brought me safely home from Harvard was very memorable. It was the second week in January when I returned to my former company's headquarters. The main factory of the company I had just sold was located in the Foreign Trade Zone Industrial Park, which is behind the Wilkes-Barre/Scranton International Airport. I walked into the lobby, hung a left, as I had done thousands of times before, only to promptly bang my nose into my locked office door. I turned and looked at my executive secretary asking, "What's up with this?"

Looking at me sheepishly, she didn't answer. I demanded to know what was going on. With the look of a deer caught in the headlights, she dropped her head and spoke into her desk. "You'll have to talk to Harvey about that."

"Who the heck is Harvey?" I was about to find out.

Harvey was the "Texas" brother of the principles who bought my company. The family owned aerospace company was based in St. Louis, but Harvey spent most of his time in Texas as a "Business Consultant." I would come to find out much later why I had been told that he had been sued for malpractice and why his family bought him a business to run as far away from St Louis as possible.

I heard the lock on my office door click and then a slightly effeminate male voice from the other side said, "Come on in!" Not knowing what to expect, I opened the door slowly. Instead of being greeted by the outstretched hand of a businessman, "Harvey-from-Texas" was high-tailing it to the other side of his desk, and what an impressive desk it was! The best description for it would be something only a Texas Cowboy "wannabe" who had no taste or style, but lots of money, would choose. I can still see that hideous desk like it was yesterday.

I stood in front of this massively ugly, no doubt, extremely expensive desk, like a schoolchild who had been sent to the principal's office after a spitball incident. It was as if the desk held some invisible power or "Texas Force Field" for Harvey. Behind the protective "No Man's Land" of his desk, Harvey finally extended his hand in greeting. I shook his cold, clammy hand. Unfortunately, mine was one of those handshakes that missed the mark. You know the type, where you shake more fingers than hand, and you wish you could do it over for fear of leaving a wrong impression. After the handshake, we sat down.

I felt like I was about to get a speech about him being the "New Sheriff" in town when, low and behold, he kicked back in his chair and swung his extremely expensive ostrich cowboy boots onto the desk. Besides the boots, Harvey was wearing a cowboy dress shirt and cowboy dress pants. A very expensive cowboy sports coat (if there is such a thing) was hanging on a coat hook behind his head. You know, a "Texas" sized coat hook that was probably installed when the desk arrived. Folding his hands across his stomach, Harvey announced that he was the "New Sheriff in Town."

During our forty-five minute conversation, he kept annoyingly, wiping his upper lip with a white handkerchief. I thought to myself, "A real cowboy wouldn't even own a white handkerchief. Even I knew a white handkerchief would simulate a deer flashing its tail to warn all the other deer (and antelope) of danger. It would scare off the animals before any real cowboy could ever fire a shot." That thought made me chuckle to myself.

After our conversation concluded, I clenched his hand in mine, giving Harvey an example of what a good, ole Northeastern Pennsylvania Coal Cracker handshake was. I immediately went and washed my hands.

Cowboy Harvey

CHAPTER FOUR

Set for Life

I believe at some point in everyone's life we all have thought about what it would be like to come into a huge amount of money. You know, winning the lottery or being a beneficiary in an inheritance. Well, it really did happen to me......... My fortune was the fruit of hard work and yes, a little luck.

Imagine the good fortune of having over a million dollars in the bank with no real debt. Add to that a $100,000 per year for 5 years for my non-compete contract. Add to that my $100,000 yearly paycheck that I didn't even have to work for. Let me correct that statement. I *couldn't* work for. Let me try that one more time. I wasn't allowed to work for. Without getting into all of the nit-picky details, Harvey had relegated me to punching a timecard and restricted me to my new office. I was then required to log all the phone calls that I made or received. The problem was that no one called me, and I had no one to call.

My office had changed from the largest in the building to the smallest in the building. I was instructed to wait until Harvey came to me with a new project for me to work on. A few days into it, a maintenance person showed up with a new clock for my new office. I didn't need or ask for a clock, but I was getting one anyway. It was the kind of big-faced clock where you can hear each second tick away as well as see it happening. You know the type, with the large red second hand that loudly clicks one second at a time. Second after second, minute after minute, hour after hour. My door was ordered closed at all times. I was allowed to use the bathroom, but I had to record the event as a special notation in my empty phone log.

The situation became a matter of wills, and I was a very strong willed person. I would punch my timecard, smile, go to my office, smile, go to the bathroom, smile, go to lunch, smile, punch out my timecard, smile again, go home, smile, cash my paycheck, and then really smile. After a few weeks of this situation, it just wasn't funny anymore.

I returned from lunch one day and after punching my time card (and smiling), I walked through the warehouse section of the building and noticed a safety issue. I brought the situation to the attention of the shipping manager and returned to my office to watch the clock. That's the day when all hell broke loose. Within a few minutes of the "incident," I was standing in front of Harvey's mammoth "Texas Desk" watching him wipe his upper lip with his white handkerchief until I thought he would make it bleed.

He didn't even ask me to sit down. Harvey just informed me that he was preparing a formal written warning for insubordination that would be inserted into my permanent employment record. Previously I had been told, in no uncertain terms, that I was not to give any instructions to any employees to do anything.

Calmly, I acknowledged his prior instructions and stated since what I saw was a safety issue, I felt the company would want me to address it. I furthered my explanation by telling Harvey that I had not instructed anyone to do anything about what I had seen. I simply advised the shipping manager of the problem. I was promptly told that if the building were to catch on fire, I was not to yell "Fire!" out loud, but to come to Harvey's office and make him aware of it. Knowing full well what he was doing, I asked Harvey in as serious a voice as I could muster, "What should I do if the building was on fire and you are not in your office?" Being the rocket scientist that Harvey is, he made a funny face, paused, and then said, "Wait for me to return."

Larry Hohol

That was the day I learned the legal term, "Forced Resignation."

Hohol Resigns from Company He Founded

The Sunday Times, September 3, 1989 — Page B-6

Larry Hohol has resigned his management position with Penox Technologies Inc., a firm he founded in 1983 and built into a leader in the home health care industry.

Hohol was owner and president of Penox in December 1988, when the business was sold to Big Ben Corp., a St. Louis investment company which acquired the assets of the Luzerne County-based company.

Hohol had was a consultant to the president of the new ownership until his unexpected resignation.

Hohol said his growing responsibilities with his medical equipment leasing firm, LeasCor, and a conflict of management styles with the new owners prompted his action.

"Officials of the acquiring firm obviously saw fit to utilize a different corporate philosophy than the one which was in place under the original ownership," Hohol said.

He added that he recognized the need for organizational change as his former firm grew and realized that a more structured management system was essential to continued growth and success at Penox.

Penox, specializing in portable liquid oxygen systems, began as a small business in Hohol's Shavertown home. As it grew, Hohol moved to Wilkes-Barre and opened another facility in Swoyersville.

Looking for a larger site, the former Luzerne policeman was contacted by Northeastern Bank of Pennsylvania, which held the mortgage on the former RCA building in Pittston's Eastern Distribution Center.

Hohol built a prototype of his portable liquid oxygen unit in 1981, following a stunt with an ambulance service when he recognized the need for better machine than what was available at the time.

Hohol perfected the device by creating a coupling unit to make refilling easier and reduced the unit's weight from 12 to 6.5 pounds.

In 1981 with fiscal year revenues of $2.3 million, Penox management turned thumbs down on a $5.3 million buyout offer from Healthdyne Corp.

Two years later, Hohol was involved in an unrelated but equally interesting endeavor. He collaborated with Thomas Kinter of Broadway Design Works, in supplying the paraphernalia for a battle game for King Juan Carlos of Spain.

During a trip to Spain to discuss health care and Penox's European operations with the kind, Hohol mentioned *Skirmishes*, a game in which players test their skills by firing guns filled with paint pellets at each other, in a quest to capture the opposing team's flag.

The king was quite interested in the concept, and Hohol supplied the needed equipment as a gift during a follow-up visit.

LARRY HOHOL

As you can read in the Press Release, I didn't bad mouth anyone when I resigned. As a matter of fact, I even attempted to explain away Harvey's bad behavior. As tough as it was to leave the company I had founded, I was content that I had secured my family's financial future "forever." Nothing in the world was more important to me than MY FAMILY.

    I had proven time and time again that I was a very productive individual with a real drive to accomplish things. After waking up in the morning for many weeks after my resignation with nothing to do and no place to go, I understandably became very restless. At this stage of my life, my two daughters, who were twenty-four months apart in age, were very young and in grade school so jumping on a jet and heading off to some tropical island to live out the rest of my life was not a realistic option. While my paycheck and healthcare insurance had stopped, I certainly had everything covered. I began to wonder what I should do next. This couldn't be all that Larry Hohol was to accomplish in his life. Could it? A unique idea for a "Sales Company" began to formulate in my brain. To this day, the concept for this sales company still rings true as a good idea.

CHAPTER FIVE

A Friend Indeed

---

*I*n the early days of my company I had hired a high school buddy and made him a sales representative. His name was Matt. Matt and I still met and talked after my resignation. Matt had proven himself to be very good at what he did. Whether it was his God-given talent as a salesman or direction from me, I don't know, but he eventually became the Vice President of Key Accounts for my company. He handled the big customers, thus the big deals. He was a part of my inner circle. I had confided in him and considered him as one of those friends you can count on one hand. We had history. So much for my instincts.

Once Matt had learned I was selling the company, he freaked out. He begged me not to sell. When that didn't work, he tried to convince me to sell the company to anyone but that particular family from St. Louis. I didn't understand why he was so upset and he wouldn't tell me. After weeks of his pressure and a few adult beverages, I got him to tell me what his problem really was. Matt told me he could never, ever, work for people of …"That Religion." You could have knocked me over with a feather. "What???" I exclaimed.

Matt opened up and nothing but the nastiest nouns and pronouns spewed forth. I was in shock. It took a while for everything that Matt had said to settle into my brain. One thing was for sure, he was not going to work for the new owners, or so he convinced me. After my resignation, Matt again told me, in no uncertain terms, that as soon as he could, he was moving on. He had a wife and baby, but he was out of there ASAP.

At one point, Matt finally hit critical mass. He said he would do anything to go into business with me and just needed to get out of there. I shared my idea about the sales company concept that I had. Matt went into orbit with enthusiasm. This was just what he had been hoping for over the last year. I became excited and energized at the idea of getting back into a business, any business, especially with everything looking so promising. After all, we had a hell of a proven track record together.

We put together a structure for the new company to operate under and I assigned a number of tasks to Matt. I was willing to actually make him a partner in the new venture. After a few weeks of Matt's excitement, but no action, I quietly backed away from him and went in a totally different direction. Matt's testimony under oath, at a later date, will shock your senses. It did mine.

CHAPTER SIX

A Plan for Action

M_y attorneys were "outside counsel" to Subaru of America and represented the likes of Gloria Estefan when she had her almost fatal bus accident. They had handled my company's legal matters for close to a decade, as well as these specific buyout contracts. I showed up at their office with a detailed business plan for another idea I had and asked them to research the "non-compete" contract that they had co-written. I felt it was prudent to find out if there was "any chance" I could be in violation of my contract with any new business idea I had. After a lot of questions and research, they provided me with a written opinion that I would "not" be in violation of the non-compete contract through my new activities. They setup my new corporation and I named it, Cryco Inc.

My attorneys further offered two pieces of advice. The first was do not try to steal away any of my former employees, even though that issue was not addressed in the contract. If former employees came to me looking for a job that was okay, but if I tried to steal them from my former company that would make for a bad appearance. The second piece of advice was not to sell anything to any of my old customers no matter what the product was. This advise was offered even though selling to my former customer base would be acceptable under the terms of the "Non-Compete" contract, as long as I sold them products that were not sold by my old company. They insisted it was best to avoid contacting my old customers for any reason to eliminate any perception of a "gray area."

Speaking of "gray areas," there were none and I mean exactly that. My old company sold products that were regulated by the

FDA as class 2 medical devices. My new company was repairing and manufacturing products that were not manufactured or controlled by the FDA and could never legally be used for medical purposes. My products were regulated by the Federal Department of Transportation and were used for transportation and industrial applications. My new company operated under totally different federal compliance standards as well as had totally different customers. No overlapping whatsoever. This is an extremely important point.

I felt my attorney's advice was reasonable and appropriate: don't steal employees and maintain a totally different customer base. It was best to play it safe since legal action was imminent. Harvey and his family were in serious default for some substantial payments due to me. All of the required default letters had been sent to them via my attorneys. The only thing left was to file suit against them. I hate lawyers and I sure hate lawsuits, but I had no choice.

After successfully starting a multi-million dollar medical equipment manufacturing company on a shoe string, I thought it would be wise to start my new company the same way. I had a massive garage at my home that I could utilize. To make room, I started off by backing out all of my toys, stretch limo and all.

I began to fabricate machinery in my garage and boy, it didn't take long to discover that I had gotten rusty. It was a very humbling experience. I didn't stay in my garage very long and before I knew it, I had rented a pretty nice facility downtown. My toys were returned to where they belonged.

Not only did we send the new owners of my old company written notice of my activities, but we put out press releases as well. We weren't trying to hide anything from anyone.

One day while at my new office, I looked up from my desk and saw a good friend of mine standing in my doorway. He was a short, stocky fellow with a very bald head. Although his sheriff's uniform was neatly pressed, it seemed a little unnatural on his slight frame. His lieutenant's bars stood out brightly from the rest of his otherwise drab uniform.

"Felix, how the heck are you?" I said. "I haven't seen you in, well, let's see, it's been hours."

Just the night before, we had spent some time together at a local Irish watering hole, "Flaherty's" with his wife and some other friends. Felix's big grin quickly changed to a more serious professional expression.

"Well Lar, I need you to sign here," he said in a very gruff voice. "I saw this coming through this morning at roll call with your name on it, so I grabbed it before anyone else could get their hands on it."

I had just been served. To this day, I think it would have been better if a stranger had served me.

The new owners of my old company had stopped making any and all payments to me, including rent payments. Because they were in serious default for some hefty amounts, they knew I would have to take legal action. They simply beat me to the punch. But what could they possibly sue me for? They were the ones in default.

Two of my attorneys read the complaint as I nervously watched for their reactions. The two of them were passing pages back and forth like they were hot potatoes at a Cub Scout cookout.

Finally, the senior attorney of the two smiled and laughed out loud. Even though he was also slight in stature, he bellowed like a big man.

"Is this the best they could do? This is pitiful."

His subordinate nervously chuckled, still reading the documents.

"The only problem I see with this is that we have to be ready for trial in two days," he said. TWO DAYS!!

"What the heck are you talking about?" I asked. My attorney replied, "Cowboy Harvey" and his friends have filed for a Preliminary Injunction asking to close your new company down because they claim you are in violation of your non-compete contract. First of all, you are not in violation…..are you?"

My response was, "You tell me!" We reviewed everything I was doing with the new company and my attorneys said, without hesitation, that there was no violation.

"Secondly, they did not make a number of payments as required via the contract. We have the notices of their defaults right here," he continued, while producing the paperwork. "Even if you were in violation of the non-compete, which you are not, they are not entitled to the relief they are seeking because they violated the very contract that they are trying to enforce."

How on "God's Green Earth" could something appear so clear and yet worry me so much? Why would they pick such a loser of a reason to come after me and my new company? I didn't sleep well the next two nights.

We showed up bright and early for court. I had two trial attorneys with me, Rick and Norman. Additionally, a senior partner of my law firm, Bruce, who actually wrote the contracts, showed up for moral support. The President Judge of the County, Judge Patrick Toole, Jr., was presiding over the matter and even made a joking comment about Bruce, the senior law partner, being up so early.

After hours of nonsensical testimony from my adversaries, we knocked off and reconvened late the next morning. Attorney Piccone put into evidence my press releases and letters from my attorneys outlining my new manufacturing activity. The President Judge then asked some pertinent questions. He asked Harvey how many customers and how much money had they lost due to my activities? Harvey looked at his Attorney, Arthur Piccone, pulled out his handkerchief and whispered something into it. My attorney chimed in and said, "I'm sorry, Your Honor, but I did not hear his answer."

"Neither did I," remarked Judge Toole.

Harvey wiped his lip like he was sanding a piece of furniture, and then said clearly, "We have lost no customers and lost no money…yet."

The President Judge looked over at my attorneys and said, "We will reconvene after lunch at 1:30 pm." Still looking at my attorneys, he went on to say, "If at that time you wish to present a defense, I will hear your witnesses."

We walked out of the courtroom stunned. "IF" we wanted to present a defense was repeated by all four of us as we were on our way out of the courtroom.

We reconvened after lunch and gave the appearance that I was going to take the stand. The courtroom was called to order. President Judge Toole looked at my attorney and said, "You may call your first witness."

My attorney stood up, turned to look at me, turned back to the judge and said he would not be calling any witnesses and that the defense rested.

The President Judge then said, "That's what I thought."

Opposing counsel, Attorney Piccone, rose to his feet and started objecting. After a brief time the judge asked Attorney Piccone to be specific as to what he was objecting to. Piccone tried to convince the judge that it was not fair that he could not cross examine me under oath. The judge's response was very fitting. He said, "If you are here trying to tell me that you need to put Mr. Hohol on the stand in order to prove your case, then maybe you should have called him when you had the chance."

After very brief closing arguments, the judge turned, looked around the room and said, "I will render my decision in due course. He then looked directly at me and said, "Go forth and prosper. Court is adjourned."

Within a couple of weeks we received the judge's decision. The Preliminary Injunction was denied. The President Judge of the county had ruled 100% in my favor. He ruled that my activities were not in violation of my non-compete just as my attorneys had advised. Beer and chicken wings for everyone! We were back on track... or so I thought.

An appeal was filed by my adversaries. It read just as badly as the original complaint. I thought about how much money Harvey was spending on attorneys and how little he was getting in return. The thought also occurred to me that since this wasn't his money, just how dangerous he could be.

CHAPTER SEVEN

In the Clear

Eight months had passed since President Judge Toole had ruled in my favor. My new business started taking off. New customers, the likes of Union Carbide, Air Products and Air Gas, to name a few, were sending work our way. I had taken a lot of time to build special machinery rather than buy it and "no," none of the equipment was proprietary. In doing so I saved hundreds of thousands of dollars. Phones were ringing, trucks were delivering and, most importantly, invoices were being mailed. My life was once again back in balance, or so it seemed.

Take notice that the following press release is very specific as to the application of my "new" product. Nowhere is it written that the helium tank could be used for oxygen therapy. Again, by Federal Law, none of the products built or repaired by my new company could be used to compete in the FDA regulated and controlled market place.

Liquid helium supplier launches line of transportable vessels

Cryco, Inc., a new Wilkes-Barre based manufacturing company, has launched a line of transportable vessels for shipping the coldest substance known to man. Because liquid helium is only seven degrees from absolute zero it is the most difficult fluid to store and transport, according to Larry Hohol, the company's president and owner.

Hohol says the fact that Cryco's products will be distributed worldwide and the entire manufacturing process will occur in the Wyoming Valley translates into new jobs for the area.

"Cryco has developed some innovative techniques that make our helium tanks series the most durable and thermally efficient tanks available," says Hohol. He added that "the introduction of liquid helium vessels marks a major milestone for our company."

In addition to thier use for transporting helium, the containers manufactured by Cryco have other applications, including use in super conductor research and in magnetic resonance imaging (MRI) equipment.

Hohol said his firm's name is derived from the work "cryogenics," the science of low-temperature phenomena. The company operates from offices in the Jeweler Center Building on Pennsylvania Boulevard, Wilkes-Barre.

Larry Hohol, president and owner of the Wilkes-Bare based Cryco, Inc., is pictured with a "transportable cryogenic helium vessel" which his firm manufactures. The high tech containers are used for shipping liquid helium, the coldest substance knwon to man.

Cryco owner Larry Hohol

Somewhere in all of his quotes Attorney Piccone tried to allude to the fact that his client Essex Industries, (AKA Big Ben Corp) actually purchased "Cryogenic Technology" from me, thus anything to do with cryogenics was protected by the non-compete. There are two HUGE problems with this statement. First of all, it was a lie. If Essex Industries purchased my company so they could acquire cryogenic technology, you can bet that their protection on this matter would have been clearly spelled out in the contracts that we both signed. Certainly, they would not have allowed me to keep my U.S. Patent 4,783,969 which is a Cryogenic, High Flow, Heat Exchange Manifold that had both medical and industrial applications.

Essex could have purchased this patent for a single dollar just as they did with my "Cryogenic Coupler" patent number 4,909,545 which was used exclusively for the medical marketplace. They chose not to buy it for a reason: There was never any intent to restrict my activities outside of the medical equipment field, and that is a fact. They bought my medical equipment product line and my 6000 Homecare Medical Equipment customers. I had signed a "Non-Compete" contract. That means I agreed that I would not COMPETE.

The second major problem with Attorney Piccone's statement was that Essex already had a full fledged cryogenics division that had been in business for decades before their acquisition of my company. Yes, I said decades. If anything, they could have taught me a few things about cryogenics (they did not). For any of you non-believers, feel free to Google "Essex Cryogenics." Make sure that you use quotes around the company name. Even with the quotes, you will get over 33,000 hits. Better yet, read the following:

Home ▶ NEWS ▶ Story

ST. LOUIS POST-DISPATCH

Essex Industries Subsidiary Pleads Guilty To Test Falsification

SOURCE:
PUBLICATION: St. Louis Post-Dispatch
SECTION: NEWS

DATE: February 9, 1992
EDITION: L5
PAGE: 2D

A subsidiary of Essex Industries Inc. has pleaded guilty of falsifying results of tests on oxygen tanks used by crews of Air Force refuelling planes.

The firm, **Essex Cryogenics** of Missouri, could be fined as much as $500,000 when it is sentenced April 3 by U.S. District Judge Clyde S. Cahill.

Lawyers for Essex entered a guilty plea Friday to one count of falsifying test results for production of low-pressure oxygen tanks used by crews. In exchange for the plea, prosecutors dropped other charges that were in an indictment returned in May.

Keith B. Guller, president of Essex, said in a statement that the charge to which the company pleaded guilty resulted from an allegation in 1989 over tanks shipped to Tinker Air Force Base.

Investigators found no evidence of defective welding of tanks, said Guller, adding that the company's top management told supervisors to cooperate with the government.

Sure, I could have used some other document to prove that Essex Industries had a Cryogenic Division, but this one serves two purposes for me. Nuff said.

CHAPTER EIGHT

Déjà Vu, All Over Again!

"*F*elix! Buddy! What the heck are you doing here?" I called out to my Sheriff friend.

Felix once again stood in my office doorway, holding more papers. I jumped up from my desk, shook his hand and made some smart ass comment about how handsome he looked in his uniform. He didn't laugh. I signed his paper and opened up the envelope while he stood there.

Yes, I had been sued again. I read the complaint and laughed out loud, just like my attorney had the first time I got sued. The new suit looked exactly the same as the old suit. I looked at Felix and said, "This is pitiful. What a joke."

Felix looked at me and said with the most serious face I had ever seen on him that it was not a joke and that I had better take it very seriously. I stood there waiting for the punch line. I waited for him to crack up and bust a gut laughing. He didn't.

Instead, he looked me straight in the eye and said, "The President Judge, who heard your first case, went on vacation this morning. It is not a coincidence that I am serving you with this suit on the very first day that he is gone." Felix continued, "The judge who is filling in for him is best friends with your opposing counsel, (Attorney Piccone). Whenever that attorney gets in front of this judge, he has NEVER lost a single case……. EVER! The judge and opposing counsel are godparents to each other's grown children. They were law partners together in at least two separate law firms before the judge became a judge."

Felix had a look on his face like that of a police officer who was telling a parent, one of their children had just been killed in a horrible car wreck. In my case, it was a "Train Wreck." The Luzerne County Railroad had just dispatched an "Express Train to Hell" and I had a First Class Ticket.

CHAPTER NINE

One Hell of a Coincidence

*T*hat was a Monday morning. By Wednesday I was standing in front of the most evil person I had ever met in my life. I was certain that Satan himself steered clear of this man. Judge Gifford R. Cappellini is a name that will forever be intertwined in my family's DNA. Two hundred years from now a gene will be identifiable in a Hohol blood sample, if you will, a Cappellini Chromosome. Here we were, having an emergency hearing for something that had already been ruled on and was presently under appeal to the Superior Court of Pennsylvania.

Judge Cappellini

Immediately, my attorney, Rick, asked to approach the bench. He presented a copy of the first lawsuit as well as a copy of the pending appeal. He stated quite loudly that opposing counsel was not entitled to a "Second bite of the apple."

"How can I possibly know if these two actions are the same unless I hear testimony?" queried Judge Cappellini after glancing at the paperwork.

"Thank you, Your Honor, you have just proven my point," my attorney said. "Since you were not present at the first hearing, you couldn't possibly be able to compare the two cases by having a second hearing. You simply were not there, President Judge Toole was."

To say Judge Cappellini was pissed doesn't come close to describing his reaction. After he gathered himself, Cappellini said, "I guess I will have to read the transcripts of the first hearing when we are done and compare them, won't I? Motion to dismiss is denied."

My attorney wasn't done. "Since I am already up here, I would like to ask for a continuance. Your Honor, we were just served with this suit less than 48 hours ago," Rick said. "To properly defend my client, we really need to have some time for discovery. You know depositions, document production and the like."

"Additionally, President Judge Toole will be back from his "scheduled" vacation in two more business days. Surely, since eight months have passed since we last addressed these issues, waiting two more days for his return would harm no one. If that's not enough, I can show correspondence from over a year ago where opposing counsel was put on notice of Mr. Hohol's specific activities which are being addressed in this lawsuit. Here it is more than a year later and out of the blue they are asking for an emergency hearing. It just isn't right," he concluded.

Cappellini almost looked cross-eyed with anger. He spoke loudly, clearly, and as controlled as possible. Here is what he had to say:

"The matter before this court today is so important, so urgent, and the damage potentially so great, that I cannot, in good conscience, wait another minute to hear this matter."

Everyone in the courtroom, except for Attorney Piccone, kind of looked around as if to say, what the hell is he talking about? I thought to myself, "How could he possibly come up with that conclusion on his own?" No evidence had been presented. All he had in front of him was a complaint. Judge Cappellini then declared, "Motion for continuance is denied." Attorney Piccone did his best to conceal his approval. As my attorney turned to walk back to my table he said out loud, "Yeah, what a surprise." Naturally, the judge warned him about his comment.

For some unknown reason, and my good fortune, a newspaper reporter was present in the courtroom that day. I hadn't contacted anyone from either one of the local papers, so I wasn't sure why she was present. She approached us at our table after the day's testimony was finished.

The reporter commented that she thought it was very odd that the judge refused to wait until the original trial judge returned from vacation, especially since that trial judge was his boss. I didn't know it yet, but her presence and that of other reporters in the courtroom, going forward, was going to directly help me keep my sanity.

We were scheduled for trial mid-morning on the following day. Rick had another plan up his sleeve. He had burned the midnight oil to prepare a formal motion for a Stay of the Proceedings. A "Stay" is simply a court ordered stopping of the trial. He presented his motion to the Motions Judge first thing in the morning. After a brief hearing, the Motions Judge agreed with Rick and issued a formal order stopping or "Staying" the proceedings. Attorney Piccone was present at this hearing and objected strenuously to the motion. When I met up with Rick outside the courtroom, he was beaming from ear to ear.

There is no doubt in my mind that Attorney Piccone contacted his friend, Judge Cappellini, immediately after the Interim Stay was signed. This is called an Ex-parte communication and is against the rules of both civil and criminal procedure. What was about to happen would dramatically demonstrate just how far these two train conductors would go to get me to my final destination.

Rick could hardly control his happiness. He had a spring in his step that could best be described as boyish. Even though he tried desperately to remove the smile from his face, even his attempted frown made him look happy. The court was called to order. Before anyone else could speak, my attorney sprang to his feet and asked Judge Cappellini if he could approach the bench. The judge told him there was no need to do that.

"Oh, yes there is," Rick exclaimed, waving the court ordered Stay high in the air.

The judge then said, "I am assuming you want to discuss the Stay of Proceedings you have in your hands." "Yes, sir, I do," was his reply. Suddenly, we both realized that we had not told the judge what my attorney was holding in his hands, but somehow the judge already knew.

"No need to get so excited, counselor. You see, earlier this morning, I heard a rumor that you had filed your motion for a Stay of these proceedings, so on my way to my courtroom I swung by the judge's chambers that issued the order." Judge Cappellini was now looking down his nose as if he was wearing bifocals even though he wasn't and continued on by saying, "He really didn't mean it."

"What?" asked Rick?

The judge repeated his statement, "He really didn't mean it."

"He really didn't mean what, Your Honor?"

"He really didn't mean to Stay the Proceedings."

"He most certainly did, Your Honor," argued Rick, "and I have the proof right here in my hand."

With the court order now bending limply in his hand, Rick stood there for what seemed like an hour before he said, "For crying out loud, Your Honor, I have a real, honest-to-goodness, Stay of the Proceedings signed, sealed and now delivered."

Cappellini responded once again, but this time slower and with more deliberation.

"He—really---didn't--- mean---it."

Rick sat down and as quickly as he hit the seat, he sprang back up to his feet.

"Your honor….until I have something in writing to the contrary from the Motions Judge, I am advising my client not to proceed. As a matter of fact, we are all going to leave right now."

With that, he began to put papers in his briefcase. If evil has a face it was now the face of the judge before us. Pointing his index finger like it was a poison dart and looking down his nose as if he were looking through those make-believe bifocals, he raised his voice to the point that any school children getting off the bus for a tour that day could hear him bellow.

"Sit down, right now, or I will find you in contempt of court and you won't be spending time with your children tonight. You got that?!"

Rick froze, and I mean froze. You could see his brain pulsing. You could almost hear the gears evaluating whether he should call his bluff or not. He was one, big, raw nerve. Just when it looked like he was going to say, "I dare you," the judge said just two words. These two words made it sound like he was ordering the world's most disobedient dog to listen.

"DOWN...... NOW!" he said, pointing at Rick.

Very slowly, Rick lowered himself into his seat as if he were afraid it was loaded with thumb tacks. He turned, leaned over to me and whispered, "This freaking guy's nuts."

I responded intentionally loud enough for everyone to hear my remark, including the judge. "No, he's crooked."

The Stay was written in such a form that only the issuing judge could rescind it and then only in writing. To this day, neither has occurred.

CHAPTER TEN

What to do about a Rogue Judge

We finished out the week by hearing nothing of any consequence during testimony. Over the weekend we needed to plan a counter attack. We knew that the original trial judge and the boss of all the county judges would be coming back from vacation bright and early Monday morning. Man, was he going to be pissed. Not only had one of his judges completely rescheduled most of his week by delaying cases that were already in sequential order to be heard, but this same judge was interfering with a case already disposed of by the President Judge himself.

It was important to inform the President Judge so he could become involved as soon as possible. After investigating all of the formal ways to do this, we concluded, there were none. We knew that we had a rogue judge on our hands who was hell bent on helping his friend and former law partner.

My attorney finally directed me to write a letter to President Judge Toole outlining everything that had happened while he had been away on vacation and simply ask him, as President Judge of the county, to investigate this situation. We drafted a simple one-and-a- half-page letter. At the last minute my attorney, told me to hold off faxing the letter to President Judge Toole. Rick was going to try to convert our Interim Stay into a more permanent form. After arguing and receiving the new Stay of the proceedings he presented it to Judge Cappellini. Cappellini promptly rejected the second stay and ordered the trial to continue. At that point Rick told me to fax my letter to the President Judge, as well as opposing counsel. It is important to emphasize that the letter clearly showed that I had copied opposing counsel. What happened next could never have been predicted.

It wasn't an hour later following the faxing of the letter that my fax machine began humming. I received a scathing response from President Judge Toole. The gist of his response was, how dare I question the integrity of the court and how dare I contact him, ex parte, which means without advising opposing counsel, and how dare I try to say that this new action was the same as the old action. Keep in mind that the President Judge was never given a copy of the new action so how the heck would he know if it was the same or not? I had sent a copy of the letter to Attorney Piccone via fax which went through as received by his office. President Judge Toole no longer had any action before him that concerned me or my company. His previous ruling (in my favor) had been appealed to the Superior Court, so it was out of his hands. The best part was that Attorney Piccone faxed President Judge Toole a letter complaining about me faxing President Judge Toole a letter. Unbelievable!

We were correct in predicting that Toole would be pissed. He was pissed, all right, but not at Cappellini. He was pissed at us. I immediately wanted to file a formal complaint against both of these judges for misconduct. At that point I found out something very interesting regarding my own legal counsel.

"Larry, I make my living by practicing law in front of these judges," said Rick. "If I file a complaint with the Judicial Conduct Board, nothing will happen to the judges, but they will all remember who hit the hornet's nest with the stick."

My law firm was not going to file a complaint against any judge from Luzerne County, regardless of what travesties the judge committed or what anguish it would cause any of their clients. They were more worried about their future ability to represent clients that they hadn't even acquired yet than they were about my best interests. To this day, I am still amazed that attorneys cannot comprehend why no one likes lawyers, even the good ones.

At this point my attorneys tried to convince me that this case was so pitiful that the judge could never grant a Preliminary Injunction against me for violating my non-competition agreement. We would simply win on the merits of the case. The way they explained it was, even a crooked judge couldn't turn this sow's ear into a silk purse. I, however, was not so optimistic.

By law, a Preliminary Injunction is an action taken that is so urgent that it bypasses all other pending litigation. Cases that have been scheduled for months or even years will be pushed to the side and delayed because of the emergency nature of this action. Because the aggrieved party is seeking decisive and immediate relief, the action is so urgent that failing to act in such haste would surely harm the petitioning party so egregiously that monetary damage from inaction could not be calculated nor fairly compensated.

None of the above applied to me, my new company or my activities. Certainly, if I were stealing customers, sales and, ultimately, profits from the new owners of my former company, all of that could be found out through court-ordered discovery, not to mention, their customers advising them about my conduct. I was doing none of this. I was selling and repairing new products for totally new customers who had never purchased anything from my former company. So, where was the rub? What was going on?

There was a very interesting strategy in play here, but it would be years before I figured it out. This situation was not about winning or losing on the merits of the case. Heck, it wasn't even about winning the case at all. This case could have been heard and a decision rendered in three days—if it had merit. They could have won the case, closed me down, game over. No, this was about deep pockets and punishment. This was about taking no prisoners and leaving nothing but scorched earth behind.

Unfortunately, that old saying, "He who has the deepest pockets, wins," is very true. My adversaries knew they legitimately owed me big money and that if I were successful in getting them to trial, they would lose. They also knew that through court-ordered discovery, we had uncovered material fraud perpetrated by them to purposely defraud me out of large sums of money. Further, the "Big Eight" accounting firm from Philadelphia that had discovered and documented the fraud would be indisputable in court, should I have them appear. The actual photographs of the massive fraud along with their detailed accounting would be a challenge they could never overcome. They stood there and watched as my accountants photographed and documented the evidence. They knew firsthand what they were in store for should we get to trial. Then there was the way they treated me after the sale of the company. Imagine me testifying to a jury about the safety issue or being isolated in my office on top of all of the documented fraud.

Because the fraud issue I am addressing would have allowed huge multiples of damages to be awarded to me for punitive damages, they could never have allowed me to bring them to court. What should have been a normal three day trial took seventeen days stretched out over a nine month period. So much for their demand for, "immediate relief." When everything was over, my case became the longest lasting Preliminary Injunction case in the history of Pennsylvania and possibly in the history of the United States.

Judge Toole   Attorney Piccone   Judge Cappellini   Judge Augello

CHAPTER ELEVEN

The Merits of the Case

There were absolutely no merits to this case. Rather than retrying the entire case in this book, and bore you to death, let me just hit on some of the highlights.

The day I sold my company, we took a snapshot, if you will, of the products that the company manufactured and sold up to that date, as well as the list of 6,000 or so current customers. This was to protect me from being accused of violating my non-competition agreement should I ever want to, for instance, start selling "ANYTHING" down the street. After the sale of my company, the new owners could not decide to start selling "ANYTHING" and then find me in violation of my non-compete agreement. Even if I thought about selling "ANYTHING" before the company was sold, or if they thought about selling "ANYTHING" before they bought my company it wouldn't have mattered. ==My former company had to have been in the business of selling "Anything" or had definitive plans that they shared with me in order to restrict me. They could not just say that they were thinking about it. They also had to prove that they shared those specific plans with me in order to restrict my activities.== It turns out that the new owners shared absolutely nothing with me as far as their future plans were concerned because I simply wasn't a part of their plans. The contract wording was VERY specific.

Very exact language was used so that at a later time no one could say, oh, we were thinking about that awhile ago, so you can't do it.

CHAPTER TWELVE

*P*rivate Eyes

---

*O*ne morning while working at my new company, one of the employees came to my office. He informed me that a guy was sitting in a pickup truck across the street from our parking lot, next to the town playground. The truck had a short cap over its bed and a small aluminum boat turned upside down on the roof. My response was... so? Well, he advised me, this guy is video-taping us. "No way," I said.

We went into another office that had the shades closed so I could peek out the window. Sure enough, there he was, video-taping whatever he could. I got my camera and took some zoom pictures of him filming us. As I sat back down at my desk, I was thinking, what the heck is this all about?

My attorneys had given my adversaries proper notice via a letter over a year ago as to what we were doing. Everything was in black and white. We weren't denying or hiding anything. It made me feel very uneasy.

Sitting there, I started getting angry. I was going to pay a visit to that truck and confront the jerk, and just maybe kick some ass. As I headed towards the door, a thought struck me like a hard fist. I had a better idea.

Grabbing the phone, I called the local police department. I gave the dispatcher a description of the truck, told her that the guy was parked next to the kids' playground and that he was video-taping activity while sitting in the cab of his truck. Everything I said was true. My office staff and I snuck into the closed office to watch the fun unfold.

A marked police car drove by slowly, at first, like he was just on patrol. Evidently, the guy in the pickup thought it would be a

The Luzerne County Railroad

good time to vacate the area, so he drove off. That's when the patrol car spun around after him and we were off to the races. Two unmarked cars joined in the pursuit before everyone traveled out of our sight.

About twenty minutes later, a good friend of mine who was a detective with that police department, showed up at my office. He told me what had just happened in my parking lot.

After a short chase, they surrounded the guy in the truck, told him get out of the cab with his hands up and then proceeded to jack him up, spread-eagle across the hood of his truck.

The officers made him replay the video tape for them. The detective told me that it turned out the guy was video-taping me and my operation. I confessed to my detective friend that I was the one who had made the call to his department and that I was aware of what he was doing. He got a big chuckle out of that and told me he wished he would have known what was going on earlier so he could have had more fun with it. Well, that's where the fun stopped for me.

I found out later that the man in the truck was a private detective who had been following me for months, plus my wife, and even my children as they went back and forth to school. This situation was getting way out of hand.

During one of the days of trial, the same private detective testified on the stand. He rattled off dates, times and places of my movements both during work hours, as well as after work. Months of my activities were put into the record. Obviously, if I had a mistress, my wife would have become aware of it at this time.

He also reported to the judge on the rest of my family's movements. He produced pictures of my house and the vehicles we drove. There was no apparent reason for this information to be shared with the court, but, of course, the judge allowed it. I guess this invasion of my privacy was supposed to scare me, but it had the opposite effect. It made me really angry. You know, violated angry. The same Private Detective produced dozens of file boxes filled with papers that he had personally removed from my dumpster. A few neatly dressed men in coveralls entered the courtroom, pushing and pulling hand trucks that were half loaded with boxes. They strategically deposited the boxes, one after another, on a table in front of the judge, stacking them as high as they could reach. The men appeared to struggle with the overwhelming "weight of the evidence." It was as if they had practiced the entire drill the night before in the closed courtroom. No one had to tell them where to put anything, they automatically knew.

It was a large courtroom with a seating capacity sufficient to hold a murder trial, but the boxes were stacked directly in front of the judge for dramatic effect, which obscured Cappellini's view. All of their movements were exaggerated and labored. There is an old saying, "What you don't have in evidence, make up for it in volume."

Judge Cappellini not only allowed this charade, he participated in it. The charade would begin with a loud knock on the chamber's door, followed by the courtroom door being swung open by the judge's tipstaff. The judge would acknowledge each entry by performing some sort of hand gesture or shaking his head in disbelief and locking his eyes on the handcart. All the while smiling......his satanic smile. At one point he even combined the two gestures and put his hand to his shaking head as if to record total disbelief.

Now, after all that stacking of boxes, the trial could not proceed until a Maytag Repairman-look-a-like moved this mountain of boxes once again so the judge could see the courtroom or, more importantly, be seen in the courtroom. The boxes were placed in the jury box on top of the jurist chairs. Each chair was stacked to a height sufficient to resemble a person seated in the Jury Box. It was as if they were intentionally stacked in this bizarre and creepy manner to give the appearance of bearing witness.

When the theatrics were finally over, everyone acted exhausted, especially opposing counsel, even though Attorney Piccone hadn't lifted a finger the whole time. He did, however, accompany each and every delivery from the courtroom door to the judge's bench; logging miles walking back and forth as he personally escorted this "mountain of evidence." I am sure that if he were a car, he would have been due for an oil change.

Upon the resumption of testimony, the private detective described how he entered my covered dumpster at night with a flashlight in his mouth. He described how quickly he found exactly what he wanted. The dumpster was completely full of "cold, hard evidence." Sure, there were also some coffee cups, empty lunch bags and used feminine hygiene products but if he could have, I'm sure the private detective would have shrunk-wrapped the entire dumpster in order to have it sitting here before the judge. He all but apologized for only being able to provide this "small sampling" of what he had found. His eyes lit up like a four-year-old boy on Christmas morning as he described exactly what it was that he had discovered:

1. Actual copies of a mailing we had done.
2. Names, addresses, with full zip codes.
3. Hard copies of a promotion we were running.

Yes, sir, right here in these boxes was the mother of all mailings!

The private detective spent time telling Judge Cappellini how he almost got caught by the local police patrol, but in the end had outsmarted them by parking his surveillance vehicle (camper truck with aluminum boat on rack) in an area that would not cause suspicion. Remarkably, he was even able to lay still while surrounded by all of this evidence when the police patrol shined its spotlight directly on the dumpster while he was inside. Great detail was given about how he bagged and tagged the evidence before us and how he and his secretary selected the most readable, relevant and unstained pieces for inclusion in the boxes.

What he actually found and claimed was so revealing was a preprinted, multi-layered promotional mailer I had purchased that was similar to a rebate check you get in the mail. It allowed us to print a promotional message on the outside of the sealed document with a dot matrix printer. We simply removed the outside layer after it ran through our printer and threw it away. The discarded paper showed the message that was now inside the mailer via carbonless transfer as well as the address of the recipient. It was a slick promo piece and it worked very well.

I told my attorney that this whole thing was bullshit and not to even bother cross examining the detective. I wanted Harvey on the stand.

CHAPTER THIRTEEN

The New Sheriff Takes the Stand

One of the things we were focusing on when Cowboy Harvey took the stand was all of those boxes. I was really tired of those damn boxes. They were actually left in the courtroom for months. While other trials took place, everyone was required to work around this mountain of boxes. Eventually they were removed from their priority seating, although they didn't go far.

I was told that the judge explained to each new batch of litigants, as they came through, that he was involved in a very complicated civil matter and to please excuse the mess. He was also heard telling stories to the school children who were on tour about the seriousness of the evidence before them. Now it was our turn to bring attention to those boxes.

When Harvey finally took the stand, it was sweet. He was so nervous; you could have bottled the sweat pouring off his upper lip. My attorney Rick walked towards the stand and asked Harvey if he had looked at the papers in the boxes. As he wiped his upper lip with his white handkerchief, he replied that he had. At first wipe of his lip, I pictured all of the deer and antelope running away again. I think it was some form of gallows humor.

Rick asked, "What did you see?"

"Copies of a massive mailing list that had obviously been mailed out by Hohol and his new company," Harvey exclaimed.

"So, tell us why that list was so relevant to these proceedings?"

Harvey bit, hook, line and sinker. He proudly announced that, "Its proof positive as to the companies Hohol is targeting with his marketing," as he pointed at me like I was an accused murderer who had just been pointed out from the stand. I wanted to snap off that finger and stick it in his ear, but I digress.

I had previously asked Rick to open a few boxes, hold up numerous papers for the judge to see and have Harvey repeat more than a couple of times why these documents were so important. I also had Rick agree with Harvey to the point that he eventually stated, "Let the record show that we totally agree with the witness as to the scope of the marketing my client's company is undertaking. It is truly massive, as well as very specific."

Piccone quickly exchanged glances with Cappellini, followed by an objection to Rick's statement. The two of them realized that my counsel agreeing with a hostile witness could not be good. Attorney Piccone didn't know what to say after his objection, so he entered into an argument about some legal nonsense.

Harvey sensed something was amuck, but he wasn't bright enough to figure it out. Piccone again started objecting to us being in agreement with his client. He also objected to Rick repeating what Harvey said. Finally, Cappellini had heard enough and stopped everything. As my attorney walked towards our table, he turned to the judge with one final suggestion.

"Your Honor, how about this?" Rick slowly walked back towards Harvey. He reopened one of the precious boxes, instructing Harvey to take his time because this was very important.

"Please go through the boxes carefully and show the court how many of these customers belong to you. Show the court the names of your customers that are right here in these boxes."

Piccone objected, stating that the evidence was so massive it would be impossible and unreasonable to go through the boxes to find all of their customers. After the dust settled and the shouting was over, Rick quietly agreed that he had made an unreasonable request. Again, he walked slowly back to our table.

Just as you would have expected Rick to say, "I have no further questions, Your Honor," he stopped dead in his tracks. Rick didn't want to do what he did next, but I had demanded it. He turned to Harvey and said, "It appears that these boxes are an extremely important part of your case. You have spent a lot of time and money to acquire these documents. You paid a lot of money to have Mr. Hohol and his family followed by a private detective. His surveillance ultimately led to the discovery of these boxes of exhibits. Didn't it?"

Harvey proudly exclaimed, "It sure did."

"After these documents were discovered and retrieved, you had to pay someone to go through them and put them is some kind of order. Isn't that right?" Rick queried.

"Sure did," replied Harvey.

"You then had to store them, transport them and deliver them to this courtroom," Rick continued.

"Yes."

"As you know, they have been sitting in this courtroom for months now, because they are so important."

"That is correct."

Rick paused as if to suggest he didn't know what he was going to say next. Oh, but he knew. He just didn't want to say it.

"Rather than go through all of these boxes to show the court all of your customers…just show the court one…."

There was a very long pause then Rick repeated……..."Just one of your customers….just one!"

All hell broke loose. Piccone sprang to his feet, yelling, "Objection!"

Rick kept repeating "one" while holding his index finger high in the air. Cappellini started banging his gavel while instructing Rick to stop repeating himself. Rick didn't stop. He kept saying, "Just one," with his index finger held high in the air.

Cowboy Harvey wasn't able to identify one single customer who was his for the court in all of those boxes because there were none. Not one. They had proven beyond a doubt that our marketing was massive and specific, yet they could not show one single incident where we even tried to sell anything to a single one of their customers. They basically had proven our defense which was the fact that I hadn't taken, or even tried to take, a single customer away from my old company. Do you think this mattered to the judge? It was simply an obstacle to look past.

Rick demanded that all of the boxes of exhibits be stricken from the record as evidence. They were not, but they were referred to in the future by Attorney Piccone as a part of the massive record of evidence against me.

One other quick story; during discovery I was required to produce records from all of my other companies in order to have these records photocopied by the opposition. It was a harassment tactic that backfired on them. My adversaries even went after my equipment leasing company, which was not part of the sale and it was something that I was phasing out. In order to be compliant, we loaded up our truck with thousands of dead files, which we delivered to the printing company located in Wilkes-Barre. My adversaries copy bill for just these documents was over $10,000 and there wasn't a single scrap of useful information in any of it. We even told the printing company that we didn't want anything back after they copied everything, so they had to get a dumpster to dispose of everything. There weren't many times I felt good during all of this, so it is important for me to share some of those rare moments.

CHAPTER FOURTEEN

Testifying Turncoats

As I stated much earlier, my friend Matt was very upset that I was selling my company to the family who purchased it. He had repeatedly told me after the sale was final how he was leaving the company as quickly as possible. However, not only did Matt remain with the company, he became Harvey's right hand man. They became joined at the hip, business-wise, as well as socially.

During one day of testimony, Matt was called to the stand as a witness. He raised his hand, swore to tell the truth, the whole truth and nothing but the truth. I still shake my head in disbelief over his statements. Matt testified to the conversations we had had about my idea for a sales company during the time he was in panic mode, except, he turned the incident completely around.

Matt testified that after the sale of the company, I had badgered him to leave his employment and to come work for me in my new company. He also stated that I had tried to extract sensitive and confidential information from him about the inner workings of my former company. I was flabbergasted. Being betrayed by a life-long friend has few equals.

My former Executive Vice President, Joel Guerin, also testified against me. Joel was a very honest and straightforward type of guy. Judging from his mannerism, Joel was not at all comfortable giving his less-than-accurate testimony. I could understand a person spinning the details, but what I couldn't understand was flat-out false testimony. He had a very difficult time. I thought to myself, I sure wish this guy was still on my side. Little did I know, my wish would come true. Shortly after his testimony, Joel's employment was terminated by Harvey.

Joel and I talked extensively after his termination and he agreed to retake the stand to not only correct the record, but to testify that he was forced to stretch the boundaries of honesty. Further, he was willing to state that he had been personally coached by opposing counsel regarding "touchy" testimony and was "required" to misstate facts. When we put Joel on the stand he did and said everything as promised. Piccone told the judge to simply disregard the testimony because Joel was clearly a disgruntled ex-employee. Cappellini followed counsel's advice. Joel went on to become the President of Tempurpedic Mattress Company's institutional division and retired a multi-millionaire. We still stay in touch.

We presented expert witnesses from my Philadelphia based "Big Eight" accounting firm, that clearly showed we had a defense of "unclean hands." In other words, we showed that my adversaries had, in fact, perpetrated material fraud against me. By law, this issue alone would bar them from pursuing the action they were undertaking, regardless of the merits. Cappellini totally disregarded their testimony, even though they were certified as expert witnesses and no rebuttal was offered.

As time went by, days turned into weeks. The next thing I knew, the months were adding up. My new business was doing very well, but occasionally it was necessary for me to go to court for another day of testimony. Both newspapers were present every day I was in the courtroom. Many dozens of stories were written about my case and the judge's escapades. As the reporters began to realize what was going on, they became more and more alarmed. They even went to their editors to explain what was happening in this charade of a trial. The newspaper editors wrote extensively about Cappellini and his friend Attorney Piccone. The Editors of the papers zeroed in on the judge and attorneys incredible lack of concern over appearances. But I knew it was all about the destination. The train was chugging along and they were in complete charge of the locomotive. Nothing was going to stop this excursion.

8A The Times Leader, Wilkes-Barre, PA, Tuesday, November 10, 1992

Judge should recuse himself from this case

Cryco, Inc.

The Times Leader doesn't often give its competitors around the corner a pat on the back. But in the matter of Cryco, Inc., and Larry Hohol, the Citizens' Voice has earned it.

The Voice laid out a story last week that made even cynical observers of Luzerne County politics shake their heads in dismay. It was the rags-to-riches-and-back-to-rags tale of Larry Hohol, a Wyoming Valley businessman. The dismay arose from the apparent zeal with which Judge Gifford Cappellini pushed Hohol down the back-to-rags slope.

Hohol, 36, is a former borough patrolman who made millions in the 1980s through his offbeat inventions. His tinkering with "cryogenics" — the science of extremely low temperatures — won him three U.S. patents and a solid niche in an expanding, high-technology industry.

To make a very long story short, Hohol got sued twice by a former employer, a cryogenics competitor. Luzerne County Judge Patrick Toole dismissed the first suit. An appeals court upheld the dismissal.

The second, similar suit had better luck. Judge Toole was out of town on vacation. In stepped — barged? — Judge Cappellini, who took the case and began a whole new round of hearings. Months later Cappellini ruled against Hohol, effectively shutting down the man's fledgling business.

The appeals court now voided Cappellini's decision. But that must have been small consolation to Hohol, who, by then, was broke.

Oh, by the way. Hohol's nemesis, the attorney representing the competitor in this ordeal — who was he? None other than Arthur Piccone, Judge Cappellini's former law partner.

Judge Cappellini is still handling the case. He shouldn't be. We strongly agree with the Citizens' Voice that Cappellini should turn the case over to another judge. The appearance of a conflict-of-interest is bad enough. The seeming confirmation of it, through Cappellini's eagerness to find in favor of his former partner despite the decisions of Judge Toole and the state appeals court, is worse.

We urge the judge to recuse himself for the next round, and to put Hohol's interests where they have belonged all along: in the hands of a neutral party.

Citizens' Voice Editorial Board
EDWARD P. HOURIGAN — Publisher and President
PAUL GOLIAS — Managing Editor
JUSTIN O'DONNELL — Assistant Managing Editor
JAMES B. GITTENS — Editorial Editor

Editorial

Hohol (Cyrco) case should be given to different judge

Eliminate the appearance of conflict of interest

When a man's livelihood is at stake in a court case, details matter.

That's why the case of "riches-to-rags" local businessman Larry Hohol — and questions about how it has been handled by Luzerne County Court Judge Gifford Cappellini — is drawing attention.

Hohol, a former policeman who invented medical and welding technologies worth millions of dollars, has been bankrupted by lawsuits and a court injunction that closed his company.

He says the lawsuits amount to harassment.

He says the injunction — issued by Judge Gifford Cappellini — raises some suspicion.

What are the concerns?
- An almost identical request for an injunction against Hohol's company was denied by Judge Patrick Toole in 1989.
- The decision of Judge Toole to allow Hohol to stay in business was upheld by a higher court, the Pennsylvania Superior Court.
- Judge Cappellini began his own proceedings in the Hohol case hurriedly during a few days in 1990 when Judge Toole was on vacation.
- Judge Cappellini granted the injunction despite an "interim stay" of the request by yet another county judge, Joseph Augello.
- Judge Cappellini is a former law partner of Attorney Arthur Piccone who represents the company pressing the case against Hohol.
- Another attorney, in another legal case, has held up the Hohol case as an example of a pattern of possible conflict of interest in the relationship between Judge Cappellini and Attorney Piccone.

It is possible, of course, that Judge Cappellini's opinion on the injunction has merit — although it runs totally counter to that of two other county judges and the state Superior Court.

It is also important to point out that Judge Cappellini's decision has not been questioned in any official forum.

However, it can be said that there are enough questions about the divergence in the case and the relationship between Judge Cappellini and Attorney Piccone to call for turning the entire case over to a different judge. A man's livelihood is at stake.

CHAPTER FIFTEEN

I Was **NOT** the Only One

---

*I*t turns out that the "Tag Team" of Judge Cappellini and Attorney Arthur Piccone had been busy making hay with other cases besides mine. Case # 1238-L of 1991 just screams of judicial misconduct. Attorney Piccone and Judge Cappellini were both accused of a number of serious improprieties by Attorney Louis J. Sinatra of the firm Lesser & Kaplin, P.C. located in Blue Bell, Pennsylvania. In this case, once again, Piccone was ruled against by President Judge Patrick Toole. Not being happy with the outcome, Piccone simply did what he did best. He went to his buddy Judge Cappellini.

I have a ton of documents surrounding this case. In an effort to save trees, I have scanned excerpts from the actual Supreme Court documents and included them in the next chapter for your viewing pleasure. I must say that Attorney Sinatra had demonstrated he had a pretty big set. He came into Luzerne County and was getting "home towned" all over the place. Did he roll over, take his fees and go home like most attorneys would have? Nope. He went right after Judge Cappellini and Attorney Piccone.

What is especially striking is the fact that in Attorney Sinatra's Motion for Recusal, he makes the claim in writing that Judge Cappellini was so biased that the judge should not even preside over his own recusal hearing. I told you he had a set.

The Law

Beltrami-Hazleton Bank case takes another detour

By RENITA FENNICK
Citizens' Voice Staff Writer

Proceedings in the ongoing legal dispute between Louis J. Beltrami and the Hazleton National Bank took another detour Friday.

Judge Gifford Cappellini ruled at the scheduled hearing on the contempt of court order filed against Arthur A. Tarone, a bank officer, to postpone further proceedings until Friday, Oct. 23, at 1:30 a.m.

Acting on a request by Tarone's attorney, Louis J. Sinatra of the Blue Bell law firm of Lesser & Kaplin, the jurist delayed further action on the case because Tarone had not yet been served the contempt of court order.

The order was filed July 15, 1992 by the firm of Hourigan, Kluger, Spohrer & Quinn on behalf of Beltrami and one of his holdings, the Concorde Coal Co., Inc.

The actions stem from a complaint for confession of judgment for $1.9 million filed April 18, 1991 by the Hazleton National Bank against Concorde and Beltrami. Tarone, a co-respondent in the case, is the senior vice president of the bank.

Attorney Walker Grabowski of the Hourigan firm, representing Beltrami, offered Friday to dispose of the contempt position if the bank agreed to continue with the proceedings at the time. Attorney Bob Marsh, representing Hazleton National Bank, said he was not ready to proceed since he had been out of the office for six weeks due to a death in the family.

The contempt against Tarone is the result of the bank's decision to freeze $300,000 which was in a checking account that Beltrami maintains with the bank.

Well, as fate would have it, Judge Cappellini felt that it was in the best interests of fairness and justice that he remain the trial judge. Even though all of the dots had been connected by Attorney Sinatra, there was no other judge (according to Cappellini) in Luzerne County who could be fairer. Not only was he the fairest judge in all the land, he now had to decide if Attorney Sinatra should be sanctioned and removed from the case. Oh, yes, you are reading correctly.

Not only was Attorney Sinatra's client found in contempt of court (while he was out of town on vacation), but now Sinatra himself was the one who could be removed. This is called "putting manners" on a hostile attorney. Cappellini wasn't about to bounce this attorney. It had become personal and Cappellini had "ALL" the power. Cappellini's ruling now set the stage for a "Supreme" showdown.

Cappellini won't withdraw, allows Philly law firm to remain in case

By RENITA FENNICK
Citizens' Voice Staff Writer

Both the jurist and the attorney for one of the co-respondents in an ongoing legal dispute between a Hazleton area business and a financial institution will remain involved in the proceedings.

In an order handed down by Judge Gifford Cappellini, filed Monday at the courthouse, the jurist denied two motions stemming from the April 18, 1991 confession of judgment complaint for $1.9 million, filed by the Hazleton National Bank and Arthur A. Tarone against Concorde Coal Co., Inc., and Louis J. Beltrami.

Judge Cappellini denied a motion to disqualify the Philadelphia area law firm of Lesser & Kaplin, and one of its members, Attorney Louis Sinatra, from the case.

The jurist also denied a request filed by Sinatra on behalf of Tarone to have Judge Cappellini removed from the case. Tarone, senior vice president of the bank, is a co-respondent in the case.

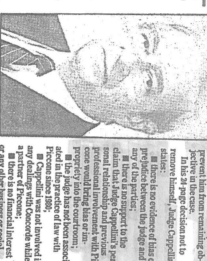

Judge Cappellini

Sinatra on July 28 filed a motion for the recusal of Judge Cappellini, charging the jurist's prior associations with Beltrami and his attorney, Arthur Piccone, would prevent him from remaining objective in the case.

In his 24-page decision not to remove himself, Judge Cappellini states:

■ there is no evidence of bias or prejudice between the judge and any of the parties;

■ there is no support to the claim that Judge Cappellini's personal relationship and previous professional involvement with Piccone would bring any bias or impropriety into the courtroom;

■ the judge has not been associated in the practice of law with Piccone since 1980;

■ Cappellini was not involved in any dealings with Concorde while a partner of Piccone;

■ there is no financial interest or any other business or social relationship between Piccone and Cappellini that would justify recusal of the judge;

■ a judge is not required to disqualify himself when there is insufficient cause to do so.

> If I, applying objective standards, had any doubt as to my fairness to preside, it would not require a recusal motion... I would recuse myself.

During the hearing on the recusal motion, Sinatra pointed to Judge Cappellini's professional and personal association with Piccone and asked the jurist to recuse himself from the case on the grounds that "no fair-minded person could learn of the facts and circumstances surrounding the Piccone/Cappellini relationship and the judge's actions in the Beltrami case) without becoming extremely suspicious of the propriety of the proceedings and the impartiality of the court."

In the decision, Judge Cappellini states: "If I, applying objective standards, had any doubt as to my fairness to preside impartially, it would not require a recusal motion by Tarone; I would recuse myself."

Beltrami's lawyers on Aug. 24 filed a motion asking Judge Cappellini to disqualify Sinatra and his firm from the case on the grounds that Beltrami had been in contact with David N. Bressler, a member of the Lesser & Kaplin firm.

In a hearing on Sept. 2, Attorney David Grabowski of Flourigan, Klinger, Spohrer & Quinn, argued that a 7¼-minute, June 24 telephone call between Beltrami and Bressler is in violation of the Rules of Professional Conduct.

In a four-page decision, Judge Cappellini rules that the testimony of Beltrami did not contradict Bressler's testimony that "no conflict of interest can reasonably be found."

Attorney Grabowski said he would comment on the denial of his motion for disqualification until he had read the decision. Attorney Sinatra could not be reached for comment.

CHAPTER SIXTEEN

I'm a "SUPREME" Example

Well, it is not often that a lawsuit in which you are the main focus is dissected and used as evidence in front of the Supreme Court of Pennsylvania. Attorney Sinatra had his request for an un-bias judge (anyone other than Cappellini) to hear his original Motion of Recusal of Judge Cappellini denied by who else but ------------Judge Cappellini. Imagine that. Judge Cappellini then held a hearing on the motion itself as reflected by the previous newspaper article.

Attorney Sinatra was apparently outraged by the judge's decision and actions so much so, he took an "EXTRAODINARY" measure.

Attorney Sinatra filed a "King's Bench Petition" with the Supreme Court of Pennsylvania!   WOW!

Talk about taking your gloves off. A "King's Bench Petition" is a rarely used measure that takes a matter directly to the Supreme Court for their intervention. The petitioner must show that the ruling in question has a reversible error and that the ruling was made in a form that was not appealable.

The following are actual scanned excerpts of Sinatra's Petition to the Pennsylvania Supreme Court requesting "Extraordinary Relief, and the Recusal of the Trial Judge" (Cappellini). This document contains some VERY SERIOUS allegations and, yes, my case is specifically addressed. Enjoy!

ARTHUR A. TARONE,	:	SUPREME COURT OF PENNSYLVANIA
and	:	
THE HAZLETON NATIONAL BANK,	:	
Petitioners,	:	NO. 1238 L 1991
v.	:	
CONCORDE COAL COMPANY, INC. and LOUIS J. BELTRAMI,	:	
Defendants/Respondents	:	

PETITIONERS', THE HAZLETON NATIONAL BANK AND
ARTHUR A. TARONE'S, PETITION FOR EXTRAORDINARY
JURISDICTION UNDER 42 Pa.C.S.A. §726 AND FOR RECUSAL OF TRIAL JUDGE

TO THE HONORABLE JUDGES OF SAID COURT:

Petitioners, by their attorneys, hereby move the Court to assume plenary jurisdiction pursuant to 42 Pa.C.S.A. §726, to recuse the Honorable Gifford S. Cappellini

8. Defendants are represented by Arthur R. Piccone, Esquire ("Piccone"), a member of the law firm of Hourigan, Kluger, Spohrer and Quinn located in Wilkes-Barre, Pennsylvania (the "Hourigan firm").

9. Prior to his ascending to the Bench as a Judge of the Court of Common Pleas of Luzerne County, Pennsylvania, Judge Cappellini was a member of the Hourigan law firm, and he and Piccone were both partners in the Hourigan firm from 1979 until July 1980; as above, Piccone continues to be a partner in that law firm.

10. Prior to their association in the Hourigan firm, Judge Cappellini and Piccone were also law partners in the firm, Cardoni, Coslett, Cappellini, Sobota & Piccone ("the Cardoni law firm") from 1972 until 1977.

11. While Judge Cappellini and Piccone were both partners in the Cardoni law firm, that firm represented Defendant Louis J. Beltrami, and at least two of his affiliated companies, in substantial matters involving millions of dollars in transactions.

12. Judge Cappellini and Piccone are close personal friends.

31. During the same conference in chambers, however, Judge Cappellini admitted that Defendants' attorney came into his chambers (without the appearance of Plaintiff's counsel) and requested an expedited hearing.

32. Based upon statements from Judge Cappellini evidencing that he had substantial personal knowledge of facts relevant and indeed critical to the disposition of the recusal motion, Tarone's counsel requested that Judge Cappellini not hear the recusal motion but instead recuse himself since the averments in the motion and the statements made by Judge Cappellini in chambers evidenced that recusal was necessary and appropriate. Counsel for Tarone requested in the alternative that the Court assign another Judge to hear the recusal.

33. Judge Cappellini refused to recuse himself during the conference and instead advised that he would schedule a hearing; he denied Tarone's counsel's request that the matter be assigned to another Judge for hearing and instead, as more particularly noted below, presided over the recusal hearing.

34. The recusal hearings were conducted on August 11, 1992 and August 14, 1992 and were marked by colloquy from the Judge indicating that he had knowledge of critical, relevant facts; indeed, the proceedings were marked by Judge Cappellini's interrupting counsel to provide the Judge's version of the history of his relationship with Piccone and the history of the proceedings.

35. Counsel for Tarone, Louis J. Sinatra, Esquire, confirmed certain of the statements made by Judge Cappellini during the chambers conference on the record during the recusal hearing of August 11, 1992 and relevant portions of the transcript of the recusal hearing reflecting certain of the colloquy between counsel and Judge

present an application for stay to Judge Cappellini (N.T. 8/11/92 at 175-180). Accordingly, when pressed on this issue, it became undisputed during the cross-examination of Piccone that Bank was not present when Defendants' lawyers met with Judge Cappellini and obtained the stay of the Bucyrus-Erie equipment and that Bank's counsel had no notice of the requested stay.

U. That Judge Toole did not grant the request for expedited hearing (N.T. 8/11/92 at 187).

V. That on July 17, 1992, Piccone presented a Motion for Expedited Hearing to Judge Cappellini (N.T. 8/11/92 at 187-188).

W. That the Motion for Expedited Hearing with respect to the Second Petition for Contempt was presented to Judge Cappellini on an ex parte basis without notice to Bank's counsel (N.T. 8/11/92 at 188).

X. That Bank's counsel's office was (and still is) located less than two blocks from the Courthouse; notwithstanding the proximity of Bank's counsel's offices to the Courthouse, no notice of the application for expedited hearing was given in the case (N.T. 8/11/92 at 191). Accordingly, this witness fully admitted to two occasions when defense counsel met with Judge Cappellini on important matters where Plaintiff's lawyers were neither present nor afforded notice of the intention to seek relief from the Court.

BB. Piccone also acknowledged that he represented plaintiffs in two separate companion cases, viz, Essex Industries, Inc. and Penox Technologies, Inc. formerly Big Ben Group Limited v. Larry Hohol (Hohol I) and Essex Industries, Inc. and Penox Technologies, Inc. formerly Big Ben Group Limited v. Larry Hohol and Cryco, Inc. (Hohol II) (N.T. 8/11/92 at 208-209, 213,219-220).

CC. That both cases, to wit, Hohol I and Hohol II, were brought against Hohol (the second case also included a company purportedly owned and controlled by him) based upon restrictive covenants Hohol had granted and delivered to Piccone's clients when those clients purchased Hohol's business from him (N.T. 8/11/92 at 220-223).

DD. Piccone's clients sought a preliminary injunction in both of the foregoing cases enforcing the restrictive covenants and enjoining Hohol from competing with Piccone's clients in alleged breach of the restrictive covenants (N.T. 8/11/92 at 211-212; 8/14/92 at 5; T-26, T-29).

EE. Hohol I was assigned to President Judge Toole and came before the President Judge for hearings on the application for preliminary injunction; following those contested hearings, the requested preliminary injunction was denied (N.T. 8/14/92 at 5-6).

FF. Approximately eleven months later, Piccone filed Hohol II on behalf of the exact same plaintiffs involved in Hohol I (N.T. 8/11/92 at 220; 8/14/92 at

GG. That case also included a request for preliminary injunction and the preliminary injunction matter in Hohol II, based upon the same restrictive covenants at issue in Hohol I, came before Judge Cappellini for hearing (N.T. 8/11/92 at 221-223; 8/14/92 at 10-11).

HH. Prior to the hearings conducted by Judge Cappellini on the requested preliminary injunction in Hohol II, plaintiffs had filed an appeal to the Superior Court in connection with Hohol I (N.T. 8/14/92 at 8).

II. That contrary to the decision of President Judge Toole in the first case, Judge Cappellini granted the request for preliminary injunction (N.T. 8/14/92 at 18-19).

JJ. That Judge Cappellini's initial Order granting the preliminary injunction afforded plaintiffs in Hohol II a preliminary injunction without requiring the filing of a bond in contravention of Pa. R.C.P. 1531. (N.T. 8/14/92 at 20-22).

KK. That the Superior Court of Pennsylvania has affirmed President Judge Toole's denial of the requested preliminary injunction in Hohol I (N.T. 8/14/92 at 8-9). (The Superior Court has now reversed Judge Cappellini's grant of preliminary injunction).

LL. Relevant portions of the Notes of Testimony containing the foregoing admissions are attached hereto as Exhibit "D."

41. Accordingly, there was no good faith question but that Tarone's allegations were accurate, providing a substantial basis for recusal. In addition to the foregoing admissions by Piccone, the evidence at the recusal hearing was also uncontroverted on the following issues:

A. That Judge Cappellini failed to dispose of the Petition to Open for a period of sixteen months (N.T. 8/11/92 at 45) (following the recusal hearing, the Judge entered an Opinion and Order opening judgment);

-14-

F. That Judge Cappellini entertained ex parte applications from the defense on no less than two separate occasions (N.T. 8/11/92 at 56-57, 68);

J. That defense counsel in Hohol II asked Judge Cappellini to defer decision in the preliminary injunction matter in that case as a consequence of Judge Toole's denial of preliminary injunction and the appeal in the prior pending case (Petition for Stay filed in Hohol II and denied by Judge Cappellini was made exhibit T-44 at the Recusal Hearing);

K. Judge Cappellini refused to stay proceedings in Hohol II (T-44).

42. Canon 3 of the Code of Judicial Conduct provides:

> The judicial duties of a judge take precedence over all his other activities. His judicial duties include all the duties of his office prescribed by law. In the performance of these duties the following standards apply
>
> . . .
>
> (A) (4) A judge should accord to every person who is legally interested in a proceeding, or his lawyer, full right to be heard according to law, and, except as authorized by law, must not consider ex parte communications concerning a pending proceeding.
>
> (5) A judge should dispose promptly of the business of the court. (Emphasis supplied).

43. Canon 3(C)(1) provides in pertinent part:

> A judge should disqualify himself in a proceeding in which his impartiality might reasonably be questioned. . . .

44. Despite the overwhelming evidence of substantial bases for recusal, on September 28, 1992, Judge Cappellini entered his Order denying the Petition for Recusal (copy of Opinion and Order attached as Exhibit "E").

45. As your Honorable Court will note from a review of the Opinion and Order of September 28, 1992 denying, inter alia, the Motion for Recusal, that Opinion itself raises serious issues for the following reasons:

A. Judge Cappellini's acknowledgement at two separate parts of the Opinion of his personal relationship with Piccone (see pages 6 and 7 of the Opinion);

B. Judge Cappellini's failure to adequately take into account the seriousness of the ex parte discussions and ex parte relief afforded by him to Defendants. More particularly, the Opinion addresses only one of the two ex parte applications known by Petitioners to have occurred in the case. Accordingly, the Opinion ignores one of the two ex parte applications and literally attempts to excuse the second ex parte disposition afforded by Judge Cappellini to the defense.

C. Among other matters, the Opinion states: "The stay was only predicated upon a hearing to be held as expeditiously as possible. Substantive rights of

46. Recusal is required whenever there is substantial doubt as to a jurist's ability to preside impartially. See Commonwealth v. Darush, 501 Pa. 15, 459 A.2d 727 (1983).

47. In the present case, there is substantial doubt as to Judge Cappellini's ability to preside impartially over the remainder of this proceeding for the following reasons:

    (A) Judge Cappellini's relationship with defense counsel and their prior legal association both in the Cardoni firm and the Hourigan firm;

    (B) The prior representation of Defendants or those associated

48. Serious public issues concerning questions relating to Judge Cappellini's fairness and impartiality have also been raised in another proceeding in Luzerne County, to wit, a criminal case styled Commonwealth of Pennsylvania v. Henry Rush ("Rush Case").

49. The Rush Case has become a public issue in the Luzerne County area

resulting in widespread media attention as evidenced by the newspaper articles attached hereto as Exhibit "G."

50. As the Court will note from the media articles on the Rush Case, Judge Cappellini's son, Gifford Cappellini, Jr., an attorney practicing in Luzerne County, obtained a work release order from his father for the son's client, Henry Rush.

51. The work release order was signed by Judge Cappellini on behalf of his son's client, notwithstanding the fact that Mr. Rush was at the time of the work release order a prisoner incarcerated for a violent crime, to wit, attempted homicide and aggravated assault occurring where Mr. Rush stabbed one Thomas Day of Wilkes-Barre in the throat, apparently damaging his trachea and esophagus and causing his lung to collapse.

52. Mr. Rush had served just three days of an eighteen month sentence at the time of the work release issued by Judge Cappellini.

53. Furthermore, Judge Cappellini entered the work release order notwithstanding the fact that the case had previously been presided over by another judge in Luzerne County.

62. It is respectfully submitted that any hearing in connection with the contempt should be stayed pending your Honorable Court's review and disposition of this Petition, especially since the King's Bench Petition raises very serious questions with respect to the appropriateness of Judge Cappellini disposing of any further issues in connection with this case.

WHEREFORE, Petitioners respectfully request this Honorable Court to enter relief in the form attached hereto.

Respectfully submitted,

LESSER & KAPLIN, P.C.

By: _____
LOUIS J. SINATRA, ESQUIRE
MICHAEL P. COUGHLIN, ESQUIRE

Please keep in mind that the proceeding document was actually presented to the Supreme Court of Pennsylvania.

I spoke to Attorney Sinatra in 2010 and discussed this case with him. Turns out he remembered my name. I told him I was flattered that after all these years, he remembered me even though we had never met. I also told him that it concerned me that soooo many attorneys remember my name. He got a chuckle out of that.

Turns out the Supreme Court denied his King's Bench Warrant with not so much as a comment. A simple "Denied" was all he got. It amazes me that an attorney could include so much information about outrageous misconduct and the Supreme Court of Pennsylvania did nothing and said nothing. If the attorney was lying, something should be done about the attorney. If the judge was doing half of what is claimed, something should be done about the judge. For the Supreme Court to do nothing about either just sounds plain wrong to me, but that's just me.

I have taken great pains to insert actual copies of newspaper articles and excerpts of court documents into this book for a reason. It would be one thing for me to make outrageous claims and then quote from these documents. It is quite another to present the documents to you in all their glory. It is my goal in doing so to attempt to remove or dramatically reduce the amount of "interpretation bias" I possess. It is my hope that you, as the reader, do not have to rely entirely on my tainted opinions. I have bias and I am tainted, but the facts are the facts.

CHAPTER SEVENTEEN

Back To My Case

---

*M*y adversaries knew how much money they had paid me. They were aware of what the hourly rate was for my attorneys and they also knew how much I had to pay in income tax. Anyone could take a guess at my living expenses, and then there was the funding of a startup company. They knew it was just a matter of time before I would be out of money. I strongly believe that is why my trial intentionally lasted seventeen days and stretched out over nine months.

I finally hit critical mass financially. My wife of twelve years sat me down and said, "Honey, I will always love you." I could hear a "but" coming. "It has been one hell of a ride on the way up, *but* you are now going down the backside of the rollercoaster and I'm not going down with you." Enough said on this subject.

My attorneys called a special meeting at the ten story office building they owned in downtown Wilkes-Barre. All of the senior partners were in attendance. After a lot of discussion, the most senior of the partners spoke up, stating he was speaking for everyone in the room. The entire firm had been following what was happening to me, and it was certainly a travesty of justice. He acknowledged that they all valued me as a client, as reflected by our ten year history. Then he pledged all of the resources of the firm to continue the fight, even without getting paid. They, as a firm, would not abandon me or my company no matter how long the battle, especially when confronted by such an injustice. Everyone clapped their hands and yelled, "Here, here!" It was sort of a mini pep rally.

As the last partner shook my hand on his way out of the board room, the "Master of Ceremonies" asked if I would come to his office. Once I got there he stated that since the firm was going to commit whatever resources it would take to win, he was wondering if I would have any problem signing a document that allowed the firm to place a lien against my million dollar home. I stood there absolutely stunned. I was not prepared to be blindsided in this fashion. I signed the lien papers, all the while feeling I was not doing the right thing. I wasn't.

Within a few weeks of perfecting the lien against my home, the law firm filed to withdraw as my counsel from all of the litigation that they were involved with on my behalf. They were allowed to withdraw from everything with the exception of the injunctive hearing. The noose was tightening and now I was almost completely on my own.

I still had hearings to attend, documents to prepare and asses to kick. You have got to be kidding me, I thought. I didn't even have a place to live. At the request of my soon-to-be-ex-wife, I had moved out of my own house. I was down, but I was not out.

You know that old saying, "He who represents himself as a client, represents a fool." I still had a number of other cases that were active and winnable, such as a mortgage foreclosure on my old building and material fraud charges against these fine people. Thank God, one of my friends was a Paralegal. He not only helped me, he did it for free. As he put it, this was the way for his law firm to give back to the good people of the community. I never asked but I suspected that he did most, if not all, of the typing of my motions and responses on company time using the law firm's computers.

Everything I submitted looked as good as my high priced law firm's paperwork and it was properly researched. My friend apparently received some sort of joy out of that part. The lawyers he worked for were so lazy that they did not even sign most of the official papers that they were required to, he did. He often told me that if any of his attorneys actually signed anything, it would probably be rejected as a forged signature. The judge knew I was secretly getting help from someone out there, and he didn't like it.

To say things were desperate at this point is an understatement. I had more than one friend tell me how much they admired the fact that I had neither killed the judge nor committed suicide. All kidding aside, they really said that and meant it.

For a brief time during the beginning of the trial, my attorneys had half-heartedly convinced me that we were going to win this case on the merits. In my heart, I didn't believe them, but I had no other alternative but to follow their lead. I knew, without a doubt, that this judge was going to rule against me. I was also beginning to figure out why he was taking so long to do it. After all, Cappellini was really taking a beating in the press. Why would he continue on for so long without a motive? Maybe there was the hope that I would commit suicide or get killed in a car wreck after drowning my sorrows at the local watering hole. Obviously, neither happened.

CHAPTER EIGHTEEN

*B*rass Tacks

On the bright side, my new business was booming. We had built sales up to just over $80,000.00 per month and I had fourteen really good, full-time employees. The company was paying its own bills and, due to a deep discount program for prompt pay, even the cash flow was good. I had dramatically reduced most of my personal living expenses by living at my brother David's house. I thought that if things keep going this way, I could hire a new law firm. That's what I get for thinking.

It was like they knew I was getting stronger instead of weaker. I didn't put out press releases or even brag to my friends about how well the company was doing. Maybe that private detective had traded in his truck and aluminum fishing boat for a fake tree trunk. I imagined him reporting back to Harvey like Maxwell Smart, obscured from view by a phony tree. He would call Harvey from his shoe phone while hidden amongst the maples of the playground he enjoyed so much.

There was a lot of activity at my business for him to observe. Trucks constantly could be seen pulling up to our loading docks and the employee parking lot was overflowing. Then there was the fact that many of my former employees at Penox were approaching me for a job.

Under Harvey's stewardship, things had slowed down considerably at my old company. There were rumors of layoffs. I was sure that somehow Harvey was telling his brothers in St. Louis that I was responsible. I could almost hear him saying, "I know Hohol has been gone for over two years, but we are still finding things that he screwed up."

Then one day, as abruptly as the lawsuit had started, opposing counsel rested its case. Nine months of hell, in which there were a total of fourteen days of testimony to date, finally their case came to an end. Now it was our turn for the defense.

We called our witnesses and attacked the issues head on. Since they really hadn't proven their case at all, we needed to be careful. We didn't want to validate nonsensical evidence that never should have been allowed into the record by defending each and every bullshit point. On the other hand, in cases where they lied in order to make their point, we needed to act. We had to provide hard evidence and rebuttal testimony.

I was probably still working under the misconception that there was no way the evidence could support their claims, so this judge couldn't or shouldn't rule against me. We put Harvey back on the stand for a re-cross examination. I had come up with my own legal theory. The fact that I had started thinking like an attorney still bothers me.

We put a copy of the original non-competitive agreement into Harvey's hands. He had already testified to the existence of the document and its validity. Out came the white handkerchief. Rick asked him to read into the record the "requirements" of the contract. First, my requirements as the seller, which were written using standard contract terminology, but were very specific.

Harvey spoke clearly and loud enough for tour groups in the hallway to hear him. He appeared to enjoy reading the specifics of my requirements. Then he was told to read the buyer's requirements. Piccone kept objecting, but couldn't come up with a reason that could remotely work for him. After all, this contract was the basis of the action before the court. Even Cappellini was getting fidgety. The newspaper reporters were writing down every syllable.

It has been established by the Supreme Court of the United States that in order for a non-competition contract to be valid, the person who is being restricted must be fairly compensated. That is again like non-compete law 101. Rick had Harvey read the compensation portion of the contract into the record. It was simple:

they were required to pay me $100,000 per year and in exchange for that compensation, I agreed not to compete.

Rick then took Harvey back to the day the company was sold. Harvey was not present at the closing, but in prior testimony he had been allowed to testify as to the events of that day. Rick had to remind the judge of that fact after opposing counsel objected to Ricks question once again.

Harvey testified that he knew for a fact I was paid $100,000 on closing day in compliance with the non-competitive agreement, and I was. Rick then had him work the timeline. Harvey testified that the first $100,000 payment covered the period from December 28, 1988, till December 27, 1989.

Piccone was getting very agitated and demanded that the judge stop this line of questioning as there was apparently no point to it. Cappellini looked at the reporters who were writing feverously. He had to, at the very least, give the appearance of fairness. So, the judge declared that he would allow Rick to continue, but he needed to get to the point quickly or he would order everything stricken from the record. I thought; imagine that, after all of the crap he allowed the other side to put into the record, here he is threatening to strike this portion.

Rick continued on by asking Harvey to identify the dates for the second year of the five year contract. He answered, matter-of-factly, "That would be December 28, 1989 to December 27, 1990."

Rick said, "Thank you," and stopped talking. He walked back to my table, shuffled some papers and wrote a note on my tablet. The note read, "This is great!" As he slowly walked back to Harvey, I believe I saw Harvey change to a new handkerchief. Opposing counsel was fit to be tied. If Piccone could have, he would have objected to us breathing.

Rick spoke loudly for my two reporter audience. "As we are all aware, you and your counsel have entered into the record a literal mountain of exhibits," Rick said, pointing to the stacks of silent jurists.

"Objection, Your Honor, I didn't hear a question," Piccone yelled out.

The judged looked down his nose through the non-existent bifocals and said in a scolding tone, "This is your last warning. You need to ask questions and get to your point quickly."

Piccone stood up to proclaim, "I want the record to show that Attorney Russo is providing argument and not cross examination. These proceedings have drug on long enough. This court's time is very valuable and it now appears that Attorney Russo is just trying to prolong these proceedings while his client is hoping for a miracle. This is just ridiculous."

We knew what he was doing and as much as Rick and I wanted to run down that road to expose what was really going on, we didn't. Piccone had just finished up his fifteen days worth of testimony and we were on our second. Unbelievable!

The thought occurred to me that the other side must have just paid a large legal bill and said, "No more." Rumor on the street was that my old company was now losing money like there was no tomorrow.

Rick looked at Cappellini and said, "Your Honor, I promise to phrase my next statement in the form of a question and I promise to get to my point as I am now aware that your time is very valuable."

It was obvious that both reporters caught the sarcasm because they smirked. Rick wasn't making any points with the judge, but we both knew that didn't matter.

Rick turned quickly to Cowboy Harvey. Harvey had gotten caught up in the attorney bashing festivities, so Rick caught him off guard and off balance.

"In that entire mountain of paperwork, or anywhere else for that matter, can you show the court a copy of the second $100,000 payment that you made as required by the contract you are holding in your hand?"

If you think all hell breaks loose when a piñata is finally smashed open at a 5 year olds birthday party, you should have been there for this reaction. Not only was Piccone up on his feet objecting, but Judge Cappellini half stood up himself, also objecting. I couldn't believe it. He was banging his gavel, trying to bring the court to order while loudly objecting to the question. It was like they were both moving in slow motion, but speaking in double time. They were falling all over each other while Rick stood motionless without saying another word. Cappellini continued to bang his gavel until he realized that the only two people in the courtroom who were out of order were his best friend and himself. After an awkward moment they both looked at each other and stopped. The courtroom remained silent for a few moments but Rick knew he needed to head the judge off at the pass.

"Your Honor, if I may," Rick attempted to say.

The judge shook his poisoned dart finger at him and said, "You may not."

Rick knew Cappellini was going to shut him down, but he had more to say, so he spoke loudly. He turned away from the judge and addressed the reporters.

"I am simply trying to show that they are only entitled to the amount of protection under the contract that they have paid for. They paid for one year and they got one year. That fact is not even in dispute."

Other floors of the Courthouse could probably hear Cappellini smashing his gavel as if he were using it to crush walnuts. He demanded that Rick stop, but he didn't.

"Until they pay for the second year, they are not entitled to a second year of protection, no matter what. They are here in this courtroom trying to enforce one part of the contract while they are in material breach of another section of the same contract."

At that point Rick spun on his heels and very dramatically pointed his own poisoned dart finger at the judge and said, "And you are allowing them to do it!"

He then stopped talking and just stood there. Cappellini ceased smashing his gavel, and even Piccone shut up. For a few seconds, it seemed like one of those moments in a second rate TV series where the brilliant lawyer finally confronts the real killer and brings him to confess on the stand. But there was no confession and this was not one of those moments.

"I know what you are trying to do here and I will not permit it," Cappellini stated, turning to the stenographer. "Strike this testimony from the record."

The stenographer started flipping back through her cash register-style papers extending out from the back of her little mini typewriter looking machine. She looked up at the judge and asked, "How far back, Your Honor?"

Cappellini looked at both of us and declared, "All the way back to, please rise." Well, that went well, I thought, sarcastically to myself.

I have always been outraged by the above "highlighted" quote. The judge tried to make it sound as if we were trying to do something illegal or unethical. We were simply pointing out a fact that a first year law student would probably know and understand. The fact was that even if I was competing directly with my old company, Essex was not entitled to protection from the court because they simply hadn't paid for the protection "AS REQUIRED." That fact alone made the ENTIRE trial a moot point and Judge Cappellini knew it.

Well, we put our expert witnesses on the stand from my Philadelphia "Big Eight Accounting Firm" as well as myself and a few other witnesses. We countered EVERYTHING of substance that they had presented as evidence. Since they hadn't presented much of a case, the defense portion of the trial was over in a day and a half. Now we had to wait.

CHAPTER NINETEEN

Game Over

I almost think Piccone typed the order himself and simply had the judge sign it. Of course, I have no proof of that, I just had that feeling. Even though I was mentally preparing myself for the inevitable, the shock that flowed through my nerve tips was unexpectedly stunning.

According to the order, not only was I shut down, I couldn't even finish the repair work that was in progress. That meant I would have to crate up hundreds of pieces of industrial cryogenic tanks that had been disassembled for repair and ship it back to all of my customers in pieces. Those companies would never do business with me again, no matter what.

When my secretary heard about the court order, she freaked out, literally running from the building. Nothing I could say to her was sufficient to convince her that she would not go to jail if she stayed to help me clean up.

"I see what the judge is doing to you and I'm out of here," she said. That was the last time I ever saw her. I even had to mail her last paycheck to her because she wouldn't come to the office to get it.

I gathered together my remaining thirteen employees to give them the bad news. Some employees offered to work for nothing, thinking if I didn't pay them that somehow we could skirt around the court order. I thanked them for their offer, but I wasn't going to do that. No, even though the situation was unfair, we were going to play by the rules.

I kept looking at the court order like it wasn't real. It seemed impossible that here, in America, something like this could happen. On the positive side, it seemed that everywhere I turned I had the support of the local community. I made new arrangements with my landlord. He allowed me to store my equipment in a considerably smaller space than I was originally renting from him, at a fraction of the price. Even my accountant, Gene Rich, wouldn't send me a bill. I couldn't go anywhere in the county without total strangers stopping me to say how they had been following my story in the papers and that this was a shame. Most everyone told me to give those bastards hell and keep up the fight. I surmised they watched a lot of Disney movies, too.

About a week after all the dust settled, I sat down with my copy of the court order. I needed to start working on the appeal since I had only thirty days to file my "Notice of Appeal." I thought about how counterproductive it was to expend all this energy. If only this effort could go into building or fixing something. It was during this time in my life that I lost all interest in one of my lifelong favorite sports, hunting. I just couldn't kill anything for sport anymore.

I read and re-read the brief court order as if by doing so I could find an error in it. I was completely overwhelmed with the task at hand, an appeal to the Superior Court of Pennsylvania. I thought about the difficulty of this endeavor. I was a businessman not an attorney. Seemingly outrageous claims would have to be made about not only judicial misconduct and judicial error, but also judicial incompetence and conspiracy. I had all the evidence in writing. I could show the court example after example. Then I had an unnerving thought: If I hadn't been there to see this with my own eyes, I wouldn't believe a word of it. Would the court believe what I presented?

The fact that both newspapers basically reported what I saw, gave me great comfort. The problem with that was, their observations and articles could not be considered as evidence in a court of law. I had this sick feeling that Superior Court would think that I had ridden off the rails of the Crazy Train. My job was to show them it was really an *Express Run* of the "Luzerne County Railroad."

I had heard through the grapevine that there was a law firm in town that had more than a few run-ins with the Cappellini and

Piccone "tag team." Maybe they could help. I met with one of the namesakes of the firm. Surprisingly, I didn't have to fill in many blanks for him. Apparently, not only had the general public been following my story in the papers like it was the hottest soap opera on TV, but the legal community at large was quite interested as well. My case had been the topic of many a legal gathering, both official and social.

It wasn't until then that I realized the volume of information that had been printed about me and my case. I spent seventeen separate days in trial. Each newspaper wrote a minimum of one new article for every day I was in court. Feature stories were written about my meteoric rise into the local, state, national and international business communities. There were personal stories about my family and investigative stories about the judge's prior "outrageous" rulings that exposed the common thread between Piccone and Cappellini, as well as Cappellini's bias.

Each and every press release that I had issued was in print, not to mention the "Letters to the Editor." Then there were the incredible editorials written by the two competing newspapers. If one paper took a position on any given issue, the other could be expected to take a contrary view, but not in this instance. The only time these two newspapers even acknowledged that the other existed was when they were able to write negative stories about each other. The union strike that had divided the two papers had pitted brother against brother and father against son. One of the newspapers was actually a spinoff of the other. The Wilkes-Barre Times Leader Unionized and went on strike. The strike was long and very ugly. The Citizen's Voice was born of this strike and became the "union" paper and the Times Leader then continued as the non-union paper. Coal miners and their children are not a very forgiving group. We make the best friends in the world, until we are wronged.

It gave me confidence to see that I wasn't crazy. A whole lot of people who were smarter than me were sharing the same observations as I was. I can honestly say that without the support I received from the community, I probably would have lost it. For as alone as I felt at times, I knew I wasn't. We may get off track once in a while, but there are no finer people in the world than the residents of Luzerne County, Pennsylvania.

It wasn't long before I realized that the attorney I was sitting in front of was willing to commit his law firm to represent me in my appeal. "Pete" was a very conservative man, both in dress and in his mannerisms. He was a Deacon at his church and very active in the community. A large man in stature, he had a melodious voice that would have been well suited for radio or TV commercials. When Pete spoke, people listened. Pete was well respected by all.

Instead of getting right down to the nuts and bolts of my situation, Pete started telling me some stories about cases in which he had experienced similar situations with Attorney Piccone as opposing counsel. He spoke about multiple cases that had no business coming in front of Judge Cappellini, but magically ended up in Cappellini's courtroom anyway and how the judge ruled in his friend's favor every single time. Pete looked me square in the eye and said, "These two sons' of bitches have been getting away with this shit for way too long," without looking embarrassed after he said what he did. Over the next few years, I never heard another bad word come out of his mouth. That statement came from his soul.

After Pete finished his stories, he looked at the court order that I had been holding in my hand for the last forty-five minutes. It had become more than just a little wrinkled. Apparently, listening to his stories struck a nerve with me and without realizing it I had taken it out on the paper.

"Ok, where is a copy of their bond?" Pete asked.

I looked at him and shrugged my shoulders and said, "As far as I know, they don't have one."

He looked at me and said, as if to scold me, "You know that they are required to post a reasonable amount of bond *before* this order can be enforced to shut you down?"

I looked at him, puzzled at first, and then I wanted to hit myself in the head like that commercial, "I could have had a V8!"

Now I remembered. The subject was even broached during my trial. At some point we put it in the record that if for some outrageous reason the court were to issue the Preliminary

Injunction, a substantial bond would be required by my adversaries. We even went onto explain to the court in detail the scope of the success my ongoing business was enjoying. My adversaries had all of my financial information through expedited, court ordered, discovery. We figured we would just cover our bases. Judge Cappellini had acknowledged that he understood what we were doing and why.

Pete declared, "This court order is not enforceable without a bond in place."

I was stunned but then my brain clicked into hyper drive. That meant that I shouldn't have closed. That meant I could re-open. "Go forth and prosper." More than anything, it meant that I could show just how biased the judge was because he had granted opposing counsel extraordinary relief by knowingly not requiring my adversaries to post a bond or risk a single penny of their money in order to shut me down. I had to make some calls, I needed to reopen.

Pete said, "Before you go off the deep end, let's think this through."

I told him that I found it hard to believe that the judge could have forgotten about the bond requirement. Pete assured me that he hadn't forgotten because even a law student knows that you cannot shut down an ongoing business with a Preliminary Injunction without covering all possible financial harm should the Injunction be reversed on appeal.

"It is a requirement that has no exceptions," he said. "It is like Preliminary Injunctions 101, if you will."

The judge was not a law student. He spent many years in private practice (with Piccone) and had been a judge for over 10 years. Additionally, we reminded him of this specific requirement during the trial. No……..he hadn't forgotten.

CHAPTER TWENTY

The Horns of a Dilemma

---

*N*aturally, I wanted to call my workers back to the factory as soon as that afternoon and issue a press release. Pete told me to do neither. He didn't want to tip our hand because we needed to get the notice of appeal filed in order to lock Cappellini out of the proceedings. Once my case got bumped up to the higher court, Cappellini couldn't screw around with it anymore, no matter what his inclination. Jurisdiction would be officially transferred and the case would be stripped away from Cappellini's influence once the appeal was formalized. I was ecstatic. Not only could I reopen, but I could get this entire matter out of Judge Cappellini's hands. Beer and chicken wings for everyone!

Pete moved quickly. Within a day or two our Notice of Appeal was filed. Cappellini was officially out of the picture. Not only that, but this insured that one of the conductors on the "Luzerne County Express" had been removed by the forces of good. We would now be dealing with only half of the evil. Maybe there was some hope after all. Maybe Disney had the right idea.

I couldn't wait to hand deliver my press release to the newspapers. As you can imagine at this stage of the game, I still was haunted by a sub-conscious warning transmitting in the back of my mind.

Pete and his firm were now officially on record as my attorneys. The appeal was officially acknowledged as received and docketed in Philadelphia. Not only had the press releases been printed in both papers, but major, very favorable stories about me and my situation were published. It was almost as if the newspapers and their staff were celebrating the end of World War

II. The injunction was not only unenforceable but it was unenforceable due to a biased omission by the "Judge from Hell."

When I stated earlier that no matter what happened going forward, my customers would never do business with me again, I wasn't kidding. I pondered my dilemma. Now that I could reopen, where the heck would I draw business from? Before I could call my employees back, I had to make some contacts. I began dialing the phone, but didn't have any success. Just as I was trying to figure out who to call next, the phone rang. I thought maybe it was a customer who had heard we were back in business. I answered the phone like things were really hopping at my end. It was Pete. He asked if I had re-opened. I told him, no. Before I could tell him that I was having a hell of a time with my old customers, he told me, don't.

I asked, "Don't what?"

"Don't reopen."

Oh boy, I thought, what now? Pete started reading me a copy of a "Motion for Reconsideration." I stopped him and asked, "Why would we file a motion for reconsideration since we already filed an appeal?"

He politely, but firmly, told me to be quiet as he continued. After he was done, I was really confused.

"Why the, who the, where the, what the....?" I just didn't understand.

It wasn't *our* "Motion for Reconsideration" that Pete was reading. Attorney Piccone had filed this motion following our appeal to Superior Court, but before the thirty day window had expired where such a motion could be filed, or could it?

I asked, "How could a party to a lawsuit file a "Motion for Reconsideration" after the judge has already ruled 100% in their favor? What is there to reconsider? They had won."

Pete told me that it obviously had everything to do with the bond issue. He added that he had never seen or heard of a party who had totally prevailed request that a judge reconsider his or her decision. Once again, it was unprecedented. Pete said that we were in uncharted waters and that he would file an objection. He also told me the objection would be denied because this judge was going to do what he wanted to, regardless of the rules. Pete repeated his earlier instruction. "Don't reopen."

I thought to myself, I guess it was good that I didn't get any business while I was on the phone. I thought what an optimistic twist I had just put on a bad situation. It also entered my mind that I was a very stupid optimist. I stopped making phone calls.

CHAPTER TWENTY-ONE

*N*ot You Again

I walked into the courtroom as I had so many times before. I thought to myself, "Murder trials don't last this long." I now had a new legal team. I was still alive, but just barely. The judge thought he had pulled the plug on me three weeks ago, but everything was still on life support. Hey, I am the stubborn grandson of a Czechoslovakian coal miner. I was too strong to die. I am sure Cappellini felt that I was just too dumb to die. After all, his father was a boss in the same coal mines where my grandfather had worked as a low-life laborer. Cappellini's father made enough money off the back of my grandfather and people like him to send this future judge to college as well as law school. I felt he looked at me just as his father probably looked at all the other low life laborers. You could just feel the contempt.

After a few minutes, everyone settled in. I noticed that the judge was sitting differently than was usual in his lofty "God-like" perch. His body was sort of sideways, facing away from the two senior reporters who had sat through all of the previous proceedings. He considered them the enemy and knew they had their microscopes clearly focused on him and what he was about to do. The judge also knew what he was about to do was not only wrong, but that it was outrageously wrong. Although he realized he was going to get extremely bad reviews for his conduct, that didn't seem to matter.

As I have stated previously, it's all about the final destination. That's the only thing that matters and there is nothing anyone can do to change the course of the train no matter how bad it looked. The two reporters were not only competitors of each other they were at war with each other and had been for years. These two reporters had been reporting to the public everything the judge had done and said in this courtroom for the past nine months. Everything that Judge Cappellini was accustomed to normally getting away with, was now published in black and white for all to see. Even though almost all of the articles written about the case sounded similar, they came from two totally different perspectives. In almost all cases, the judge's actions were brought into question.

Today would be just one more story. Besides, the reporters weren't judges, they weren't even lawyers. These were common folk with no real understanding of the complicated world of law. They were incapable of understanding the law even if the judge were inclined to explain it to them. If the coal mines had still been open, reporters would have been ranked lower in standing than the mules that pulled the coal cars, that is, if they had the good fortune to be reporters rather than miners. When a miner was killed, there were a hundred more just like him that were more than willing to take his place as soon as the body was pulled out of the way. But if a mule came up lame, it was truly a tragedy. It was as if this distain for the lower class had been placed permanently in this judge's genetic code, in one single generation.

Pete was unable to be at this hearing due to a prior trial. He left my defense in the very capable hands of one of his partners, "Glenn." The judge wasted no time before getting right to business. After all, the morning was getting late and I'm sure the judge didn't want to miss the Thursday Lunch Special at the Uptown Restaurant. It was like he was sure that after today's festivities his good buddy would insist on picking up the tab.

Glenn asked if he could address the court. The judge looked at him with a half smile and said, "Sure," adding half a wink.

"As you know, Your Honor, we have filed an objection to these proceedings. Opposing counsel produced this Motion for Reconsideration only after we had perfected our appeal. Our adversaries insisted on enforcing the Preliminary Injunction with full knowledge and understanding that the bond requirement had not been satisfied. Additionally, after extensive research, we have found no case law that supports a prevailing party being entitled to a Motion for Reconsideration under these circumstances," said Glenn, pausing to look at his notes.

The judge spoke up. "Objection denied." He looked at opposing counsel and said, "Call your first witness."

This was proceeding just as Pete had predicted.

Harvey, as president of the company, was placed on the stand. He jabbered on about how the dollar amount of the bond should be minimal. His contention was that they had proven that they were the aggrieved party here and that requiring a large bond would be a form of punishment. I thought to myself, that my friend is a great argument. I had looked at a copy of the bond requirements for the issuance of a Preliminary Injunction before today's festivities began. The requirements were very clear and specific, not giving the judge a lot of discretion.

"The amount of bond <u>required</u> <u>shall</u> be equal to the amount of <u>all</u> damages both actual and projected should the prevailing party be reversed on appeal. The words "<u>required,</u> <u>shall</u> and <u>all</u>" leaped off the page at me.

I had previously taken my K-Mart calculator and figured the bond should be between five and fifty million dollars. The five million represented a realistic number while the fifty million had a touch of that optimistic side of me. Regardless, I was already doing over $80,000 per month and was showing a very healthy profit. The business was on track to show minimum sales of at least a million dollars over the next 12 months. If you looked ahead five or ten years and then combine that with the fact that I had a proven track record of taking my first company to 2.3 million dollars in sales during the first year of production, the calculations were a no-brainer. Add to that, the fact that I had receipts and invoices for hundreds of thousands of dollars in paid and unpaid legal bills. If nothing else, there would be money set aside to go after once we reversed this debacle in a higher court.

I am positive that when they started this journey the intent was to dry me up financially so I could NEVER even think about filing an appeal. I am sure that no one ever asked the question before it started, "What do we do if Hohol appeals?" It just wasn't part of the plan and would never be an option for me, or so they thought. That is why this hearing lasted 17 days and why thousands and thousands of irrelevant documents and hours and hours of nonsensical testimony was allowed into the record.

I thought to myself that maybe this bond hearing wasn't so bad after all. My opposition was about to be required to post a substantial amount of money and gamble all of it on this outrageous ruling. For a moment I thought about what it would be like to cash that check. It was just a moment, mind you.

Unlike the past nine months of testimony, Harvey's time on the stand was short and to the point. It appeared Harvey knew he didn't even need to be there or say anything. Glenn put me on the stand and I testified to the above facts and figures. I made a point of reading the bond requirements into the record, again. Opposing counsel objected strenuously, but Glenn insisted that the rule was used as the basis for our calculations and therefore we should be able to read it into the record.

The judge didn't seem to care one way or the other and allowed it, probably to show that he could be fair. Besides, he would have needed some sort of reason not to allow it since it was the rule. I stepped down.

The judge looked at his watch and almost forgot to call for closing arguments. He was cutting it close on that lunch special. He called his Tip Staff to the bench and whispered in his ear. I swear I heard something about reserving the lunch special and that he may be running a little late. Nobody needed to be a Rocket Scientist to know what the closing arguments were going to be.

I thought we would have a decision in a day or two. The only question was, how much of a bond would Cappellini require? More than a week later, late in the afternoon, Pete called me. He said that he had heard through the grapevine that the judge had issued his ruling. Unlike last time, opposing counsel did not fax Pete a copy. Pete told me he was on his way to the courthouse. He couldn't get anyone there to fax him a copy of the order and the courthouse was closing in a matter of minutes. I sat and waited by the phone. Pete didn't call me back.

The next morning I called Pete's office before it had opened. As usual, Pete was there. He told me that the person he needed to see at the courthouse to get a copy of the order had left a few minutes early because of a personal emergency. Since he was unable to get a copy of the order yesterday, he was going to get it as soon as the courthouse opened today and that I could meet him back at his office.

Pete's office was in a spectacular, old building. It was a converted mansion that was once home to a Coal Baron. How fitting, I thought. I heard Pete come in the back door of his building. I was anxious to read his face. One quick look and I knew he wasn't happy. I hurried into his office. The news wasn't good.

The bond required was a total of $100,000 which meant it would only cost my adversaries pennies to close my business down. They could purchase the bond through their insurance company. Pete was pissed and I was dejected. $100,000 didn't cover a third of my legal bills let alone business losses. Pete exclaimed loudly, as he slammed his desk with his fist, that we were going to file our own Motion for Reconsideration and that he was going to make a fool out of this judge. Pete rolled up his sleeves, and before lunch, he had the motion finished and delivered to the courthouse. It was direct, to the point and scathing. A few days passed. Then it happened.

Pete received a notice in the mail from the courthouse. He was sure it was a notice of the hearing date for our motion. Instead, there was a brief letter explaining that Cappellini had rejected our motion without a hearing because it was not filed in a timely manner. It went on to explain that any Motion for Reconsideration was required to be filed within thirty days of the judge's initial ruling. We looked at the calendar. You may have guessed it; thirty-one days had passed. Cappellini had waited until the end of business on the thirtieth day to issue his ruling. Talk about reaching into your bag of dirty tricks. If questioned, I am positive that Judge Cappellini would state very nonchalantly that it was simply a coincidence and that he was not aware of the timing issue. I am equally sure that if I pointed this problem out to President Judge Toole, I would be chastised for questioning the integrity of the court.

But Pete wasn't done. He filed another "Motion for Reconsideration" by writing a motion to reconsider the rejected "Reconsideration Motion." He argued that the thirty day period should have restarted when the judge had released his new ruling. It made sense to me. Weeks later he got another letter from Judge Cappellini stating that after "exhaustive researching of case law," nothing was found to support Pete's argument. The reason that Cappellini, or should I say his staff, could find no case law to support Pete's argument was because in the history of Pennsylvania there had never been a judge who was so, "In Your Face" blatant with an unjust ruling. The first motion Pete wrote was dismissed due to an untimely filing and now his second motion was thrown out as well. This not only stopped us in our tracks, but it kept Pete's scathing rebuttal out of the official record.

Instead of being dejected and down in the dumps, Pete was invigorated. He confidently stated that he had never had a case on appeal that was this winnable. He told me that he had received more than his fair share of reversals. Never in his decades of practice had he represented a potential reversal of a case where a judge was as blatant and outrageous with his rulings as in this case. Pete told me that one of the reasons he had taken on my case with only a $5,000 retainer and no chance of future payment was that he had had enough of this attorney and this judge.

"These two have been pulling off this scam for years and enough is enough," Pete declared. "Superior Court is going to get a hefty serving of "to the point, verdict reversing evidence" that will propel them into action." I wasn't as confident.

To add insult to injury, we found glaring errors in the reproduced transcript of Cappellini's trial. By glaring, I mean, verdict changing errors. An extremely important question was transcribed as being answered yes when in fact the transcript should have shown it was answered no. This particular question was asked of Harvey. It was as follows.

"Can you show this court a single customer that has been taken from you or a single dollar in sales or profit you have lost due to Hohol's activities?"

After objecting to the question, a long verbal battle ensued with Piccone, after which Harvey was required to answer. He answered very sheepishly, "No." The official transcript stated "YES."

I have often thought about the coincidence of one of the most critical and damaging questions, out of the thousands of questions that were asked, ending up being transcribed incorrectly. We contacted opposing counsel in the form of a mutually signed stipulation correcting and amending the record. Opposing counsel said they would review the matter and let us know. They never responded, even after extensive prompting. They knew just how important that answer was.

Cappellini was made aware of the error and asked by us to require a correction. He responded by stating that it was not his duty to insert himself into such matters. We finally got the Chief Stenographer involved and threatened some sort of court intervention. Only after she reviewed the shorthand tapes of the proceedings herself, was the transcript corrected. I got a nice bill for services rendered, even though it was clearly their error. To make matters worse, the official transcript correction would not be released to me for our appeal until I paid that bill in full. Nice group of folks.

CHAPTER TWENTY-TWO

A Long Time to Get Here

The next step took close to a year. Thousands of dollars were needed to prepare the appeal, as well as the court record. It took forever to read and re-read all of the transcripts while working through all of the corrections. After everything was submitted for the appeal, we waited.

Unfortunately, no one gets a date certain to have a civil appeal heard. Eventually, you are placed on a list of cases that could possibly be heard during certain weeks. Then you must make yourself available for oral argument on short notice. Lists come out and time marches on. When a new list comes out, you wonder why you are still close to the bottom. The right to a speedy trial only exists in criminal court, not in civil.

At this point I had given up on any thoughts of reopening my business. As far as I was concerned, my company had been killed in a tragic train wreck. The problem was that train was still chugging along. I knew all along that it was never the company they were after; it was me.

Well, as fate would have it, Pete was not available on our trial date. He really wasn't, and that was okay. I had worked enough with Glenn to know he was very capable. Naturally, we showed up early in Philadelphia for our day in court. This gave us the opportunity to listen to other cases as they provided their reasons why they were adjudicated incorrectly and unfairly.

Everything sounded extremely timid and namby-pamby compared to what we were about to unleash onto the court. We were destined to be the main attraction of the day, if not the month. I couldn't wait.

I was shocked when Piccone didn't show up for the appeal. In his place was a very junior member of the firm who was not yet a partner. His name was Ron. Ron had briefly participated in my trial by presenting a witness or two.

Glenn was not surprised at all by the no-show of Piccone. Apparently, Piccone had appeared before Superior Court many, many times and had been reversed on a higher than normal percentage of those cases. My guess was that opposing counsel never thought I would financially be able to mount an appeal. If it hadn't been for Pete, I surely wouldn't be here, so he wasn't far off the mark. I guess the last thing the firm and Harvey wanted was for this case to be connected with Piccone in any way at the Superior Court level.

Superior Court reminded me of a semi-automated butchering line, such as is used for poultry. The judges were like FDA inspectors who had been paid off. Instead of showing the inspectors the live poultry, you showed the judges all of the documentation. They didn't have the time, manpower or interest to inspect the actual birds. They didn't even check to see if the birds were breathing.

They had the attorneys stand at a podium that was facing their lofty perches. Prominently displayed in front of their bench were a digital countdown timer and three lights that reminded me of an oven or microwave. As soon as the green light was displayed, the attorney had fifteen minutes to argue an entire case. When the yellow light came on, closing argument needed to be stated, and when the red light came on, your goose was cooked.

Just like a production line, one attorney after another was processed. I don't know if it was once again, dumb luck, or one hell of a coincidence, but we were picked to go dead last. I tend to think we were last because there would be no witnesses left except for the justices themselves and their loyal staff.

Ron went first and, I must say, what he offered was pitiful at best. He had to know what we were going to go after once he concluded, but he didn't even try to head us off at the pass. When he was done, I thought, this guy is toast. It was now our turn.

Standing there, Glenn was a large man with presence, well groomed and, as they would soon find out, well spoken. The green light was illuminated and we were off to the races. We had clearly listed seventeen reasons why this verdict should be reversed, but we didn't have to prove all seventeen issues. It would only take one fatal flaw.

The first reason was a no-brainer.

The trial judge failed to stipulate in his order any "reasonable geographical restrictions." The United States Supreme Court has ruled that in order for a non-compete contract to be enforceable, reasonable geographic limitations must be specifically included. In other words, no one could restrict someone from the entire world if, in fact, they sold to only four countries. In my particular case, my former company sold products in nine countries as of the day I sold the business. A reasonable and enforceable restriction would have been to simply list those nine countries. I would not have objected to that.

However, restricting my new company was not the goal of this lawsuit, remember. The object was to destroy me so I could not hold them accountable for defaulting on payments and their material fraud. Also, keep in mind that if the trial judge would have listed those nine countries, the only product restriction would have been products that were actually sold by my old company as of the date of the company's sale. I could have sold anything else into all the countries of the world, including those nine, as long as the products were not sold by my former company. It really was that simple.

As Glenn got into his second or third sentence, a justice stopped him. He asked a simple question to which Glenn answered. I thought, "this is odd." In all of the other appeals that we had heard, the justices didn't ask a single question until the end. Even then, they didn't ask many. The usual format was, thank you, next.

Glenn picked up right where he left off without missing a beat. I told you he was good. He didn't go but one or two more sentences and another justice piped up. Damn it, I thought. We had sixteen more points to go and time was clicking away. I could see Glenn was now getting a little nervous.

"Your Honor, I will be glad to answer your questions, but I am concerned for my client that my time will run out before I can cover all of my material."

At that the chief justice stopped everything. He looked at both Ron and Glenn and said, "We kept your case for last today because of its complexity. If both counsels will agree, we can waive the time restrictions on both parties and get right to it."

Ron definitely didn't want to agree to that suggestion, but he couldn't say no to the Chief Justice. My thought was, this is good…This is really good.

The justices could see that something was amuck, so they had a general discussion about the Geographic Limitations. I heard one justice say out loud, quote, "This whole thing is a mess, one big freaking mess." Then he slammed his papers back on the bench in disgust. I was ready to jump out of my skin. If they were that upset about the Geographic Limitations, just wait till they get onto the good stuff.

The Chief Justice looked at Ron, saying, "Is there anything else you would like to add?"

Ron replied, very matter-of-factly, "No."

The judge looked at Glenn and said, "Thank you."

Glenn then proceeded to point number two on the list. As he started talking, the Chief Justice said, "No, I meant thank you as in, we are done."

Glenn quickly said, "But, Your Honor, I have sixteen more points to cover for my client."

The Chief Justice looked around at the other justices and said, "I am sure that as the Chief Justice I can speak for everyone here when I say that we have seen enough and that we know what needs to be done." Everyone kind of chuckled at his reminder to everyone in the room that he was the boss. BINGO, BABY, BINGO!

Lack of Geographical Limitations is a fatal flaw in any Preliminary Injunction, as clearly addressed by the U.S. Supreme Court. After all of this, after all these years, after all of the heartache, the system does work. Yes, Virginia, there is a Santa Claus.

I couldn't even breathe because I was afraid that I would wake up. Everyone stood up, the justices left the room and it was over. I looked at Glenn and he looked at me. We must have looked like two young boys who had just shared their first peek at a picture of a naked woman, the magic and the mystery of it all. We couldn't stop talking all the way back to Wilkes-Barre, which was almost a three hour drive. The fact that the court stopped us on our very first point made it a slam dunk. We both agreed that we had over a dozen better reasons for the injunction to be reversed, but we would take what we had been given.

I reported to the newspapers that things went very well at the appeal hearing and that we were cautiously optimistic. Man, was that an understatement. I was on cloud nine. To top it off, a large company from Korea had just contacted me regarding terms for a very large order, as well as a long-term supply contract if they were happy with our quality. I started thinking about what to do next.

CHAPTER TWENTY-THREE

Superior Court Mystery

---

*W*eeks and weeks went by before I finally got the call that Pete had received the Superior Court decision. The Superior Court had in-fact ruled in my favor. It vacated the original order and declared it unenforceable. What the Superior Court did next defies any reasonable explanation. They further ordered that the matter be sent back to the trial court in order for the trial court to correct its error. *What?*

Pete told me not to panic just yet. For some reason the rest of the Superior Court decision was missing and that he was going to call the court to find out about receiving the rest of it. Later, he called me back with bad news.

The clerk he spoke with at the Superior Court in Philadelphia told him, "What you see is what you get."

Pete was baffled. The Superior Court had treated the "Fatal Flaw" of no geographic limitations as if the lower court had just forgotten to include the required language. In other words, like it was a clerical error that simply needed to be fixed. Nothing could be further from the truth. We had shown the Superior Court that we had addressed the issue of geographical limitations during the trial, just as we had the bond issue. I had previously testified to the countries that my former company was selling to, as of the day the company was sold. There was no clerical error at all. They couldn't even make a remote connection to error, but somehow they did.

In the twenty plus years that Pete had practiced law, he told me that he had never seen an appeal where the Superior Court did not address all of the issues presented, unless it found the old "Fatal Flaw" first. Not only were we going back in front of our trial judge, but we were back at square one as far as all of our other appeal issues. This whole thing could not have gone worse. Damn those Disney movies.

Pete immediately filed a motion for reconsideration. He simply asked the Superior Court to review the remaining 16 issues that they should have ruled on as a matter of standard procedure.

Superior Court refuses to rehear Hohol case

By RENITA FENNICK
Citizens' Voice Staff Writer

Local entrepreneur Larry Hohol, whose rags-to-riches existence crumbled in the wake of an arduous legal battle against a Missouri corporation, was dealt another setback Monday.

A spokesperson in the prothonotary's office at the state Superior Court, Philadelphia, told the Citizens' Voice that Hohol's Sept. 21 request to have his appeal reargued before the court en banc (full panel of judges) was denied. No reason for the denial was given.

"I anticipated this denial but it doesn't make it any less painful," Hohol said. "When we applied for the reargument, my lawyers told me it would be difficult to get the Superior Court to allow us to reargue the numerous points contained in our appeal."

Hohol said the issue eventually will end up before the higher court again when he files a new appeal with the Superior Court, asking it to address the other points of the appeal.

Meanwhile, Hohol said he plans to ask Judge Gifford Cappellini to excuse himself from Thursday's 2 p.m. hearing on the issue of geographical limitations regarding a non-competitive agreement between Hohol and Essex Industries, Inc., the St. Louis-based firm that purchased Penox Industries, Inc., from Hohol in 1988.

Hohol, who is without legal representation, said, "If Judge Cappellini does not step down voluntarily, I will request him to do so."

On Sept. 8, the state Superior Court nullified an August 1991 decision by Cappellini which granted a preliminary injunction against Hohol's company, Cryco, Inc., Kingston, a manufacturer of cryogenic vessels used in welding and light industry.

In its ruling, the three-member panel of Superior Court judges vacated Cappellini's August 1991 order on the argument that a restrictive covenant, like the agreement that Hohol would not compete against Essex and Penox, cannot be enforced if it lacks geographical limitations. Hohol's lawyers argued the non-competitive agreement, which was part of the Dec. 27, 1988 purchase agreement between Essex and Hohol, was void since it was "overbroad" and maintained there was no reason for a court to impose a worldwide, non-competition requirement against Hohol.

Less than two weeks after the Superior Court ruling, Attorney Richard Russo, Hohol's former counsel who wrote and approved the contract in question and approved Hohol's founding of Cryco, filed an application for reargument with the higher court.

In a related matter, Hohol is preparing to file a suit against Penox to enforce Hohol's rights under the terms of the agreement. At issue is the term of the purchase contract in which Essex/Penox agrees to pay Hohol $100,000 a year for five years. Records indicate Hohol has received only one annual installment.

Hohol, a self-made millionaire at age 27, who has become virtually penniless during the lengthy legal dispute, said Monday's decision does not damper his enthusiasm to continue his fight against what he calls "a frivolous lawsuit that was enhanced by numerous improprieties in the courtroom.

"No matter what happens in the legal process, I still feel that Essex/Penox set out to destroy me and they did it with the help of the Luzerne County court system," Hohol said.

At the center of the Hohol saga is an allegation that the long-time personal and professional relationship between Judge Cappellini and Attorney Arthur Piccone, who represented Essex and Penox against Hohol, affected the outcome of the local court's decision.

"Now that the story is out in the open, I hope that it will help others who are in similar situations," Hohol said. "Hopefully, these kinds of things won't happen again. My war is far from over. My eventual plan is to seek punitive damages for the suffering I endured during this improper lawsuit and court proceedings."

Hohol has been without legal counsel since Oct. 20 when Judge Toole issued an order allowing Russo of the Rosenn, Jenkins & Greenwald firm to withdraw from the case. Russo would not disclose the reasons behind his withdrawal but Hohol, who admits he owes the Rosenn firm several hundred thousand dollars in legal fees, said he believes the move was related to his outstanding bill.

Hohol said he is concerned that if Cappellini steps down, President Judge Toole, who already has expressed an opinion in the matter, will take over the case.

Midway through the series of hearings on the preliminary injunction (between Aug. 6, 1990 and April 26, 1991), Hohol wrote to Judge Toole, asking him to intervene in the case before Cappellini.

We prepared ourselves for battle once again. I was still talking to the folks in Korea and at least that looked good. I knew my old company had never sold anything to Korea and my old company never sold any of the products that Korea was looking to buy from me now. Their potential orders amounted to hundreds of thousands of dollars in sales and tens of thousands in profit. More importantly, that cash flow would help keep me and my company alive.

Then it happened. I got a fax from Korea telling me that they were no longer interested in pursuing a relationship. After a few letters back and forth, they told me they had found out about the lawsuit and the injunction and did not want to get caught up in any of it. I didn't blame them. I believe, to this day, that my opponents were the ones who made them aware of the litigation.

I suggested to the Koreans that if I could demonstrate to them at a future date that all legal issues were properly addressed and finished, that maybe we could reopen our talks. They halfheartedly agreed to that. Eventually, I felt I would be able to show them a future court order that clearly showed the countries I could not sell to. Korea would not be on that list. Or would it?

Without divulging the name of the Korean company, I now put out a number of press releases concerning my negotiations with them. The press releases served two purposes: To give my now unemployed employees some hope and to drive my adversaries bonkers. Potential orders like this would keep me in the fight, which my adversaries would not find acceptable because their intent was to annihilate me.

I knew in my heart that no matter what I did or showed the Koreans, they would never do business with me in the future. I had come to learn a lot about the Asian culture over the years. Back in 1986, I had officially represented President Ronald Reagan on an official trade mission to Taiwan. The oriental culture hates lawyers and litigation. They don't understand how we, as a culture, allow the lawyers to dominate both our business and personal lives. In many respects, they are a very smart culture.

I decided to keep the Korean cancellation of negotiations quiet. I told no one. I also decided to conduct an experiment. I was going to play the Korean card for all that it was worth, since it was gone anyway. The judge could not possibly include Korea on the restricted list of countries without showing extreme bias and favoritism. He would, in fact, have to rewrite the contract in order to accomplish this and that was not allowed by law. Although I knew the judge would do whatever it took to get to the final destination, if he did this, it would be blatant and transparent enough that the whole world could see what he was doing. Man, had I underestimated this judge. The world was about to see the Luzerne County Railroad in all its glory blazing full steam down the tracks of tyranny.

I continued playing up the Korean connection to the press. In separate interviews, I discussed that once I got the clarification from the judge as to which countries were restricted, it would be "Full steam ahead" (Pun intended) for Korea. I mentioned calling back employees and gave details about ramping up of my production. I must say, I put on a good one man show.

Well, here we were again, in front of Satan. These hearings had gone on for so many years now that I even noticed the judge had aged in the process. I know I had.

Pete had agreed to handle my appeal but as far as going back in front of Judge Cappellini was concerned, I was on my own. I knew in my heart that Judge Cappellini was bias and would take an extreme position concerning the Geographic Limitations issue that was before him. I felt that I had enough. I was going to go "All In."

CHAPTER TWENTY-FOUR

All In

---

*T*he first thing on my To Do List was to go directly after the judge. My original attorneys had not only refused to file a complaint with the Judicial Conduct Board, they would not even file a Motion for Recusal against Cappellini. Recusal is a motion to have the judge removed from the case due to a conflict of interest or for some other impropriety and I was not afraid to file it. While the motion I prepared contained fourteen conflicts, it actually only takes one valid reason to require a judge to be replaced. I believe two of my reasons were possibly a stretch, but the remaining twelve were dead on accurate.

I prepared the motion myself on my computer at work. I wrote it in the proper format, made the proper number of copies, filed them within the courthouse as required and waited for my next date in trial. On that day I would be representing myself Pro Se (without an attorney).

Of course, the thought occurred to me, "What the heck was I doing?" I had prepared a document that publicly stated it was my belief that the judge who was hearing my case was a crooked judge. So much so, that he should be removed from the case. And I wasn't merely suggesting that there might be a slight conflict of interest, I was listing fourteen reasons why he should be replaced. The best part was, I had to present the formal motion directly to him. As nervous as I was, I was still looking forward to entering battle directly.

You would think that if anyone had a problem similar to mine, another judge would step in to hear your complaint and rule on it. It doesn't work that way here in Luzerne County. The trial judge can and does hear their own recusal trial and rule on themselves. I am not kidding. They have that right.

As soon as the courtroom was called to order I asked to approach the bench. I walked up to the judge, handed him my motion, turned around and returned to my seat. He fanned the pages like a product catalog that he had no interest in. The two newspaper reporters were taking notes and he knew both of them would write feature stories about this motion.

What's a judge to do when his bluff is called? He looked at me and said, "I was expecting this." He paused and slowly said, "There is nothing in here that I haven't already seen before."

That statement caught me off guard. I didn't know what he meant by that comment. Before he could say, "Motion denied," I jumped to my feet and blurted out, "Yes, there is, Your Honor!" I almost choked on the "Your Honor" part. "There is plenty of stuff you haven't seen before."

I already had my copy of the motion opened, so I picked a random number from the list of fourteen. I didn't wait for him to ask for an example and I don't remember the order in which I selected my choices, but I sure remember my reasons.

"How about the fact that on Thursday, April 16th, at 12:15 pm (time and date here is not accurate) you had lunch with opposing counsel at the Uptown Restaurant during a break in these proceedings? Isn't it true that you were eating lunch with opposing counsel at your table while my opposition, including the President of the company, sat at the table next to you?"

Judge Cappellini knew I was going for his throat. His dark, piercing, bat-like-eyes locked on me like laser beams. His voice, however, sounded like it was coming from someone else's body. His physical expression was defiant, but his voice had softened and became Grandfatherly.

"I surely don't recall such a lunch. Are you positive that you are not mistaken?" He asked.

Boy, that pissed me off, but I finally had the upper hand and I wasn't going to blow it. I walked closer to the bench, but rather than address him, I turned and addressed the reporters.

"Well, Your Honor, since you cannot recall this lunch, I would like to ask for a brief recess so I can get my two witnesses to come over here to testify. They are right down the street at my old law firm."

His response in this new found Grandfatherly tone was, "Are you telling me that I can't have an innocent lunch with a life-long friend? For goodness sakes, we are Godparents to each other's children."

"Thank you, Your Honor, for admitting to that fact," I responded. "I am not telling you that you cannot have lunch with your life-long friend and Godparent to your children. You most certainly can, but you cannot do so and also hear this case."

Now I turned and looked directly at him, saying, "More times than not, you have asked opposing counsel to come to your chambers at the end of the day's testimony without inviting my counsel along."

Cappellini's response was surprising.

"Oh, all of those times were to discuss personal matters and had nothing to do with your case. Surely, your counsel would not have had any interest in such matters."

"Thank you, again, Your Honor. But you can't do that either."

I felt that I was really making some good, solid headway, so I pressed on. I went after what I believed to be the best of the best.

"How about the fact that you were law partners with opposing counsel in two separate law firms before you became a judge? One of the firms even had both of your names in its title."

Even he knew there was no reasonable defense for that issue. This wasn't my word against his. This was a hardcore, provable, conflict of interest. The judge sort of slouched down in his chair. He extended both of his hands over the bench like the Pope would when he saw a handicapped child in a wheelchair. It was subtle, yet dramatic, all at the same time.

"As I told you, Mr. Hohol, opposing counsel and I go back a long way. I am proud to have him as my friend, but what you are talking about is ancient history. Everyone in the law community knows about our old ties. Neither one of us have ever tried to hide our history."

Cappellini knew we had a ways to go because my list was long and he wasn't doing well at all. In his most sincere, respectful voice, Judge Cappellini stopped everything in its tracks by saying, "I want to assure everyone in this courtroom that I would never allow my personal relationship with anyone, including my friend seated in front of me (Attorney Piccone), to influence any decision I must make to properly carry out my duties. Mr. Hohol, I shall make my ruling on your motion in due course."

Cappellini then looked at his friend, Piccone, and said, "Counsel, you may call your next witness."

It took weeks to receive his written decision. It consisted of one word: Denied. I finally had his ruling in my hand and was ready for my much anticipated appeal. There was one problem. He issued his order in a rare form called an Interlocutory Order, thus making the order final and not appealable. I am not making this up.

A flurry of newspaper articles about my case hit the street. The first article you are about to read was on the front page of the Citizens' Voice. President elect Clinton's picture was in black and white while the story about my case and this judge was in full color. My story had taken on a life of its own.

I want to take a moment here to discuss an issue that is near and dear to me. It is exposure. Just because something is exposed, it doesn't mean it is then corrected. Both the Citizens' Voice and the Times Leader newspapers exposed in great detail what was going on with my case in the Luzerne County Court System, as well as many other cases. To their credit both papers went above and beyond when it came to reporting their observations. Both papers did so at great risk. The Citizens' Voice was sued for slander for reporting on another case and lost. Their case has been re-opened by the Pennsylvania Supreme Court as it may have been illegally influenced by a reputed mobster. I will be writing about their case in my next book. What happened to their 1st amendment rights, you ask? This is Luzerne County and the Citizens' Voice was chosen to also be a passenger on "The Luzerne County Railroad". The following article was in full color and on the front page of the Citizens' Voice newspaper. It was pretty incredible.

CITIZENS' VOICE

72 Pages
30¢

November 5 1992

Washington faces a big shake-up

With the election of Clinton, big change is in the offing...page 10

Clinton and Vice President Gore at press conference yesterday

A question of justice

One judge said 'no' but a second said 'yes,' ending a rags-to-riches tale

Larry Hohol went from small-town cop to millionaire, only to have a Luzerne County Court judge shut down his business after another judge refused to do so. This is Larry Hohol's story.

...page 5

What one judge denied, another granted, apparently ending a rags-to-riches tale

A question of justice

By RENITA FENNICK
Citizens' Voice Staff Writer

In 1979, **Larry** Hohol was patrolling the streets of a small West Side community, supporting himself on the $9,400 salary of a Luzerne Borough police officer.

He began tinkering with cryogenic technology, and, in 1981, reinvented a respiratory therapy device used in the home health care industry.

Hohol's business flourished over the next few years as his company expanded into a prosperous worldwide venture. He became a self-made millionaire at age 27, met with heads of states, garnered business awards and he and his family settled into their $1.1 million customized dream home in Hunlock Creek.

It was a rags-to-riches tale of a local boy who made it big.

But two civil lawsuits and two appeals to the state Superior Court have twisted Hohol's Great American Dream into an American Tragedy.

Hohol's business, Cryco, Inc., was closed by a court order, causing him to lose millions of dollars in projected sales. He spent more than $300,000 fighting what he calls a frivolous lawsuit — not once, but twice. He and his wife are in the midst of a divorce. He has no money. And his dream home recently was acquired by the bank in a sheriff's sale.

Hohol blames it all on an improper lawsuit brought against him by a Missouri firm — a suit that was dismissed by one Luzerne County judge, only to be filed a year later with another county jurist. In the second case, Luzerne County Judge **Gifford Cappellini** ruled against Hohol, shutting down his company and major source of income.

The state Superior Court sided with Hohol twice — affirming Luzerne County Judge Patrick Toole's 1989 decision and nullifying Judge **Cappellini's** ruling against Hohol in September.

In its Sept. 8 decision, a three-judge panel of state Superior Court judges declared Cappellini's preliminary injunction unenforceable on the grounds the agreement entered into by Hohol and Essex/New Penox lacked a geographical limitation and remanded the case to Cappellini to "take whatever steps necessary to determine the extent of protection necessary to protect the plaintiffs."

The geographical limitation issue, one of 16 arguments filed with the higher court, also was addressed while the case was still in the county courts. Hohol recalls

Larry Hohol and daughters
Michele, at left, and Sara

his attorney, Richard Russo, asked Cappellini, on numerous occasions to institute a geographical boundary so that Cryco would be able to fill a $150,000 order from a Korean firm.

"We asked the judge for geographical restrictions for two reasons," Hohol said. "First, an agreement cannot be enforced unless there are some boundaries and secondly, we wanted to try to keep my company in business."

Hohol said that each time Russo argued the geographical limitations issue, Judge Cappellini listened attentively and took notes. The transcripts of the hearings indicate Cappellini did not address the issue and allowed Attorney Arthur Piccone to proceed with his case.

Though the Superior Court ruling allows Hohol to reopen his business, located at Korn Street, Kingston, the arduous legal battle has drained Hohol of most of his assets, making it nearly impossible for him to pick up the pieces.

"It's so unbelievable," Hohol told the Citizens' Voice in an exclusive interview. "The lawsuit was unfounded to begin with but the court's conduct in the second case was improper which just made the whole thing incredulous. I have nothing, absolutely nothing. Not because of anything I did or did not do, but because of a lawsuit that should have been thrown out before it ever reached the hearing stage."

Hohol's attorneys, a Superior Court panel and a Philadelphia area lawyer not involved in either case agree the charges brought by Essex Industries, Inc. and Penox Technologies, Inc., against Hohol and Cryco, Inc. are without merit.

Relationship questioned

During a recent hearing concerning a motion for recusal, or dismissal, of Judge Cappellini from a civil lawsuit involving Louis J. Beltrami and the Hazleton National Bank, Attorney Louis Sinatra raised similar arguments and cited the jurist's actions during the Hohol hearings as an example of "one of a series of happenings which would raise some suspicion."

In an interview with the Citizens' Voice, Sinatra, affiliated with the Blue Bell-based firm of Lesser & Kaplin, explained his inclusion of legal documents from the two Hohol hearings in his attempt to recuse Judge Cappellini from the Beltrami/bank case.

"I offered the record of the Hohol proceedings because I thought it spoke for itself," Sinatra said. "As I said during closing arguments at the recusal hearing, each incident in and of itself may not be conclusive. But when we put all of the pieces together there was a matrix of events that, I believe, raised suspicions.

"Judge Toole found there was not a reason to issue an injunction, then Judge Cappellini issued one,".

Businessman gone broke feels court system let him down

Citizens' Voice, Wilkes-Barre, Pa. — Thursday, November 4, 1992

(continued from page 5)

Sinatra said, "We saw that as very interesting and that's why we raised it."

Sinatra's attempt to have Judge Cappellini removed from the Beltrami case centered around the jurist's long time personal and professional affiliation with Attorney Arthur Piccone, Beltrami's lawyer who also represented Essex and New Penox in the action against Hobol. In the hearing on the recusal motion, Sinatra cited what he called inconsistencies with the jurist's actions concerning Beltrami, and Cappellini's actions concerning the bank.

At the two day hearing on the recusal issue, Sinatra introduced 44 exhibits, including 12 documents involving the two Hobol cases in support of his allegation that Judge Cappellini "moved like quicksilver" when an action involved the interests of Beltrami.

Sinatra also cited a lawsuit involving the incorporation of Bear Creek Village.

In all instances, Sinatra stressed, Judge Cappellini ruled in favor of the party represented by Piccone.

During the direct examination of Piccone, Sinatra explained the second petition for a preliminary injunction filed by Piccone's clients against Hobol was entered while Judge Toole was on vacation.

"Did you know Judge Toole was on vacation?" Sinatra asked at the recusal hearing.

"I don't keep Judge Toole's social schedule," Piccone said. "How would I know that?"

Later, Sinatra admitted into evidence the two motions for a preliminary injunction filed against Hobol, filed by Piccone. When Sinatra alleged they were "the same plaintiffs seeking the same relief from the same defendants," Piccone, maintaining they were not the same actions, said, "Why don't you lay them side by side and read them in?"

Sinatra replied, "I did and they are strikingly similar."

Piccone, who is affiliated with Hourigan, Kluger, Spohrer & Quinn, would not comment on the amount of money his law firm has accepted in legal fees from the Essex/New Penox case, but a legal observer estimated such a case would involve fees in excess of $500,000

Hobol maintains Essex and New Penox set out to destroy his business and "with the help of the county judicial system, that's exactly what they did.

"I feel as though I was executed without ever being given a trial," Hobol said

Attorney Piccone, contacted at his office Wednesday, said the case was an "interesting story," but would not discuss the details.

"I will not comment on ongoing litigation," he said.

Neither Judge Cappellini nor Judge Joseph Augello were in the not be reached at their homes. Judge Augello figured in the case after issuing an interim stay to halt the proceedings. Cappellini allowed the hearings to proceed despite Augello's court order.

Judge Toole, referring to the first petition for a preliminary injunction said, "It's a matter of record.

"As for the second instance in which a preliminary injunction was granted, it is not appropriate for a judge or a lawyer to comment on matters pending in the court," Toole said.

A rags-to-riches tale

Hohol, a former policeman, became interested in cryogenics around 1981 when he was proprietor of a small medical supply company, Pensee Medical. Cryogenics, the science that relates to the production and effects of very low temperatures, serves as the technologic basis for liquid oxygen tanks which are used in respiratory therapy.

While operating Pensee Medical, Hohol noticed a need for improvement in the tanks and set out to reinvent the apparatus. His new device was patented several years later and in February 1982, Hohol founded Penox Technologies, Inc., to manufacture and distribute medical equipment for the home health care market. The company flourished and boasted annual sales in excess of $16 million at its peak.

On Dec. 27, 1988, Hohol sold Penox to Essex Industries, Inc., a St. Louis, Mo.-based aerospace defense contracting company, for $1.1 million. The agreement included Hohol's patent for the cryo-ease valve but did not include Hohol's two other patents or his leasing company, Penox Leasing.

The contract included a clause prohibiting Hohol from competing with Essex in the field of cryogenic home health care. Another term was an employment agreement between Hohol and Essex.

After working for Essex for a few months, Hohol became disenchanted with his new employer. He claims he was never reimbursed for a business trip to Chile and that Penox owed Hohol over $350,000 for an inventory it received in the sale.

On March 20, 1989, Hohol founded a new company, Cryco, Inc., which is in the business of the design, manufacture, sale, remanufacture and repair of industrial cryogenic vessels used in the welding and light industrial fields.

After Hohol had invested $150,000 of his own money in the new venture, hired employees, built and purchased machinery and began accepting orders, his legal headaches began.

Essex and Penox took their case to the Luzerne County Court, filing a petition for immediate relief (a preliminary injunction) against Hohol in 1989. Essex and New Penox claimed Hohol was in violation of the agreement which prohibited Hohol from producing cryogenic vessels similar to those produced by Penox.

The case landed before Judge Toole who, following two days of testimony, dismissed the petition and ruled the defendants had failed to prove "any violation of the terms of any of the agreements or that the defendant manufactured or sold anything in violation of any agreement or that (Hohol) had solicited or enticed anyone in violation of any agreement or to the prejudice of the plaintiffs."

After Toole's ruling, Essex and Penox filed an appeal to the Pennsylvania State Superior Court.

On June 13, 1991, the Superior Court upheld Toole's decision, stating: "the appellants' (Essex/New Penox) evidence was insufficient to prove that (Hohol) was violating the agreement" and found "Hohol was not acting in competition with Penox Technologies, Inc., not manufacturing the same products manufactured by Penox and not pilfering information pertaining to Penox's customers."

Essex, Penox sue again

Before the Toole decision was affirmed by the higher court, Essex and New Penox again sought injunctive relief against Hohol and his business. On Aug. 1, 1990, a petition was filed by Essex and Penox seeking injunctive relief to shut down operations at Hohol's Cryco plant.

Hohol maintains the timing of the filing was crucial.

"I firmly believe that Essex's (See JUSTICE, page 8)

Justice

from page 6

lawyer, Arthur Piccone, waited until Judge Toole was on vacation to refile the suit," Hohol said. "Judge Cappellini was the miscellaneous court judge that week and when the petition came to him, he decided the issue was so urgent that he set hearings to begin that week.

"He could have waited two days until Judge Toole returned from vacation," Hohol said. "That would have been the proper thing to do since Judge Toole handled the first request for a preliminary injunction. I believe that since Piccone was representing the company that was suing, it hurt my cause in the courtroom."

After 13 witnesses testified during 17 days of hearings, which stretched across nine months, Cappellini granted the injunction, closing down Cryco.

Hohol's counsels, Attorneys Richard Russo and Norman Namey, point out the plaintiffs failed to name one customer that was taken from Essex/New Penox and were unable to prove any loss of business due to Hohol's activities.

In his memorandum, Cappellini said: "reasonable grounds support the issuance of a preliminary injunction." Referring to the two separate actions taken by Essex and Penox (before Toole and Cappellini), the jurist said: "The evidence before me differs from that which was presented before Judge Toole."

Cappellini order nullified

Last Sept. 8, a three-judge panel of the state Superior Court overturned Cappellini's decision, paving the legal way for Hohol to reopen his business.

In the appeals argument filed by Russo and Namey on behalf of Hohol, the actions of Essex and Penox continuously are referred to as "harassment."

Russo declined comment on the case since he no longer represents Hohol, following an Oct. 20 court order by Judge Toole allowing Russo to withdraw from the case.

"Since Mr. Hohol no longer is my client, I would rather not comment," Russo said.

Russo would not explain why he petitioned the court to be removed as Hohol's lawyer.

Hohol suspects the move is the result of the hundreds of thousands of dollars he owes Russo's firm, Rosenn, Jenkins and Greenwald for legal services. After the Superior Court ruling, Russo filed an application for reargument before the state Superior Court en banc (the full panel of judges).

The request for reargument ask the higher court to address some of the other 15 points raised in the appeal.

Saturday, November 14, 1992 — Citizens' Voice, Wilkes-Barre, Pa.

A *chance* for justice

In the movie "The Verdict," Paul Newman portrays Attorney Frank Galvin, a down-on-his-luck lawyer who narrowly escaped disbarment over a case in which he was set up.

Galvin lost his job at a major Boston law firm, he lost his wife and he turned to booze.

A lawyer friend tosses an easy-win case to Galvin. Two weeks before trial, Galvin shakes himself free from the alcohol and he opts to take the case to trial rather than accept the $221,000 settlement offered. He notes that $221,000 is easily divided by three — his fee would be $70,000.

Galvin is convinced that justice can be served only by obtaining a major damage settlement for the family of his client, a young woman who has been turned into a vegetable by the malpractice of her obstetrician.

The plot thickens. The large law firm representing the defendant plants a spy — a seductress — in the Galvin mini-operation. She begins to report back to the defense team, and Galvin's case begins to crumble.

The spy, herself a recently-divorced lawyer, falls for Galvin. A turning point in that relationship is a quiet dinner at which Galvin explains his perception of the law.

The courts exist, Galvin tells her, not to provide justice but to provide a *chance* at justice.

Galvin is correct. The courts are imperfect because they are run by humans who are subject to the same emotions, frailties and weaknesses that can be found in any facet of our society.

You don't always see justice in the courts, criminal or civil. Innocent people sometimes are convicted and jailed, and civil court judges, and juries, sometimes return unjust decisions or verdicts.

That's why we have appellate courts. Often, incorrect decisions at lower levels are reversed and corrected by appellate judges who, theoretically, are more objective because they are distanced from the political realities of the counties in which the initial decisions are rendered.

Larry Hohol has had four shots at his justice and he won three of four. Unfortunately, the one that he did lose — a Luzerne County Court decision by Judge Gifford Cappellini — has cost him his business, his home and his marriage.

Sure, another Luzerne County judge, Patrick Toole, and the state Superior Court — twice — ruled for Hohol, but his life was shot to pieces by a judge who rushed to re-hear a case brought before him by a former law partner, Attorney Art Piccone.

And then there were the Hohol company employees who lost their jobs, and the lost taxes to all levels of government.

Hohol is the former cop who invented a cryogenic device, later sold his company and then started another business. The firm to which he sold out sued him for violation of an employment agreement, but Judge Toole, after holding hearings, found for Hohol. The state Superior Court upheld Toole.

When Judge Toole went on vacation, Attorney Piccone filed a second suit. Judge Cappellini said it was too important to await Judge Toole's return and new hearings began. Nine months later, Judge Cappellini issued an injunction shutting down Hohol's business.

The Superior Court vacated the Cappellini decision, but remanded it back to him for a determination on the issue of geographic limitations. That hearing will be held next week.

In essence, Hohol is free to re-start his business, Cryco, Inc., but he's bankrupt. He's also without legal counsel because the firm that represented him has withdrawn; Hohol owes several hundred thousand dollars in legal fees.

In "The Verdict," justice *was* served. Frank Galvin found his key witness late in the game, and the spy lawyer found her ethics and didn't betray Frank. Galvin's clients won a large award.

The Hohol case still must be played out. The case remains before Judge Cappellini, who stubbornly refuses to recuse himself from this and another case in which Attorney Piccone is counsel.

Not justice, but the opportunity for justice, demands that Judge Cappellini bow out.

Paul Golias is Citizens' Voice managing editor.

Paul Golias

People Up Front

A dark, dark cloud

A cloud is hanging over the Luzerne County Court. It's a dark cloud.

•

The background: Larry Hohol, a small-town cop, invents a cryogenic vessel. His business blossoms and he becomes a millionaire. He sells the business and goes to work for the buyer. The relationship sours. He leaves and starts another business. He is sued for allegedly competing against the company to which he sold his first business. Judge Patrick Toole of Luzerne County Court conducts hearings and rules for Hohol. The state Superior Court supports the Toole decision.

Now it gets interesting: Judge Toole goes on vacation. Attorney Arthur Piccone files another suit and Judge Gifford Cappellini, motions judge and a long-time pal of Piccone, decides the case is too crucial to await Judge Toole's return, so Cappellini begins hearings. The hearings take nine months. Cappellini rules against Hohol and grants an injunction shutting down his business. The state Superior Court vacates the Cappellini decision, allowing Hohol to reopen, but he's broke and in bankruptcy. The case is now back before Luzerne County Court for a hearing on the issue of geographic limitations. Other issues raised in the second appeal have not been addressed. And what judge still has the case? Judge Cappellini.

•

I've known Judge Pat Toole for decades. As a lawyer and a judge and as president judge of the county courts, I've never known him to be anything but a fair, decent and honest man.

Judge Toole says he can't comment on the Hohol matter beyond this statement regarding his handling of the first suit: "The record speaks for itself."

It sure does.

As a layman, I can't help but wonder what happened when Judge Toole returned from vacation and learned that Larry Hohol was before the court again on substantively the same issue.

Did Judge Toole saunter down the hallway of the courthouse to Judge Cappellini's chamber and ask, "Giff, what the hell is going on here?"

Did Judge Toole meet with the court en banc (that's French for "in full court"), as he does from time to time, and say, "Geez, guys, (this happened before Ann Lokuta joined the court), we've got heavy civil and criminal caseloads. Why are we re-hearing cases?"

As lay people, Citizens' Voice editors and staff writer Renita Fennick, who has been laying out the Hohol story, have talked to several lawyers. We have endeavored to gather information that would support the court records that indicate -- to lay people -- that Larry Hohol has been snowballed.

Lawyers don't like to go on the record when sensitive issues such as integrity of the court are raised. The legal fraternity tends to circle the wagons, and this protects any offenders and all others inside the circle.

"We have to practice before Judge Cappellini," one lawyer said.

The implication is clear: "If I do anything to create the breath of fresh air that will blow away the dark cloud, then I may be in deep trouble myself when I come before the court."

And what of Larry Hohol? He has already been told that he faces an impossible task of ever finding another lawyer in Luzerne County to represent him.

Hohol, by the way, has nothing but praise for Attorney Rick Russo and the folks at Rosenn, Jenkins and Greenwald. They dropped out of the case recently and Hohol owes the firm lots of money, but Hohol says the lawyers there felt passionately that he had been wronged and hung in even as the legal bills mounted.

•

What happens next and what should happen?

As the Citizens' Voice editorially suggests today (see page 16), Judge Cappellini should not be handling the Hohol case. Just how Judge Toole goes about handling these matters is a procedure foreign to non-legal types.

Judge Cappellini also should have recused himself from the Beltrami-Hazleton bank case now lingering in his courtroom.

The bigger question: Who judges the judges?

•

Paul Golias is Citizens' Voice managing editor.

A question of justice

Geographical limitations issue slated for hearing Nov. 19 before Cappellini

By RENITA FENNICK
Citizens' Voice Staff Writer

The hearing on the issue of geographical limitations regarding a non-competitive agreement between local businessman Larry Hohol and Essex Industries, Inc., a St. Louis, Mo. corporation, will be held on Thursday, Nov. 19, at 2 p.m.

The hearing reportedly was scheduled for Thursday afternoon before Judge Gifford Cappellini but due to a misunderstanding between the parties involved, the hearing will be held in two weeks.

The necessity for a hearing was prompted by a Sept. 8 decision by the state Superior Court which nullifies an August 1991 decision by Cappellini. At that time, the county jurist ruled Hohol was in violation of a 1988 agreement between Hohol and Essex/New Penox and granted Essex a preliminary injunction, closing down Hohol's company, Cryco, Inc.

In its decision, the higher court ruled the non-competitive agreement could not be enforced since it lacked geographical limitations. The three-judge panel remanded the issue to Cappellini with the instructions to "take whatever steps necessary to determine the extent of protection necessary to protect plaintiffs."

Essex Industries, Inc., a St. Louis, Mo. aerospace defense contracting firm, purchased Penox Technologies, Inc., from Hohol in December 1988 for $1.1 million. Penox, which manufactured cryogenic vessels used in the home health care industry, was founded by Hohol in February 1982.

The purchase agreement between Hohol and Essex/Penox included a restrictive covenant, an agreement prohibiting Hohol from competing against Penox.

The agreement, drawn up and approved by Hohol's former attorney, Richard Russo, was the basis of ongoing litigation for three years.

Hohol is now in bankruptcy and a bank as foreclosed on the large house he built at Hunlock Creek.

Essex and Penox, maintaining that Hohol's activities in his new business, Cryco, Inc., which manufactures cryogenic vessels used to transport materials used in the welding and light manufacturing industry, violated the 1988 purchase agreement.

In Nov. 1989, Judge Patrick Toole denied a request by Essex and Penox to issue a preliminary injunction, closing Cryco. A state Superior Court panel upheld

(See LIMIT, page 42)

Larry Hohol on porch of the house he lost

Limit

from page 4

Toole's decision in June 1991.

Essex and Penox are represented by Attorney Arthur Piccone of Hourigan, Kluger, Spohrer & Quinn.

Hohol and his lawyers in September filed an application for reargument with the state Superior Court, asking it to review the appeal again and dispose of some of the issues raised in order to resolve any further proceedings.

In its decision, the panel of three state Superior Court justices remanded the case to Judge Cappellini with instructions to "take whatever steps necessary to determine the extent of protection necesary to protect plaintiffs and enter a new order consistent with its findings."

The Superior Court document said it was not in a position to address the defendants' remaining arguments.

In the request for reargument, Attorney Richard Russo, who represented Hohol until last month, asks the Superior Court to address the remaining arguments cited in the appeal in order to "resolve any further proceedings, on the appellate or trial court levels (to) avoid a needless waste of judicial resources and prevent duplicative legal expenses to the parties."

The highlighted sentence above to this day is still a mystery. I have yet to get a valid reason as to why the Superior Court did what they did. Their actions here fly in the face of required procedure. If the Superior Court was not going to treat the lack of Geographic Limitations as a "Fatal Flaw" it should have kept reviewing the remaining issues as presented in the appeal. For some unknown reason the court did not.

Hohol dispute includes destruction of Penox inventory

By RENITA FENNICK
Citizens' Voice Staff Writer

A major contention in the ongoing legal dispute between local businessman Larry Hohol and the Missouri-based Essex Industries, Inc., is a disagreement over an extensive inventory, including items which were destroyed in a 1991 fire.

Hohol, 36, of Sweet Valley, in a civil lawsuit filed June 27, 1990, charged Essex, an aerospace contractor based in St. Louis, and Penox Technologies, Inc., Pittston, with breach of contract and fraud regarding a purchase agreement.

The Dec. 27, 1988 purchase agreement, signed by Hohol and Essex officials, includes an asset purchase agreement, employment agreement and a non-competitive agreement. Essex purchased Penox, a manufacturer of cryogenic vessels used in the home health care industry, for $1.1 million.

Less than two months after Hohol sued the two corporations, Essex and Penox took legal action to shut down Hohol's business.

While under Hohol's ownership, the Penox inventory had been stored at the Luzerne Products, Inc., building, Courtright Avenue, Plains Township, which, according to sources, is equipped with a state-of-the-art sprinkler system and fireproof materials.

Sometime after Hohol sold the company to Essex, the Penox inventory was transferred to a basement storage area in the L.S. Skate-A-Rama and Bowl-A-Rama, East Washington and Prospect streets, Nanticoke, which was ravaged by fire in October 1991.

Photographs taken at the fire scene indicate Penox supplies and catalogs were being stored in the L.S. building at the time of the fire.

Owner of the building, George Ellis, Hanover Township, said damages from the blaze, which remains under investigation, total approximately $1 million.

The inventory, valued at $365,551.76, was included in the assets acquired by Essex at the time of sale.

A provision of the purchase agreement requires Hohol to buy back the unused or "slow-moving" inventory supplies one year after the Essex acquisition of Penox.

Hohol's lawsuit against Essex/Penox was refiled Aug. 13, 1990 to add a sixth count, an enforcement of suretyship (obligation of a person to answer for a debt, fault or failure) regarding Penox's failure to pay its mortgage debts to Hohol for the building in Pittston.

The charges of fraud involve Hohol's allegation that Penox returned defective and incomplete parts to the inventory and expected Hohol to purchase them.

In the lawsuit, filed by Rosenn, Jenkins & Greenwald, it is maintained that "Penox misrepresented and concealed material facts, discrepancies and irregularities in its inventory and with the knowledge of the falsity of its statements and with the intent to deceive and defraud Hohol."

The brief also charges Penox's actions as "aggravated, malicious and deliberate fraud and/or concealment which constitutes reckless disregard of the rights of Hohol."

Records indicate Hohol had to seek a court order to inspect the inventory which he was required to re-purchase.

"When we finally got in there and inspected the supplies, we realized many components were removed," Hohol said. "Some broken units were placed into the inventory and they expected me to buy them back. Then Essex said it would offset the value of the in
(See HOHOL, page 21)

Hohol
from page 3

ventory against the money they owed me for the non-competitive agreement, which was $100,000 a year for five years.

"It's strange," Hohol said. "I didn't get my money for the non-compete and I can't sell the inventory because it burned in the fire."

Hohol said the inventory was moved from the Plains Township site to the Nanticoke building without his knowledge or approval.

The lawsuit seeks compensatory and punitive damages on six counts, including breach of contract.

The breach of contract charges Essex/Penox with:
(1) failure to comply with a term of the purchase agreement that would allow Hohol access to certain accounting documents;
(2) wrongful offset of monies due Hohol in the non-competitive agreement which is to be paid in five annual installments of $100,000 each;
(3) fraudulent misrepresentation of the inventory;
(4) wrongful offset of a benefit that was due Hohol in a matter that took place before the sale of Penox;
(5) failure to reimburse Hohol for a business trip to Chile;
(6) wrongful offset of mortgage payments owed to Hohol

The case, which "demands" a jury trial, has not been placed on the county court docket pending the outcome of bankruptcy and preliminary injunction proceedings regarding Hohol in his ongoing legal dispute with Essex/Penox.

When Essex and Penox filed a petition seeking injunctive and declaratory relief against Hohol.

Penox asks Cappellini to bar Hohol from most of the world

By RENITA FENNICK
Citizens' Voice Staff Writer

Penox Technologies, Inc., asked the court Thursday to restrict former employee Larry Hohol from conducting business activities throughout the U.S., in Pacific rim and former Eastern Bloc countries and in all foreign nations in which Penox has sold cryogenic products.

Hohol, during the 25-minute session scheduled to hear oral arguments on the issue of geographical parameters regarding a non-competitive agreement, urged Judge Gifford Cappellini to restrict his activities solely to the borough of Dupont.

In addition to all 50 states, the Pacific rim and Eastern bloc nations, Attorney Walter Grabowski, on behalf of Penox, asked that the geographical parameters encompass the nations in which Penox and its parent company, Essex Industries, Inc., has conducted cryogenic sales, including France, Canada, Singapore, Japan, Belgium/Netherlands, Spain, Australia, Uruguay, Italy, Germany, Turkey, Colombia and Hong Kong.

Hohol, who served as his own legal counsel, reminded the court that he had asked Cappellini — during the 17 days of hearings on the preliminary injunction issue — to establish geographical parameters.

"We would not be here today if Judge Cappellini had done his job the first time around," Hohol said after the court session. "It is truly ironic that I, the defendant, had asked the court to impose geographic limitations. Anyone will tell you that boundaries are a basic component of any non-competitive agreement. My counsel knew that. If the judge didn't know it, we informed him. Yet, he still refused to address the issue in open court."

Hohol founded Penox, a cryogenics home health care manufacturing business, in 1982, and sold the assets to Essex Industries, Inc., St. Louis, Mo., on Dec. 27, 1988.

Following the acquisition, Hohol worked for Penox for a few months before establishing a new venture, Cryco, Inc., which manufactured cryogenic vessels for the light industrial market.

In addition to the asset purchase agreement and employment contract, the agreement package between Hohol and Penox included a restrictive covenant, or a non-competitive agreement. Provisions of the covenant called for Penox to pay Hohol $100,000 each year for five years in exchange for Hohol agreeing not to compete against Penox.

On Sept. 6, the state Superior Court vacated Cappellini's August 1991 preliminary injunction which closed down Cryco on the grounds it was overbroad and lacked geographical parameters. The higher court remanded the case to Cappellini to "determine the extent of protection necessary to protect plaintiffs."

Hearings on the issue of (See Hohol, page 71)

No stenographer for oral argument

Oral arguments presented by attorneys during the post-hearing phase usually are not included in the record of the case, a court stenographer told the Citizens' Voice.

Larry Hohol, defendant in a preliminary injunctive procedure, questioned the absence of a court stenographer during oral arguments Wednesday regarding geographical limitations on a 1988 non-competitive agreement.

Dan Coll, court stenographer, said, "No record is taken during oral arguments. But there is one judge, (Bernard C.) Brominski, who does like to have a reporter present. As a general rule, though, it is not customary."

The court session, held before Judge Gifford Cappellini, is the latest in an ongoing dispute between Hohol and Penox Technologies, Inc., the company Hohol sold to Essex Industries, Inc., St. Louis, Mo.

Hohol, who was representing himself, said he asked opposing lawyer, Walter Grabowski, at the onset of the oral arguments about the stenographer. Grabowski said the oral arguments are not usually part of the official record of the case.

Hohol
from page 3

geographical parameters were held Nov. 19 and Nov. 20.

During the oral arguments, Grabowski cited the Nov. 20 testimony of Harvey Guller, Penox president, which detailed the geographic areas in which (New) Penox sold and marketed cryogenic products. Guller testified that New Penox and its parent company, Essex, sold products in all 50 states and was in the process of entering the marketplace of Pacific rim and Eastern bloc nations.

Hohol, when addressing the court, said an agreement not to compete "is not a God-given right. It must be purchased."

Hohol, citing Penox's failure to make payments to Hohol for the last three years, said, "In order to have protection through geographical limitations, you've got to keep up your side of the bargain. What have they paid for?"

Grabowski said, "The payment is not the issue. The question is not whether you can do it but where you can do it."

Cappellini said he "allowed Mr. Hohol to argue whatever he wishes even though it is on record that the only issue before me is to fix the geographical parameters."

The judge said he would render a decision on the issue "in due course."

CHAPTER TWENTY-FIVE

*J*udge Cappellini Doesn't Disappoint

Good ole Cowboy Harvey was on the stand again, continually wiping his upper lip with that ridiculous white handkerchief. He started testifying as to the intent of the non-competitive agreement. I jumped to my feet and objected.

First of all, Harvey was not present during the negotiations of the contract and he wasn't present when I signed them. Secondly, his interpretation of the contract was inadmissible since he was not a party to the contract or an expert in contract law. He could not testify as to the intent of the contracts. He was merely the CEO of the ongoing enterprise.

I told the judge that I had no problem with Harvey reading the specific contract language into the record, but that's where it stopped. The contract was the contract and as a legal document, it spoke for itself. The judge would have none of it, so he allowed Harvey to continue rambling on about intent. Once again, I didn't like the feel of things.

Harvey was trying to make the case that the world was their market. It was as if he were implying that once man had established a base on the moon, they would certainly assign a sales rep to handle that territory as well. Since Harvey took over the reigns of the company, I don't think they sold a hundred dollars worth of products to anyone outside of the United States. As much as I tried I could not get Harvey to nail down a current international sales figure, he simply would not answer the question and Judge Cappellini didn't make him answer as much as I insisted. The reason for this was simple. It was a miniscule number and was possibly a big fat ZERO. I cross examined Harvey further and got him off the stand.

Now it was my turn. I took the stand as a witness and acted as my own attorney, all at the same time. Try asking yourself questions and then answer them out loud. Then try doing so in public. I tried to put a press release from my old company into the record. It was dated around the time of the company's sale. The press release contained a list of countries that we were selling to as of the date of the release. Opposing counsel strenuously objected. Piccone argued that the press release was not conclusive evidence of anything. In one sense, he was right. I was attempting to use the press release as a guide or an indicator. I pointed out that, naturally, in a press release the more countries you list, the more successful you appear and that is positive press, which is a good thing. If anything, companies have been known to stretch the truth a bit to make their company appear to be bigger and more profitable than it actually was. What was most important here was that Korea was not on the list. The judge ruled against me.

I then tried to put into the record a list of countries that I knew was correct, as far as sales. We sold to a total of nine countries when I sold my company. Most of them were in Europe. After Harvey took over the company, the number of countries they sold to went down, not up. Again, the judge stopped me. No matter what, I wanted it on the record that we never sold anything to Korea and, furthermore, never even talked to anyone from Korea. I blurted that statement out as quickly as I could, to get it on the record. Cappellini removed it. I thought this guy is really showing his true colors, big time. Basically, my adversaries were allowed to put everything they wanted into the record and other than my name I was blocked every step of the way.

It would turn out that if I had to pick out any single court session to prove, "Judge Cappellini's Bias" this would be the "Mother of all Sessions".

So far my opponents were allowed to put 100% of what they wanted into the record. Other than my name, I was not doing so well. Along the way I had developed my own legal theory that was simple yet profound. Even if it was proven that I was competing with my old company (I wasn't) my opponents were only entitled to the amount of protection that they had paid for. No pay, no protection. Rather than rehash everything now, read the following article carefully. Everything relevant to this argument is highlighted.

Judge Cappellini, Hohol spar over interpretation of Superior Court order

By RENITA FENNICK
Citizens' Voice Staff Writer

The hearing on geographical limitations regarding a preliminary injunction against a Kingston business came to an abrupt halt Friday afternoon after a witness and judge engaged in a verbal dispute over the wording of a state Superior Court document.

The hearing, which lasted approximately one hour and 20 minutes, was held before Judge Gifford Cappellini to determine the geographical limitations of an August 1991 preliminary injunction which shut down operations at Larry Hohol's cryogenics plant, Cryco, Inc.

The injunction was granted by Cappellini following 17 hearing sessions on a motion filed by Essex Industries, Inc., St. Louis, Mo., and Penox Technologies, Inc., Pittston. Hohol sold the Penox assets to Essex in December 1988.

Hohol, who was not represented by a lawyer, called himself to the witness stand and raised issues concerning other terms of the non-competitive agreement between Hohol and Essex/Penox.

Hohol, in his testimony, read a portion of the agreement which requires Essex/Penox to pay

(See HOHOL, page 41)

Hohol

from page 3

Hohol $100,000 each year for five years. When Hohol testified that he has not received the last three payments, Attorney Walter Grabowski, counsel for Essex/Penoy, objected on the grounds that the issue was irrelevant.

Cappellini, who on Thursday denied Hohol's request to have the jurist recuse, or remove, himself from the proceedings, said, "We're getting into different parts of the contract, a different issue entirely. It is not appropriate. We are here solely to address the issue of geographical parameters. Those are my instructions from the Superior Court and that is what I intend to do."

When Hohol charged that the Superior Court studied only two of the 16 arguments filed on appeal, Cappellini replied, "The Superior Court looked at all the issues."

Cappellini and Hohol then took turns reading the only sentence in the Superior Court's Sept. order which refers to the 14 remaining issues of Hohol's appeal.

According to the document, secured by the Citizens' Voice, the higher court addressed two points raised by

Larry Hohol

Hohol — the charge that the preliminary injunction was invalid since it did not include a bond and the argument that the non-competitive agreement was not enforceable since it did not contain geographical limitations.

The higher court decision states:

...we remand the matter to the trial court to take whatever steps necessary to determine the extent of protection necessary to protect plaintiffs. The trial court is instructed to enter a new order consistent with its findings. At this time, we are not in a position to address defendants' remaining charges of error.

The preliminary injunction is vacated. Case remanded for proceedings consistent with this opinion...

Cappellini, in his interpretation of the Supreme Court's

wording, said, "The Superior Court had to look at the entire record and did not address the other points. The ruling was not a reversal, it was a vacation."

Hohol then said, "For the record, I disagree with Judge Cappellini. The language is very clear. The Superior Court said it did not address the other points. To me, that means they did not address them."

Cappellini responded: "Please, be fair, Mr. Hohol. I'm telling you the court looked at the entire record. Now, proceed."

"I'm done," Hohol said, and walked off the witness stand.

Friday's session, the second of two on the issue, opened with Hohol resuming his cross-examination of Harvey Guller, president of Penox. Guller reiterated his previous day's testimony that Penox was doing business in Japan and its parent company, Essex, was involved in the Pacific rim marketplace, including Korea. Guller also said Penox had intentions of selling cryogenics vessels and related products in other Pacific rim and Eastern bloc nations.

Hohol attempted, on several occasions, to raise other issues regarding the longstanding dispute between Essex/Penox and each time Grabowski objected, Cappellini sustained the objection and warned Hohol: "We are here only to determine geographic parameters."

The jurist then told Hohol he could raise any issues during oral arguments and not during the testimony.

Cappellini told lawyers for the plaintiffs (Grabowski and Arthur Piccone) to submit a brief by Wednesday, Dec. 2., and gave Hohol until Tuesday, Dec. 15, to respond.

Oral arguments will be held before Cappellini on Wednesday, Dec. 16, at 9 a.m.

If you read the highlighted area in the previous article you will actually read a quote from Judge Cappellini asking me to be fair. We are both looking at the same Superior Court Ruling and we both read the same statement into the record. The Superior Court addressed TWO of my points and then stated, and I quote, "At this time, we are not in a position to address defendants' remaining charges of error."

At that point I became embroiled in a real pissing match with Judge Cappellini. This statement was not written in legalese or Latin. It was written in plain English. I thought to myself, "Judge Cappellini is pulling a Piccone." He is holding up something that is so plain and so simple a grade school student could read it and understand it and he is trying to tell me and the world for that matter that the sentence really doesn't mean what everyone thinks. I was LIVID! The sentence didn't say what he wanted it to say, so he was going to interpret it for the rest of us uneducated lowlifes. The arrogance of this man has no measure.

Please take a good look at the area of the previous article highlighted in the second Column. Cowboy Harvey does not state that Penox or any of his other related companies were selling anything into Korea. He actually had put into the record the fact that my old company was not selling anything into Korea. He uses the term, "involved". Their "intent" was proof that they were not doing it and "intent" didn't count. I strongly pointed this out to Judge Cappellini when I had the chance. As you might have guessed, it didn't matter.

Well, Judge Cappellini's ruling was spectacular. It was so spectacular that the Citizens' Voice Newspaper provided a map of the world for their feature article on the subject. The map contrasted the countries I could sell to against those countries I couldn't sell into. According to Cappellini, it was reasonable to restrict my ability to do business to the areas of the map that are colored in black. Everything in white was "reasonably" off limits. Specifically, I could sell to Antarctica and any country in Africa.

That was it. Everywhere else in the world was off limits, even Korea. So much for the "reasonable" portion of the geographic requirement. How much more blatant could this Judge get?

Jurist restricts Hohol's business to two continents

By RENITA FENNICK
Citizens' Voice Staff Writer

A court order filed this week at the Luzerne County Courthouse restricts Larry Hohol's business activities on five continents.

The order, handed down Monday by Judge Gifford S. Cappellini extends an August 1991 preliminary injunction against Hohol and his company, Cryco Inc., to include geographic limitations of Australia, most of North America, 11 European nations, 10 Asian and two South American countries.

"Unfortunately, I anticipated this," Hohol said. "This is nothing new. This should prove very valuable in the future as I set out to show that this judge and this attorney have a corner on the law."

Last November, Hohol publicly accused Penox attorney, Arthur Piccone, of using his long-time personal and professional affiliation with Cappellini to influence courtroom decisions.

The issue initially was raised earlier when Attorney Louis Sinatra of the Philadelphia area filed a motion for the recusal of Cappellini in a lawsuit between a Hazleton National Bank officer and Louis J. Beltrami, Hazleton area business magnate.

Cappellini was faced with two more recusal motions last year — when the Hazleton National Bank joined Sinatra's motion and in November when Hohol asked the jurist to step down.

In all three instances, Cappellini denied the recusal motions.

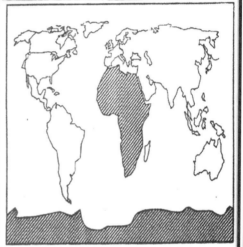

Larry Hohol gets his market — Africa and Antarctica

The request for the preliminary injunction was filed by Essex Industries Inc. and Penox Technologies Inc., Pittston. Essex, headquartered in St. Louis, Mo., purchased Penox, which manufactures cryogenic products used in the home health care industry, from Hohol in December 1988.

Harvey Guller, president of Penox, said yesterday he had not yet seen the order and, when apprised of its contents, said, "That confirms what we thought we acquired four years ago."

After the sale and following Hohol's three-month stint as an employee of Essex/Penox, Hohol launched a new business venture, Cryco, which manufactured cryogenic vessels used in the light industrial market.

In August 1990, Essex filed for injunctive relief, claiming Hohol's activities violated a non-competitive agreement between Hohol and Penox.

Following 17 hearings on the injunction, which stretched out across nine months, Cappellini granted the injunction in August 1991, shutting down Cryco.

The state Superior Court last Sept. 8 vacated the injunction on the grounds that it lacked geographical parameters and remanded the case to Cappellini.

who presided over hearings on Nov. 19-20 and oral arguments on Dec. 16.

In the order, Cappellini prohibits Hohol's firm from conducting business in Australia, all 50 United States, Canada, France, Netherlands, Belgium, United Kingdom, Spain, Italy, Germany, Turkey, Czechoslovakia, Poland, Hungary, Uruguay, Colombia, Singapore, Japan, China, Hong Kong, Indonesia, Korea, Malaysia, Philippines, Taiwan and Thailand.

Attorney Ronald Santora, affiliated with the firm of Hourigan, Kluger, Spohrer & Quinn, declined comment on the order, explaining that he "did not have the chance to review it."

Cappellini told the Citizens' Voice the "whole (Penox/Hohol) matter will be tied up this week" when he issues an order on Hohol's request to increase the $100,000 bond posted by Essex at the time the preliminary injunction was granted.

"The issue of raising the bond will be decided this week," the jurist said. "I am handling these matters in a sequence."

Hohol's request to increase the bond was argued during a July 14, 1992 hearing.

On Tuesday, Cappellini issued a one-paragraph ruling that denies and dismisses the preliminary objections filed by Hohol in 1990 — issues raised when Essex attempted to restrict Hohol's activities for the second time.

"I find it curious and interesting that it took nearly 2½ years to

Larry Hohol

render a one-paragraph decision and only a month to address the geographical parameters issue," Hohol said. "I still haven't heard anything on my request to increase the bond. That hearing was held five months before the geographical limitations hearing was over. It's strange how the judge leap-frogs over motions and decisions."

Attorney Ronald Santora, a colleague of Piccone in the Hourigan firm, said that once the judge disposes of the motions dealing with the preliminary injunction, the final hearing will be held.

"Once all of this is out of the way, we will be able to proceed with the final hearing or trial," Santora said. "With all of these objections pending, we could not go forward."

The above quote is great. "I am handling these matters in a sequence." It is a good thing he didn't say "in the proper sequence" because I would have to call him a liar again, and you know I would.

BUSINESS

Bankrupt ex-tycoon loses fight in court

■ *Businessman Larry Hohol says he will appeal the ruling*

By JERRY LYNOTT
Times Leader Staff Writer

WILKES-BARRE — A Luzerne County judge has reissued an order restricting the global business activities of Larry Hohol, an entrepreneur since bankrupted by the legal battle with the company that bought his business for $7 million in 1988.

The order issued Monday by Judge Gifford Cappellini directs Hohol, the former owner of Penox Technologies Inc., not to compete with his old company in 26 countries, including the United States, France, Germany, the United Kingdom, China and Japan.

Larry Hohol

In July 1991, Cappellini granted a preliminary injunction against Hohol and his new business, Cryco Inc.

Hohol appealed the ruling to the state Superior Court, which sent it back to Cappellini on Sept. 8, 1992, for lack of defined geographical limits.

Since then, Cappellini has held hearings, heard testimony and reviewed evidence from both parties involved in the dispute.

Hohol, of Hunlock Creek, said he believed Cappellini took an "extreme position" in the order and will appeal it to state Superior Court.

"I'm not surprised by it," he said.

Early on in the case, Hohol asked Cappellini to remove himself from handling the proceedings because of an alleged conflict of interest between the judge and one of the attorneys representing Penox, a former law partner of the judge.

Hohol has blamed his downfall on Cappellini. The former Luzerne Borough police officer, who rose to the top of the business world in the late 1980s, said he had to represent himself in the case when he could no longer pay attorneys fees.

In 1991, Hohol declared personal bankruptcy because of mounting legal and accounting bills and his investment in Cryco.

He said he was recently awarded a $100,000 judgment from an unrelated matter with Penox and planned to hire counsel for the appeal of the injunction.

Penox president Harvey Guller said he had not seen the order as of Tuesday and could not comment.

But when the part of the order concerning the geographical boundaries was read to him, Guller said Cappellini had done what the Superior Court asked him to do.

Guller said that when a group of St. Louis investors bought Penox, they acquired not only the company but "all of the areas in which it was doing business plus all of the areas it had opportunities to do business in."

In subsequent newspaper interviews, I held his ruling up high to demonstrate just how far this judge would go to help his best friend. The public was outraged.

The ruling turned into a public relations nightmare, not only for Cappellini, but also for the court in general. The competence and fairness of the court, which was already questionable, was now magnified, many fold. Prior to this, only Cappellini's fairness had been under question. Now everyone was asking, how could the court allow one of its own to behave so outlandishly? Something had to be done about it.

Judge Cappellini must have received an order from the now beleaguered President Judge to grant an interview to the friendliest of the two papers for the purpose of defusing this powder keg. It was an interview the judge would later regret. Interviewing a judge on a specific case is almost unheard of, but something had to be done to still the waters.

A simple rule to follow when being interviewed is: No matter how highly you think of yourself, never, ever talk down to the people. Statements like, "Lay people just can't understand the complexities of the issues brought before me in this court," just don't work well.

Coal Crackers are a lot of things, but stupid isn't one of them. We happen to pride ourselves in hard work and common sense but we also have our share of grey cranial matter. What this judge did, smacked in the face of common sense. Cappellini clearly appeared biased and a lot of people felt what he did was totally inappropriate. I was, and still am, one of those people.

CHAPTER TWENTY-SIX

*N*OW WHAT?

---

*A*ll hope of reopening my business was completely gone. A close friend offered to store my equipment at no charge in his warehouse. I gratefully accepted.

Cappellini "corrected" the bond issue and he "corrected" the geographical limitation issue, if you want to call what he did correcting. The only recourse we had left was to return to Superior Court to address the remaining sixteen issues of the appeal. Regardless of what Judge Cappellini said in court, the Superior Court's ruling clearly stated that they did not address the remaining issues. Or did they? You be the judge.

Believe it or not, we had to go through the same routine to get back on the list of cases, just like we did the first time around. When it was finally our day to go to court, Pete was not only available, he was eager. Pete's mood on the way to Philadelphia that day is best described as optimistically subdued. He wasn't full of fire, but he was very, very confident. I could tell he couldn't wait to expose what was happening in Luzerne County.

It was finally Pete's turn to address the Superior Court in its entirety. He confidently approached the podium. The digital clock was set to 15:00, the light turned green and once again, we were off to the races. We had about one minute per issue. Pete sang in the choir at his church. He had a deep, rich voice. Add to that the fact that he was extremely passionate about the subject at hand. His voice seemed to slightly echo off the walls of the chamber, but not in a bad way. He succeeded in grabbing everyone's attention. I thought, "Man I'm glad this guy is on my side." As I finished my thought, something very bad happened.

A louder voice bellowed out, "What the hell do you think you're doing?"

Everyone in the courtroom was stunned and shocked, but no one more than Pete. Not even me. Pete responded in a voice that had moved up an octave.

"Well, Your Honor, I am addressing the remaining issues on our appeal. These are the issues that were not addressed the last time my client was here."

The judge exclaimed in a very threatening voice, "How dare you come into this courtroom and attempt to re-argue your case. You are here to argue Geographic Limitations and only Geographic Limitations. You got that?"

"Well, no, Your Honor," Pete replied. "The remaining sixteen issues on our appeal have never been addressed by this court. The last time we were here the court addressed Geographic Limitations and that was it."

Apparently, that statement made the Chief Justice really angry.

"Now, you are going to tell me in open court that we didn't do our job? You are going to tell me that we did not follow procedure? I have a good mind to……"

A very quiet voice was trying to interrupt the Chief Justice. I thought who the heck would have the guts to do that? A very frail appearing, elderly justice, at the far end of the bench was flipping through some pages and began speaking.

"I remember this case. The attorney is right," and he continued on. "We didn't address the remaining issues. We kicked this mess back to Cappellini and told him to take care of it. Apparently, he didn't take our hint that what we really meant was for him to make it go away."

Then another justice spoke up. "He's right. I can't believe we have this thing back here, this is a mess."

A general discussion occurred between the justices. All the time the clock was ticking. Pete became animated. Most of what was being said sounded good for us, but he needed to get on the record, fast. Pete addressed the Chief Justice.

"May I continue?" he begged.

The Chief Justice still sounding very hostile declared, "You may."

"Since my time is limited, I will first address the most serious of the fatal flaws," Pete continued. "Please keep in mind that all of my arguments are before you in writing, should I not finish orally."

The Chief Justice just flicked his hand like an old man would when a young kid was bothering him and he just wanted him to go away. I liked what all the other justices had to say, but I sure didn't appreciate anything about the Chief Justice's comments or body language.

In his strong, confident voice, Pete made his points as fast as he could. When we saw the yellow light come on, he wasn't even halfway through his list. The final light turned red before Pete could even start making his closing comment. He looked at the Chief Justice and asked if he could have a little more time.

The Chief Justice had now changed his tone, ever so slightly. He said that he could not set a new precedent as it would snowball. The justices getting home at midnight every night would not make for a happy home life. Most of the justices gave a little chuckle.

We showed up at the elevator the same time as opposing counsel (no, it wasn't Attorney Piccone). He motioned for us to go first and that he would wait. That was the only time in all the years of litigation that the opposing side exhibited any form of courtesy to me. I looked at him and said, "Thank you." Pete did not speak.

After we made it to the ground floor and had gotten far enough from the elevator, I asked, "What the hell just happened up there?"

He looked at me with very, very sad eyes and said, "I don't know."

We walked to the car without speaking. Unlike the last time I drove from Philadelphia with Glenn back to Wilkes-Barre, this trip with Pete would be a lot quieter.

I really hate when an attorney says to me, "I have never seen anything like this." I couldn't begin to guess how often those words have passed through my ears in the previous three years. I offered Pete some positive observations. I mentioned how the other justices talked about how much of a mess this case was and how they had sent it back to Cappellini to make it go away.

Pete looked at me and said, "Larry, I have been doing this for a long, long time. I have never seen anything like this and believe me when I tell you, nothing good that will come of it."

I would love to tell you that Pete was wrong, but he wasn't. What was so striking about the ruling we received was the fact that the court did not dissect or address a single issue. It simply went in the order of the points listed and generically stated, for each and every one of the remaining sixteen points, the following:

Denied: This court has relied upon the judgment of the "Trial Court's review of the evidence and testimony" for this matter.

The Superior Court was flat out stating that they did not review the evidence and compare it to the argument. When I asked Pete what he thought, what do you think he said? You got it!

"I have never seen anything like this."

The best we could come up with was that the Superior Court had given us reasons to file an appeal to their decision to the Supreme Court, but even that was a stretch.

CHAPTER TWENTY-SEVEN

Judicial Safeguards

At the same time the Superior Court debacle had moved forward I had decided to also file a formal complaint against Judge Cappellini with the Pennsylvania Judicial Conduct Board. Back then it was officially called the Judicial Inquiry and Review Board or JIRB and later evolved into the JCB. If you thought what you have read so far has been incredible, hang onto your hat.

The JCB is in place to deal with exactly the type of problem I was facing. Officially, that was their sole purpose; investigating misconduct by judges was their sole mission. It was a big step, but I was raised to believe that you live by the rules and play by the rules. In my opinion, this judge and attorney were doing neither.

I sent the following "Letter to the Editor" which was published.

1 Korn Street
Kingston, PA 18704

Cappellini's Remarks "Out Of Order, Again."

I have held back commenting on inappropriate published remarks made by Luzerne County Judge Gifford S. Cappellini due to his recent hospitilization.

For Judge Cappellini to comment about ongoing litigation that is before him is not only outrageous but down right frightening. The total disregard of protocol by him can only be described as outlandish.

Why does Judge Cappellini feel the need to defend himself and his decisions so much that he would be quoted in a newspaper on why he ruled against me and my company knowing full well the permanent injunction is yet to be heard in front of him.

I am filing a complaint with the Commonwealth of Pennsylvania Judical Inquiry and Review Board concerning Judge Cappellini's handling of this entire case, as well as his preferential treatment of his ex-law partner and best friend Arthur Piccone Esquire, of the firm Hourigan, Kluger, and Spohrer & Quinn.

If anyone would like to come forward with additional information to assist in an investigation please either contact me or call directly to the Judicial Inquiry Board in Harrisburg at 717-234-7911.

In closing, if Judge Cappellini ever attempts to intimidate any local attorney by demanding the attorney immediately produce anyone that would question his integrity, as he did recently with Attorney Donald Brobst please feel free to use my name.

Sincerely

Larry Hohol
President
Cryco Inc
1 Korn Street
Kingston, PA 18704
717-288-8255

I followed through on my threat and called the Judicial Inquiry and Review Board in Harrisburg. A form letter and complaint form were mailed to me. I sat at my desk with restrained excitement. We were playing hardball and this could be my Grand Slam. I wanted to do it right. I sure didn't want to come across as a litigant who was on the wrong side of a lawsuit looking for a way to weasel out. No sir, "Just the facts, M'am....just the facts". I basically used my Motion for Recusal as a guide for my formal complaint against the judge. It didn't take long to hear back from Harrisburg.

A very official sounding man called me and identified himself as the Chief Investigator of the JIRB. His name was Ken Finnell. He told me that he had reviewed my written complaint and after a brief conversation, he asked if I would be willing to drive to Harrisburg to be formally interviewed. "I can be there in two hours," was my response.

He told me he was thinking more like next week. Since it wasn't my call, I agreed. I showed up in Harrisburg early for my interview. I remember how cold it was. It was one of those winter days where the passing snow flurries created hidden patches of ice in the shadows of the roads and sidewalks. I was dressed in a suit and tie which was not exactly winter gear. I finally found the JIRB offices and ran from my car to their front door, almost falling on more than one of those damn sidewalk ice patches.

I sat in the waiting room, hoping I was about to meet my new best friend in the world. It felt kind of like I was waiting for someone on a blind date. You know, wondering, is this going to be the one? There was a lot more at stake here, so it just amplified that sensation.

A male voice was talking loudly as he was heading towards the waiting room door. I stood up in anticipation, briefcase in hand. A rather short, slightly balding, middle-aged gentleman extended his hand and introduced himself.

"Hi, I'm Ken."

He then announced his title like he was proclaiming it to the masses at the Coliseum in Rome.

"I am the "CHIEF INVESTIGATOR for the Judicial Conduct Board."

I remember unfairly thinking, "Well, this guy is no Clark Kent." I consoled myself by remembering that the "Pen is mightier than the sword."

We then walked to his office. I noticed that Ken walked in such a way that made him look like he was sort of marching. He was rigid in his demeanor with his shoulders back, chest out, and head facing straight forward. What really caught my eye was how he squared the corners off as he walked around his desk. That was a little quirky.

His office felt like the Fraternal Order of Police's Memorial Shrine that was dedicated to all of those who had fallen and all who had served. The walls were covered with pictures of-you guessed it-Ken in his police uniform. I gazed in wonder at how grossly egotistical this sacred shrine appeared.

I started looking at the pictures, just as he had anticipated. Ken sat back in his chair to receive my questions. He actually glowed as he described his years on the force. There were pictures of him when he graduated the police academy and pictures with all the other crime fighters who graduated the academy with him. He pointed out how important some of his classmates had become and that he remained very close to them after all these years. There were newspaper articles that were hermetically sealed and framed in expensive custom frames for all to oogle over.

Sitting dead center on the wall was the picture of all pictures. I walked closer as Ken began to smile in anticipation. I acted like I was afraid to get too close because I could not believe what I was seeing. Here was a blown up picture of this yahoo straddled across the steel beams of an old-style metal bridge that was crossing over a river. Both of his arms were outstretched as he was trying to grab hold of a suicidal man. The only thing that kept Ken from simply rolling off the beam himself was his massively powerful legs, or so he implied. I acted spellbound. Please tell me more, I begged. Did you save this poor man? What kind of training did you have that could possibly prepare you for such a high risk rescue? How did you ever get him down? How the heck did you get this picture?

Ken proceeded to tell me that he was on patrol and ended up being the first one at the scene. There hadn't been any training for this type of rescue, nor had he received any training on how to talk a jumper down. Before anyone else got there, Ken had climbed the bridge on his own without safety gear and just talked to the guy. I thought to myself, if I were his Chief, I would have fired his ass when he got down off that bridge.

As far as getting the picture, well, that turned out to be harder than the actual rescue. He had to hunt down the news helicopter pilot, then the photographer and hound him for weeks before he was able to get a copy. As I could see, it was well worth it.

I shared with him the fact that I was a fellow "Former Police Officer." I wasn't able to tell any of my cop stories more than halfway through before Ken remembered a story of his own that was even better. Our first date had started out a little rocky, but we had finally bonded. I felt a bit like a prostitute.

I had a couple of meetings with Ken in Harrisburg before he came to Wilkes-Barre to do some more investigating and interviewing. He showed genuine interest and promise.

It gave me some comfort knowing that behind the scenes, a real honest-to-goodness investigation was going on by a board that was empowered to do something about this debacle. I think the judge even sensed my new found confidence. When I cross examined witnesses, I actually did so in the form of a question. You know, just like the TV show *Jeopardy*. (I love that show; it keeps me humble.)

I kept detailed notes and remembered to use them. To the untrained eye and ear of someone off the street, you might have thought I was actually an attorney. However, I can think of better things to be. In the middle of all of this carnage I still had a sense of humor as you can see by the next article.

The following is a letter that I sent to the Chief Investigator prior to his visit to Wilkes-Barre.

Cryogenics, Inc.
P. O. Box 1401
Kingston, PA 18704

(717) 288-4570

January 18, 1995

Ken Fennell
Judicial Inquiry and Review Bd
225 Market St.
Harrisburg, PA 17101

Dear Ken:

This a follow-up to our telephone conversation of last week. I am presently trying to determine the exact date that the Judge was observed sitting next to Piccone during the lunch break in our proceedings. I should be able to pinpoint the date by the transcripts. The only problem I may run into is that some of my transcripts are missing. Major portions of these proceedings cannot be found by the Stenographers office at the courthouse. See attatched.

I feel it is important that the depositions of Attorney Richard Russo and Norm Namey be taken. They will not lie under oath and I am sure they will recall the date, if pushed.

I feel that the direction you are going is good and solid, but would like to stress that my complaint here is much more serious. I truly feel that there is a pattern of conspiracy here between the judge and Attorney Piccone. There are many trials that have been put before the judge, by Piccone, using questionable tactics and verdicts,by the judge, that have been found "legally insufficient" or reversed for other reasons. Piccone and the judge living together, as well as Piconne (while under oath) swearing he no longer maintains a friendship with the judge, only to have the judge announce in open court he is in-fact very good friends with Piccone all point to a bigger problem.

Please feel free to contact me at your convenience.

"Manufacturers of the world's finest industrial cryogenic vessels."

My new buddy, Ken, finally came to Wilkes-Barre to conduct interviews. I called the two attorneys (Rick and Norm) who had witnessed Judge Cappellini having lunch with opposing counsel during my trial with my adversaries sitting next to them. I told both of them I needed to talk to them for just a couple of minutes and that I would swing by in the afternoon. I thought it best not to tell them who I was bringing with me so they wouldn't panic and suddenly become unavailable.

That didn't work. After I introduced Ken, they both had the same independent response. It went something like, I can't recall what you are talking about, but if I do I will call you immediately. Please give me your card. I have to leave now. How could they not remember, I thought? They both about had strokes when they saw the judge and Piccone having lunch together. Rick was so upset that we didn't even eat lunch ourselves that day.

Ken told me not to worry about those two. This sort of thing happens all the time when it comes to judges. Attorneys are scared shitless of them. He told me that since the judge acknowledged in open court the fact that this lunch occurred, it was probably all that he needed. It would be in the day's transcripts and was witnessed by two reporters. Ken also said that getting a subpoena for Rick and Norm to testify before the board had a way of refreshing memories. It was a shame because of all the attorneys I have known through the years, I figured these two would do the right thing when the chips were down. Wrong again, Larry!

Within a few days of Ken's visit, rumors throughout the legal community were flying big time about Cappellini being under investigation. Both newspapers dove on it. In separate interviews, I acknowledged that I had filed a formal complaint with the Judicial Conduct Board. That news hit the papers and things began to happen. Shortly thereafter, I received a very strange phone call.

CHAPTER TWENTY EIGHT

Deep Throat

A voice on the phone started out by saying, "You don't know me, but I know you. I have been following your case in the papers and I've been told that you are a man who can be trusted." Continuing on, she said, "I can help you with the problem you have with the judge and I want to meet with you as soon as possible."

I got a cold, uneasy feeling as she talked. Nothing in my life had come easy and I sure didn't expect something this easy to fall out of the sky now. It was kind of like Deep Throat. She told me her name was Debbie. Debbie insisted that we needed to meet where no one would recognize either one of us. I told her if that were the case, anywhere in Luzerne County was out. She chuckled and said maybe she was being a little over dramatic. I convinced her that we should just talk over the phone first. After I heard what she had to say I would decide whether or not we should meet. She said, "Fair enough."

Debbie told me she would have to call back later in the day and we set up a time for her return call. Debbie ended up being "The Real Deal." My initial, uneasy feeling, about her was totally wrong.

Debbie called back, as promised. I could tell she wanted to get right to it. Debbie told me that I would recognize her last name right away. I replied, "OK, try me."

Debbie's last name was Cappellini, the same as my favorite judge. I was stunned into silence.

"Just the reaction I expected," she commented.

"Oooo-kaaaay," I said slowly.

"I am married to the judge's son. The judge is Gifford Senior and my husband is Gifford Junior. I am about to tell you some things that are absolutely outrageous and absolutely true. You may want to take notes," she offered. I couldn't grab my ink pen fast enough.

"Let me start off by saying that my husband is a practicing attorney right here in Luzerne County."

I told her that I knew he was because I had seen his picture in the paper a number of times concerning lawsuits or criminal cases he was involved in.

Debbie announced, "My husband is a drug addict. Not only does he practice law while he is stoned, but he also drives the family car with our kids in it. Most of the time he comes home so "whacked out" that he can't even get out of the car to walk into the house," Debbie said. "My kids and I have had to drag him into the house or he would have frozen to death in his car many times over. This man is not a recreational user of cocaine; he is a twenty-four-hour-a-day addict."

I simply asked, "What does that have to do with me?"

"The judge knows all about the drug use," she replied, connecting the dots for me. "The judge knows his son is practicing law while he's high on drugs. He knows he is in the courtroom representing paying clients, higher than a kite. He knows that his grandchildren are scared for their lives when their daddy picks them up from school, and he knows that what he is doing to you is wrong."

There was a long silence. I finally spoke.

"You now have my full attention."

"I thought I would."

I asked her to give me a moment. I needed to process the information she had just given me and intertwine it with my situation. It finally hit me.

"Let me guess, you are in the middle of a messy divorce and you are going to use this info to get the house, the car, lots of child support and a huge settlement. Thanks, but no thanks, I'm not interested."

Before I could hang up, she said, "No, you're wrong."

"How so", I asked?

"My husband doesn't have a pot to piss in. He re-mortgaged the house to buy drugs and has screwed his Law Practice up so bad he will never recover," Debbie informed me. "He has drug dealers coming to the house at all hours of the day and night and even had one of them living with us till I told him I was going to call the cops. He got real mad, stuck a gun in my face and threatened to kill me and the kids, but he made the guy leave."

"You just don't know what it's like," she confided. "I am finding drugs all over the house. He is using so much of the stuff that he is just letting it lay around. I am worried about the kids getting their hands on this stuff, so when I find it, I flush it. If he ever knew I did that, I'm sure he would kill me. My heart stops when I know he is driving the car with the kids in it. It's not only them, but what about the car loads of kids coming the other way?"

"Okay, okay, I get it," I replied. "I'm still not sure how I work it into this mix and, by the way, how do you know the judge knows that what he is doing to me is wrong?"

"I confronted him," Debbie said. "I went to him for help. You know, in the public eye the judge is a big shot with that drug and alcohol rehab center, Clearbrook. The Judge and his wife both sit on the board of directors along with his buddy Piccone. Anyway, I went to the judge's house, begging him for help. We talked about his son's drug habit and how serious it was getting. He told me that his son was a big boy and that he needed to figure it out on his own. It escalated quickly from there. I asked him what kind of father, or better yet, what kind of grandfather was he?" I said, 'Maybe you think your son should do this on his own but what if he kills your grandkids in the process? You get your picture all over the newspapers with Clearbrook. You're Mr. Big Shot, helping all these people you don't even know. This is your son, these are your grandchildren. Why won't you help them? I'll tell you why. It's your goddamn ego! It's the family name, isn't it, you son-of-a-bitch!"

"'This family doesn't have drug or alcohol problems. That's something the "little people" have. This family helps the little people; we are not part of them. She continued, it is just like that case you are handling that has you all over the papers. You look like a fool. If you weren't smart enough to know your life-long buddy, Piccone, was using you when the case started, you must have figured it out by now. Now it's all about showing that you are smarter and that you are better and that you never make mistakes. It's always someone else that's wrong. Never you! Maybe you're just a crook like the rest of them. Maybe you never thought it would get this big and out of hand. Well, if you think that case is big, wait till I tell this story to the press."

She continued to tell her story. "Hell, at that point the judge lost it. He told me to get the "F" out of his house and never come back. As far as he was concerned I was no longer the mother to his grandchildren or a member of the family. He screamed at me that if I ever said a word to anyone, as I had threatened, he would see to it that I would never see my kids again, and that he had enough power to do it. He told me that he would bury me just like he was going to bury that punk in the papers."

We both fell silent on the phone. It was almost like we had just run down the street together as fast as we could and needed to catch our breath. Only thing was, I hadn't spoken a word for the last 5 minutes. Still, she had taken my breath away. Debbie told me that the only way she could get her kids out of harm's way was to take down the judge. Plain and simple, it was the only way out.

I told Debbie we needed to meet.

I met with Debbie many times, and we became friends. We talked about my complaint with the Judicial Conduct Board and she filled in all the blanks regarding the judge and opposing counsel. Debbie told me how Cappellini and Piccone even lived together after the massive flood in 1972 and how each other's grown children still refer to the other as uncle. She related details regarding a scam that the judge, his wife and Debbie's husband almost went to jail over. It happened before Cappellini became a judge.

The family was basically running an unlicensed adoption agency. At some point the state became involved and shut them down. They came very close to being charged with a crime. Debbie went on to say that Attorney Piccone's biggest aspiration was to sit on the Supreme Court of Pennsylvania and that Cappellini would do anything to help facilitate that dream.

Basically, Debbie told me that I was the product of bad timing. Debbie went on to tell me that Piccone had been sued for malpractice. The settlement was huge and although his firm was insured, the deductible was over $100,000, so the firm had to pay up. Piccone needed to hit a homerun, no, a Grand Slam to generate some big profits for his firm or he would be history. That's about the time when my issue came along. I sometimes wonder what might have happened to me if opposing counsel hadn't been so incompetent.

CHAPTER TWENTY-NINE

Debbie and the Judicial Conduct Board

I contacted my buddy, Ken, at the JCB and told him I had someone who he needed to talk with soon. He said, "Sure thing, Lar, no problem."

A few days later I had Debbie call Ken from my office. I trusted her totally, but I wanted to make sure she didn't skip any important details. After she had finished talking with Ken, I talked to him.

Ken told me that he already had enough evidence against Judge Cappellini and he was starting the process to bring the judge before the board on official charges of misconduct. He then told me that he had asked Debbie if she would come to Harrisburg to give a sworn statement concerning everything she had just told him and to also take a polygraph test. She had agreed. Ken considered Debbie to be icing on the cake. He told me, and I quote, "I hope this judge doesn't have any plans for his big, fat pension because he is going down."

It was necessary for Ken to coordinate a state certified stenographer and a Penna. State Police Polygraph Examiner to be available on the same day. He would schedule the stenographer in the morning and polygraph examiner in the afternoon. As fate would have it, it took a few weeks to coordinate this arrangement and I just happened to be scheduled for court on that very same day. Debbie was nervous and wanted me present for moral support, as well as to give her a ride to the JCB Office. Debbie's husband had sold her car for drug money, so I made arrangements for a mutual friend, Carolee Medico to drive her to Harrisburg since I couldn't do it.

Late on the afternoon before Debbie was scheduled to go to Harrisburg, a secretary called from Ken's office to cancel the appointment. Debbie asked why, and the secretary said she did not know. I got on the phone and attempted to speak with Ken, but it was already after 5 pm. The next morning I was in court, so I tried to call Ken during a break to find out when everything would be rescheduled. I thought this would work out better anyway because I could then attend her interview and make sure no information was skipped. Ken was not in, so I left a message. By the end of the day Ken still had not returned my call. I started to worry.

The next day I called and once again, no Ken. I engaged the secretary in conversation to try to get a feel for what was going on. I finally said to her, "Look, I hate to keep calling you, so why don't we do this? Please ask Ken for the new date of the meeting and give me a call back to let me know when it is."

She was very pleasant and agreed to do what I had asked. The secretary never called me back. Debbie had also tried to get Ken on the phone without success.

After a few weeks of no response from Ken, Debbie's husband was arrested. Debbie's disclosure to the Judicial Conduct Board about her husband's drug problem had nothing to do with his arrest. There was a separate, unconnected investigation going on at the time. According to published reports, the State Attorney General's Office had arranged a sting operation where Debbie's husband, Attorney Gifford Cappellini Jr. would have the opportunity to purchase a small amount of cocaine. The buy took place in his law office while he was "representing" the person who was selling the drugs in a legal matter. This person was actually a real client that had turned into a wired informant. I sent copies of the newspaper articles to Ken, along with the following cover letter stating that she is obviously telling the truth.

Later on in this book, I will detail what happened to her husband and, more importantly, how the judge, his father, intervened in his case.

Naturally, I smelled a rat so I sent Ken the following letter as a way of covering ALL THE BASES.

April 7, 1995

KEN FENNELL
JUDICIAL INQUIRY & REVIEW BD
225 Market Street
Harrisburg, PA
17101

URGENT

Dear Ken:

Please find enclosed two newspaper articles concerning Gifford Jr.. As you know, I put his wife in direct contact with you and your office. It appears to me she was telling you the truth about her husband's drug problem. I would like to know if the fact that she was willing to give a sworn statement about Judge Cappellini having firsthand knowledge of his son's drug problem is being pursued by your office.

I realize that if a separate investigation on this matter is being conducted you cannot discuss it with me. On the other hand, if this issue is going to be piggybacked onto my complaint we need to discuss it further.

If your office is not taking any action on this matter to date because you have not received a formal complaint, please consider this letter such a complaint.

Please feel free to contact me at any time.

Best Regards,

Larry Hohol
(717)288-4570

FRIDAY, MARCH 31, 1995 — **WILKES-BARRE, PA**

Drug bust nets judge's son

■ Prominent lawyer Gifford R. Cappellini blames his arrest on being 'set up' because police were angry with him.

By DAWN SHURMAITIS
Times Leader Staff Writer

WILKES-BARRE — Attorney Gifford R. Cappellini, charged Thursday with trying to buy $190 worth of cocaine from a client, says he was entrapped by a desperate police informant because of who he is, what he does and who he is related to.

Cappellini, 42, of Dallas Township, said during an interview after the arrest he was set up to "get to someone higher up." He refused to be specific. His father is Luzerne County Judge Gifford S. Cappellini.

"I feel used and abused and set up," said Cappellini, a former assistant public defender who has represented a number of clients in high-profile drug cases. "Let's face it, I deal with bad people. Some you can't trust."

Wednesday night, narcotics agents from the state attorney general's office and the Wilkes-Barre Drug Task Force stopped Cappellini's car on Hollenback Avenue. On Thursday police charged him with one count each of solicitation to possess a controlled substance and criminal attempt to possess a controlled substance.

The misdemeanors each carry a maximum penalty of one year in jail and a $85,000 fine, said Deputy Attorney General Fran Sempa.

Sempa, who said more arrests are expected, refused to respond to Cappellini's comments.

According to the affidavit, here's why Cappellini was charged:

■ In early March, Cappellini's client, the unnamed informant, told Wilkes-Barre police officer Joseph Coffey that Cappellini gave him $100 to buy a gram of cocaine and deliver it to his Kingston law office.

■ On March 14, investigators secretly recorded Cappellini telling the informant and another, unidentified person they could be "set for life" if they could get 1 to 2 kilos of cocaine, sell it and invest the profit.

■ See LAWYER, Page 14A

Lawyer faces drug charges

from page 1

Donald L. Batz, a narcotics agent assigned to Region VIII Strike Force in Wilkes-Barre, received information from Wilkes-Barre Drug Task Force Officer Joseph Coffay that a person who was a confidential informant (CI) to police was solicited by Gifford Cappellini, Jr., to purchase cocaine for Cappellini.

According to Coffay, the informant stated that in early March 1995, Cappellini provided the CI with $100 in cash to purchase one gram of cocaine. The informant purchased the cocaine and delivered it to Cappellini at his law office in Kingston on March 8, 1995.

Batz confirmed this information in a subsequent interview with the informant.

On March 14, 1995, in a conservation recorded at Cappellini's office, the informant, another person and Cappellini discussed that they could all be "set for life" if they could obtain a large quantity of cocaine (one to two kilos was mentioned), sell it and invest the money.

On March 16, 1995, in another recorded conversation at Cappellini's law office in Kingston, the informant agreed to purchase one-eighth ounce of cocaine for Cappellini. During the conversation, Cappellini said to the informant, "I'll give you the money." The informant answered, "I can man."

Cappellini asked, "How long?" and the informant responded, "About two hours because its kinda' hot out there."

"I know," Cappellini said, then asking: "Is it definite?"

The informant answered, "(Do you) want a gram or more? I can get a deal on an eight ball for one-ninety."

Cappellini stated, "This isn't gonna' be an all-day thing now, is it?"

The informant: "No."

Cappellini: "You promise me?"

According to the informant, Cappellini then provided him with $200. Cappellini told the person, "Keep the ten for gas."

On Wednesday, March 29, on the direction of Batz, the informant purchased one-eighth ounce of cocaine from Dawn Partington. This transaction also was recorded, the affidavit states.

Prior to the purchase, the informant was searched for money and drugs with negative results and provided with $200 of advance funds to make the purchase. The informant subsequently turned over the cocaine purchased from Partington and it field-tested positive for cocaine.

The informant, at the direction of Batz, called Cappellini and told Cappellini that he had obtained Cappellini's "eight ball." The informant and Cappellini arranged to meet to consummate the transaction and this conversation also was recorded.

Batz subsequently supplied the informant with a non-controlled substance (as a substitute for the cocaine purchased for Cappellini).

The informant subsequently met with Cappellini and handed Cappellini the non-controlled substance indicating that it was the eighth-ounce of cocaine purchased for Cappellini. This transaction and conversation was recorded.

Drug agents conducted surveillance and watched the meeting between the informant and Cappellini.

Cappellini is the son of Judge Gifford Cappellini of the Luzerne County Court.

I received my answer in the mail in the form of a letter from Mr. Vincent J. Quinn, Chief Counsel of the JCB.

COMMONWEALTH OF PENNSYLVANIA

JUDICIAL CONDUCT BOARD
225 MARKET STREET
HARRISBURG, PA 17101

VINCENT J. QUINN
CHIEF COUNSEL

(717) 234-7911

June 14, 1995

Mr. Larry Hohol
R. R. #3, Box 202
Hunlock Creek, PA 18621

RE: Complaint No. 94-093

Dear Mr. Hohol:

This letter is in response to the complaint you filed with the Judicial Conduct Board.

After conducting the necessary inquiry and reviewing your complaint, the Board has determined that there is no basis for further action. Therefore, the complaint docketed to the above number has been dismissed.

Very truly yours,

Vincent J. Quinn
Chief Counsel

The words stunned, shocked and betrayed don't even come close to describing my emotions. I had given the JCB everything they needed to take action against Judge Cappellini on a silver platter. Judge Cappellini and this drug issue was big. I don't care if it was his son. According to Debbie, who was a "Cappellini," the judge knew his son was representing clients in serious court proceedings while heavily under the influence of cocaine. On a non-legal issue, Judge Cappellini knew his son was driving his grandchildren all around Luzerne County while he was heavily "under the influence."

CHAPTER THIRTY

What Really Happened to the JCB INVESTIGATION?

I called Ken. Naturally, he didn't take my call, so I left a message. Very politely, I asked Ken's secretary if she was ready to write, telling her that it was very important that she get my message written down exactly how I relayed it. She said she was ready. I said, "You tell that son-of-a-bitch that if he doesn't return my call today, I am coming to his office to talk to him." He still didn't return my call, so the next morning I was on my way to Harrisburg.

I arrived early, but waited until I was pretty certain that Ken was in his office. I didn't picture him being there promptly at nine o'clock no matter how well he marched or how perfectly he squared his corners.

I approached his secretary and asked to see him. She asked me if he was expecting me. I said, probably, but I wasn't sure. When I told her my name, suddenly she understood. The secretary said, she'd be right back. After being gone a few minutes, she finally came back and said, sheepishly, "I'm sorry, but Chief Finnell will not be able to see you today. Can you make an appointment?"

"No, I can't make an appointment," I replied. "I am a very patient man and I will simply wait until Ken can see me. Do you know of any reasonable hotels in the area?"

The secretary obligingly gave me a few numbers to call and told me which ones she felt were the best. As I turned away she said, "Goodbye."

I turned back to her and said, "I'm sorry, I'm not leaving. I will be sitting right here until either Ken meets with me or your office closes. I will only need the hotel information if I need to come back tomorrow."

With that said, I sat down and started reading magazines.

The morning turned into afternoon. I didn't dare go to lunch for fear Ken would leave for the day. Around 3pm the secretary's intercom rang. She picked it up and acknowledged the message. She said, "Ken can see you now."

I thanked her and found my way to his door. Ken jumped from behind his desk and, while shaking my hand, apologized for being so busy.

"It's just crazy around here," he said. "I just don't know what's going on with all these judges, its nuts!" He hurried by me to use the restroom as he had been held up in his office all day waiting me out.

Upon his return, I looked him square in the eye and said, "Ken, the last judge you guys tried to do anything to was six years ago and he skipped the country. He is still laughing at you and this board. I read an article about him in *USA Today*. He called you and this board a bunch of buffoons."

Ken answered, "It's just not so easy to peg one of these guys down."

"Why don't you tell me about it," was my response.

We talked for over an hour and a half. There was one recurring sentence throughout the conversation. It was, "I'm sorry, but it is just out of my hands."

If I heard it once, I heard it twenty times. After a while, Ken started repeating himself. At one point I said, "Ken, you already told me that. Tell me something I haven't heard yet."

I believe that Ken was genuinely embarrassed by his apparent impotence. After all of the stories he had shared with me about how strong and capable he was when he was "on the department," he was now toothless and couldn't provide me with a decent explanation as to why. I worked his ego ever so slightly, acting confused every time Ken said it was out of his hands. I even questioned his Chief Investigator position. It seemed to strike a nerve or maybe it was just his ego recoiling.

I gave Ken the benefit of the doubt by asking if maybe one of the regular investigators screwed it up for him. Ken then advised me that not only was he the Chief Investigator, he was the only investigator. With that I said, "Ken, this is squarely on your shoulders. I need to know what is going on here."

I could see that I had said the right thing. He stood up, walked around his desk using those semi-military corners and closed his door. He started looking around his office like he was checking to make sure no one else was there. Ken walked back around his desk, but chose not to sit down. He became very animated with his arms.

"Larry, you probably don't know this, but your judge is a member of this Board."

"*As a matter of fact I do!*" I almost sounded like a robot, which even surprised me when I heard my voice.

"I am going to tell you straight up that if I ever get backed into a corner about this conversation, I am going to lie my ass off. You got that?" said a very agitated Chief Investigator.

I nodded my head in agreement.

"We never had this talk!"

Again, I nodded my head to indicate I understood.

"Judge Cappellini contacted the board," Ken said. "He knows all the members and they all know him. He told them flat out that he knew about the investigation. He told them that he was going to retire shortly and that "The Board" could better use their resources to serve the fine people of this commonwealth if they were to focus their efforts elsewhere. They agreed." The Chief Investigator for the Pennsylvania Judicial Conduct board then said to me, "I swear to God that if I ever get called on this, I am going to lie my ass off!"

Ken then added, "I'm sorry, it is out of my hands."

That was the last time I ever spoke to Ken Finnell. My drive from Harrisburg to Wilkes-Barre that day was long and lonely.

I am convinced that Debbie's appointment to give her "on the record" sworn statement and take a polygraph test was cancelled so that no official record would ever be created. Such a record would cause a serious problem with deniability. The name of the game that the JCB plays best is "deniability" and they have certainly perfected their game.

I am sure the judge received either a courtesy copy of my denial letter or at least a phone call from a JCB member regarding the cancelled investigation. I did my best to act like everything was motoring along just fine. Apparently, over my lifetime, I have watched too many Walt Disney movies. You know, in the end where good always prevails over evil and everyone lives happily ever after. This was no movie and Walt Disney was dead.

CHAPTER THIRTY-ONE

*L*iquidation

---

*A*s I earlier stated, the opposition had paid me $100,000 at closing for the first year of my non-competitive agreement. If you take the first year that they paid for and add it to the four additional years that they didn't pay for, we come up with a total of five years. Hard to believe, but we were about to celebrate the fifth anniversary of the sale of my company to these fine people, sarcasm intended. Even though it seems like it has taken forever to get to this place in the story, I have only touched on the highlights.

Appealing the Superior Court's decision was out of the question for two obvious reasons. One, I was flat broke. The second reason was by the time the case would be heard the non-competitive agreement would have expired. If we won we would only be entitled to a reversal and the $100,000 bond. If we wanted to then pursue additional damages, we would have to file a new lawsuit and basically start over. Yeah, right. Would you do that?

What is probably the most mind boggling part of this whole lawsuit is what it was not. It was not a final hearing. It wasn't even a Permanent Injunction. It was an emergency, temporary incursion of the court to stop an activity that was so incredibly damaging that a dollar amount of damages could never be calculated, thus damages could never be awarded should the petitioning party prevail somewhere down the road. You have got to be kidding me! Five years later?

All proceedings ended on the fifth year anniversary of the sale of my company. The non-compete that my adversaries had never paid for had died a natural and timely death. It didn't even whimper when it expired, it just vanished without a trace.

The fact that my adversaries never paid me a penny of the $400,000 balance due under the terms of the "Non-Compete" contract screams of conspiracy involving this judge. Even if he honestly thought I was competing he should have "required" payment in order to enforce the terms of the contract.

I never sold a single one of their customers anything. I never even contacted a single one of their customers and *tried* to sell them anything. They didn't lose a single dollar of sales or a penny of profits to me or my company's activities.

You would think at this point I would start to wrap up this book with some words that would sound wise and thought provoking. Folks, we are not even close to being done yet.

Bankruptcy is a very bitter pill. Not only had I always paid all of my bills over my entire life, I had grown accustomed to sharing a lot of my money. This is not to toot my own horn, so please don't take it that way. I contributed the maximum amount of money allowed by law to my employees' retirement accounts, even though I wasn't required to deposit one penny. I paid full healthcare premiums for my employees and their entire families. I secretly paid for underprivileged children throughout Luzerne County to be bused into the Dorothy Darte Dickson Center for the Performing Arts every Christmas. Here they were treated to a live ballet performance of the magical, holiday classic, *The Nut Cracker*.

I would get such a kick out of watching the local TV stations with their "Live Reports" asking who the "Secret Santa" might be and then speculating that maybe it was the real Santa himself who did this wonderful thing. I had created enough business that over 500 people had worked for me over the 7 year period I had been in business. That, my friends, is a lot of positive effect on our local community.

It was now time for me to do the unthinkable. I had to convert to Chapter 7 bankruptcy, both personally and for my business. During the Cappellini trial I had already taken the step of filing for Chapter 11 protection. Now we were talking about converting to Chapter 7. That meant full liquidation of all assets. To me, bankruptcy was proof of failure. It meant that I had done something wrong. In my mind, it is what happens when you don't take care of business. What was so ironic is, in the business world I flourished at most everything I did. But we were not in the business world here. This alternate universe allowed people who had violated the very contract they were enforcing in court to prevail. It kind of reminded me of a person stealing a new car, and then suing the auto maker for their rebate and to also perform warranty work, even though the car wasn't broken, or paid for, if that makes any sense.

My adversaries couldn't show any harm even though their burden to show harm was enormous. Not one dollar, not one customer, not one product, not one penny. The best they could do was to connect the technology. I hadn't invented Cryogenics. It had been invented 100 years before I was born. Even the products that I was manufacturing and repairing with my new company were controlled by a very different federal agency than the one that regulated my old company. One product could not, by law, be used in the other marketplace. This entire escapade was simply bizarre. Bizarre, however, so real.

I had put the company into Chapter Eleven years before in the hopes of reopening it sometime in the future. Everything hinged on my appeals. Penox now attacked those plans through the bankruptcy court. They made outlandish claims against me, thus making all of the sitting creditors very nervous. My company was forced into liquidation and you will never guess who purchased my equipment? You guessed correctly. They did.

I was bankrupt, not because I had a gambling problem or a drug addiction or a drinking problem, or any other kind of addictive behavior. It was more like playing a vicious chess game instead of participating in litigation. I was getting clobbered and checkmate was only a few moves away.

After the Chapter 7 was finalized by the Federal Bankruptcy Court, everything was gone. I was living in a thirty foot tow-behind camper trailer parked behind my brother's house I and was driving a 1982 Cutlass that had one AM station (WILK) on its radio.

CHAPTER THIRTY-TWO

Time for this "Coal Cracker" to Move On

Other than some consulting work, I didn't even have a job. My ex-wife filed to have my child support based on what I could be earning, not on what I was actually earning. After all of this, I still didn't give up. I tried to restart my now destroyed company, but after a year of total frustration, I was nowhere.

I woke up one winter morning in 1999 and out of the blue decided that I had had enough. I drove to my office that day like I was going to the funeral of my best friend. I sat at my desk and opened up my calendar. Looking seven or so months out into the future, I circled the date of Sept. 21st. Over the next few months I closed down my anemic business and found jobs for my few remaining employees. I sold everything I owned (which wasn't much) at garage and yard sales. On the very day I had circled more than half a year earlier, I found myself driving south to Florida..........alone.

Totally out of character, I moved to a small town where I knew absolutely no one. Not one single person. I may have been by myself, but more importantly, I was away from the pain. Sure, I would think about everything that I had been through from time to time, but as the years flew by and I started living my new life, the horrors of The Luzerne County Railroad felt more and more like a bad dream. There were times it felt like more of a movie that I had watched instead of a reality that I had participated in.

For many, many years, no one in Florida knew that I had been a self made multi-millionaire, not even my new best friends. Moving away from Luzerne County was one of the best things that I ever did for myself in my entire life. Additionally, after 17 years

The Luzerne County Railroad

as a confirmed bachelor, I even recently remarried, which was another good move.

I have started two small businesses in Florida. I have kept my living expenses to a minimum and have just kept plugging away. Low and behold, one day my brother Dave called me from Luzerne County with an announcement. It had just hit the news that two Luzerne County Judges had been arrested on bribery and corruption charges. Judge Conahan and Judge Ciavarella were both charged by the FBI with corruption and, shortly thereafter, removed from the bench by the Pennsylvania Supreme Court. Their arrests have become known as "The Kids for Cash" scandal. Time Magazine, 60 Minutes, and 20/20 all have done major stories about this scandal.

All of a sudden, everything came crashing back. I started having dreams (nightmares, actually) about my past life up north. I wasn't eating or sleeping right. Concentration on my work was off. My new bride began to really worry about me. I began to worry about me.

I began waking up in the middle of the night to find myself sitting at my laptop typing information about my "prior life" with such clarity that it scared me. It was like everything happened yesterday. I remembered details like bad ties, bad haircuts and bad days. Lots and lots of bad days. I would immerse myself into my typing for hours and hours without taking a break. Those hours flew by like they were mere minutes. It was like I was in a time warp. I watched the FBI investigation back in Luzerne County with the intensity of a laser beam.

Then it happened. The FBI arrested President Judge Patrick Toole's son, Judge Michael Toole, on corruption charges that were unrelated to the other two judges. Judge Michael Toole was the "heir apparent" to the throne of his father. What made this arrest so significant was the fact that it looked like the FBI was not just doing a "hit and run" investigation of two crooked judges; they were doing some real digging. To date, the FBI has arrested over 30 people, of which most are public officials who are charged with some form of corruption in this single investigation.

At one point I felt like the Richard Dreyfuss character in the movie "Close Encounters of the Third Kind." Remember when he was busy building a huge model of "Devil's Tower" in the middle of his living room and he didn't know why? I was building my own structure in my living room except I was using a laptop. Like Dreyfuss I was building something and didn't know what it was or why I was building it.

I contacted the FBI in Scranton who were heading up the corruption investigation in Luzerne County and sent them a ton of information. They were courteous and professional. After they reviewed what I had sent, their response was disappointing. I was told that the information was extremely interesting and "could" be used in the future, "but" (there is that "but" word again) everything that happened to me was out of the box of their current investigation's time frame. In other words my case was too old. I asked one of the senior agents what the statute of limitations was on violations of my civil rights. He seemed very interested in my question. He asked which one? I said the 14th Amendment, my right to "Due Process." He perked up even more when he responded. He told me that he didn't know but that I should investigate it both criminally and civilly. I am.

It was shortly after talking to the FBI that I decided that the very best thing that I could do with what I know, was to share it. It is important that the public knows what could be in store for them if they every end up in a court proceeding. Like you, I was just some schmuck off the street. I believe with all of my heart that I was simply a victim of timing, and nothing more. Unfortunately, "The Perfect Storm" was also caused by timing.

CHAPTER THIRTY-THREE

A Judge's Son in Luzerne County

$\mathcal{M}$y original plan was to write one closing chapter here and simply show examples of how outrageous Judge Cappellini could be regarding issues involving people other than myself. While the following chapters started out as being a single chapter, the more I researched peripheral issues, the more enraged I became. The following chapters took on a life of their own. It was as if the stories themselves were demanding to be written.

As I wrote about earlier in this book, Judge Cappellini's son, Attorney Gifford R. Cappellini Jr, was arrested by the Pennsylvania State Attorney General's Office for attempting to buy cocaine from one of his "wired" clients. He attempted this purchase while meeting with this client in his Law Office, which was located about four blocks from the courthouse. Cappellini Jr. was recorded by the AG's office as wanting to buy a small amount of cocaine immediately for his own use. He was also recorded as wanting to purchase a large quantity of cocaine in the near future so that he could retire from his law practice and be financially set for life..

I will cut Attorney Cappellini some slack here and express sympathy for his drug addiction. My family has been blessed in the fact that we have never had anyone suffer from such a tragic affliction. With that being said, Attorney Cappellini's request to purchase a large amount of cocaine at a future date, so that he could retire from his law practice, constitutes "Drug Trafficking," which is a whole different matter in my mind, as well as under the law.

Keep in mind that the Pennsylvania Judicial Conduct Board was advised in writing by myself and Attorney Cappellini's wife (via the Chief Investigator) of not only Attorney Cappellini's drug addiction prior to his arrest, but also the fact that he was practicing law while under the influence of cocaine. Some real Constitutional issues arise from that fact.

The JCB was also advised before Attorney Cappellini's arrest that his father, Judge Cappellini, was fully aware of his son's illegal and unethical activities. The Judicial Conduct Board is not the governing body when it comes to attorneys. They are, however, the soul governing body when it comes to judges. They did nothing about Judge Cappellini just as Attorney Rick had told me years before, nor did they advise the appropriate agency when it came to Attorney Cappellini activities. What you are about to read will outrage even the most skeptical.

Attorney Cappellini paid $190.00 plus a ten dollar "tip" for simulated cocaine from the "wired" informant and was subsequently arrested. As you can imagine, it was big news. It made headlines in both Wilkes-Barre newspapers. Naturally, he didn't go to jail. Sons or daughters of judges in Luzerne County have never gone to jail. He was charged by the Pennsylvania Attorney General's Office with two crimes. The two charges were, "Solicitation to Possess a Controlled Substance" and "Criminal Attempt to Possess a Controlled Substance."

I noticed right from the beginning that the charge of "Attempted Drug Trafficking" was missing. I believe even the drug agents were trying to limit the amount of damage to the Cappellini family as a professional courtesy to a powerful judge. I also believe that the judge didn't see it that way for one millisecond.

Because the Pennsylvania State Attorney General's Office came in to make the arrest, this case was now beyond control. If a local police department, county detective, or even the local Pennsylvania State Police made the arrest, without the states involvement, things might have been "manageable," but that's not what occurred. So what is a judge to do?

Damage control is the first order of business. Since the judge and his wife were sitting board members of Clearbrook Lodge, a drug and alcohol rehab center, I would have thought intervention would have topped the list. It did not. Additionally, Attorney Piccone was the Chairman of that board and his son, Robert Piccone, was, and as of the day of this publishing, still is the President of the same rehab center. After I wrote this portion of the book another incredible bit of information was made public by Attorney Piccone himself concerning Clearbrook Drug Rehab Center. Attorney Piccone owned the rehab center. Look it up yourself. They have a website.

Attorney Cappellini was released without cash bail or a bond requirement and allowed to simply go home. I could write a whole book on this case. Attorney Cappellini began wearing a neck brace, like Ted Kennedy did after the Chappaquiddick incident. He also started attacking the media and claimed the media and the police were out to ruin his good family name because of his prior defense of numerous drug dealers.

Judge Cappellini is not the first sitting judge to have a son or daughter who has a drug problem. However, I would venture to say that Judge Cappellini has secured his place in history as having scored a number of "firsts" as far as how his son's case was handled. I have tried on numerous occasions to count the number of "firsts," but each time I review my records I basically find a new one for the list. Just for fun, see how many you come up with. Of course the judge will tell you with a straight face that he had nothing to do with any of it. I humbly disagree.

The next thing that happened was Attorney Cappellini waived his right to a Preliminary Hearing. No big deal here. After endless delays and posturing, his day of reckoning finally came. On September 11, 1995, Attorney Cappellini plead No Contest to the two drug charges. He was sentenced to 45 days of home confinement and one year of probation with no jail time, no fine, and no community service required. Basically, he was slapped on the wrist. Yet, it was something. Because the state was involved he hadn't just walked away unscathed.

This is where it starts getting real interesting. Attorney Cappellini is confined to his home, and is required to have random drug and alcohol testing performed by the Luzerne County Adult Probation Office. Attorney Cappellini is only allowed to leave his residence for pre-authorized appointments and meetings. No exceptions. Everything was quiet for a few months and then the following article appears in the local paper.

Wes-Barre, PA, Thursday, February 15, 1996 **3A**

Steve Corbett

An update on a drug case

Nobody likes to pee in a bottle.

Still it's one of the few conditions attached to Gifford R. Cappellini's probation.

Back in September, Luzerne County Judge Michael Conahan sentenced the former county public defender to one year's probation.

The 43-year-old lawyer son of County Court of Common Pleas Senior Judge Gifford S. Cappellini had pleaded guilty to drug charges that he had tried to buy $190 worth of cocaine from a law client.

At the time, many people, including myself, believed that Cappellini was one very lucky criminal.

Cappellini's doctor testified that Cappellini suffered from cocaine and alcohol dependency and was cocaine-dependent when police arrested him.

Conahan ordered random drug testing.

So far, though, Cappellini says that nobody at the county probation office has bothered to ask for a urine sample.

Cappellini says he isn't even required to stop by the courthouse to talk to his probation officer. Instead, Cappellini says he sends his probation officer a form every month saying that he's feeling fine.

"It's sent over by one of my secretaries," Cappellini said. "It's personally delivered."

Still, according to Cappellini, that's five months without being asked to provide a sample by his probation officer, Gene Duffy, whose father serves as the Luzerne County Prothonotary.

Last week, however, somebody apparently decided to ask.

But this is where the story gets cloudy.

Cappellini danced when asked if probation officials finally tested him.

"That's for you to talk to them about," he said. "I'm not going to comment."

The lawyer also declined to say if he had spoken with Duffy last week about the drug testing.

"I don't really want to comment on what they're doing and what they're not doing."

Let me get this straight, I said. You're telling me that you didn't take a drug test last week?

"What I'm telling you is that as far as I'm concerned, this is between the probation office and myself," Cappellini said. "Whatever test they order."

Let's begin again, I said.

"**D**id you take a urine test last week?" I asked.

"I have no comment on that," Cappellini said.

How about the result?

Again, no comment.

Cappellini said he was having difficulty hearing some of my questions and statements.

"I was in the hospital last week," he said. "I have high blood pressure and I was in the emergency room. I'm having difficulties. I was in the hospital at the time. I was sick in bed. I was under doctor's care and to be quite honest, I don't really remember too much of what happened."

Again I asked about the test and the result.

"Talk to Gene Duffy," Cappellini said. "Call him and talk to him."

Duffy declined to discuss Cappellini.

Duffy's boss, Steve Wolinsky, failed to return three phone calls.

Joe Sklarosky, the lawyer Cappellini said represents him, also failed to return calls.

So did Cappellini's sister, Dotie, who also works as a probation officer at the county office.

One more time.

"Did your probation officer ask you to take a urine test last week?"

"I don't want to get into that, I really don't," Cappellini said.

Conahan declined to discuss the Cappellini case and said he never knows how often defendants he orders to undergo drug testing actually do so.

Well, Attorney Cappellini did pee in the bottle and guess what? His test came back "HOT" for not only cocaine but also for heroin. One other major problem here, according to the Attorney General's Office, his probation records were tampered with.

Since the following articles are so large, they have been inserted twice. The second insertion makes them large enough to read without a magnifying glass.

The Times Leader

THURSDAY, FEBRUARY 22, 1996 — WILKES-BARRE, PA

LUZERNE COUNTY'S LARGEST CIRCULATION NEWSPAPER • 7 DAYS A WEEK

BUSINESS
Tobyhanna Army Depot offers early retirements
Lag in electronics repair work prompts retirement offer to at least 250 workers.
Page 7B

SPORTS
Lady Argents go marching on
Bishop Hoban tops GAR in the District 2 Class AAA girls basketball playoffs.
Page 1B

KIDS
Interview with Kermit tells what's 'hop-ening
The famous frog answers questions about "Muppet Treasure Island."
Page 1C

Cappellini fails drug test; faces jail

■ Judge to decide today if lawyer violated his probation and whether sufficient grounds exist to revoke it.

By DAWN SHURMAITIS
Times Leader Staff Writer

WILKES-BARRE — Attorney Gifford R. Cappellini, son of Luzerne County Judge Gifford S. Cappellini and a probation employee, could go to jail today for using cocaine and heroin.

And, state investigators have launched a criminal investigation into possible mishandling of his probation on drug charges.

The state Office of Attorney General confirmed Wednesday it is investigating the Luzerne County Adult Probation/Parole Office, where Cappellini's sister, Dode, is employed.

His father is Luzerne County Court of Common Pleas Judge Gifford S. Cappellini. Cappellini, who pleaded guilty Sept. 11 to trying to buy cocaine from a client, tested positive for drugs two weeks ago, court records show.

The veteran defense attorney, the 43-year-old Cappellini of Dallas Township, was sentenced to one-year probation, ordered to submit to drug tests and to continue drug counseling.

That didn't happen, according to documents filed by a special prosecutor Wednesday.

Cappellini tested positive for drugs during his only drug test Feb. 8. Eight days later, the probation office reported the violation to the district attorney, said Special Deputy Attorney General Michael Kershaw, who petitioned for today's probation revocation hearing.

Neither Cappellini nor Chief Probation Officer Stephen Wolnusky Jr. returned phone calls Wednesday.

■ See CAPPELLINI, Page 10A

Wife blames system for husband's setback

■ Deborah Cappellini says the county parole office failed to check whether her husband was being treated for his drug addiction.

By DAWN SHURMAITIS and MITCH MORRISON
Times Leader Staff Writers

The Luzerne County criminal justice system failed to admitted drug user Gifford R. Cappellini, his wife claimed this week during an emotional interview.

When Cappellini pleaded guilty last fall to possessing cocaine valued at $6190, his wife Deborah hoped the veteran defense attorney would stay clean.

But, she says, the Luzerne County Adult Probation/Parole Office failed to monitor whether Cappellini was going for treatment.

He wasn't.

The county probation office also failed for five months to test Cappellini to see if he was using

■ See WIFE, Page 10A

Deborah Cappellini says the Luzerne County Probation/Parole Office failed to monitor whether her husband, Gifford R. Cappellini, was going for treatment.

Tough questions await county probation office

Steve Corbett

For five months, Luzerne County officials failed to enforce one of the main conditions of Gifford R. Cappellini's one-year probation.

Why?

The answer to that and other tough questions is why Pennsylvania Attorney General Tom Corbett on Tuesday launched a criminal investigation into employee conduct at the Luzerne County Adult Probation and Parole Office.

As part of the probe, state investigators plan to interview numerous appointed and elected county officials, including Cappellini's father, Court of Common Pleas Senior Judge Gifford S. Cappellini, and

■ See CORBETT, Page 10A

★10A The Times Leader, Wilkes-Barre, PA.

Cappellini fails drug test; faces jail

THURSDAY, FEBRUARY 22, 1996

Gifford R. Cappellini

■ *Judge to decide today if lawyer violated his probation and whether sufficient grounds exist to revoke it.*

By DAWN SHURMAITIS
Times Leader Staff Writer

WILKES-BARRE — Attorney Gifford R. Cappellini, son of a county judge and brother of a probation employee, could go to jail today for using cocaine and heroin.

And, state investigators have launched a criminal investigation into possible mishandling of his probation on drug charges.

The state Office of Attorney General confirmed Wednesday it is investigating the Luzerne County Adult Probation/Parole Office, where Cappellini's sister, Dotie, is employed.

His father is Luzerne County Court of Common Pleas Judge Gifford S. Cappellini.

Cappellini, who pleaded guilty Sept. 11 to trying to buy cocaine from a client, tested positive for drugs two weeks ago, court records show.

A veteran defense attorney, the 43-year-old Cappellini of Dallas Township was sentenced to one-year probation, ordered to submit to drug tests and to continue drug counseling.

That didn't happen, according to documents filed by a special prosecutor Wednesday.

Cappellini tested positive for drugs during

his only drug test Feb. 8. Eight days later, the probation office reported the violation to the district attorney, said Special Deputy Attorney General Michael Kershaw, who petitioned for today's probation revocation hearing.

Neither Cappellini nor Chief Probation Officer Stephen Wolinsky Jr. returned phone calls Wednesday.

■ See CAPPELLINI, Page 10A

Cappellini —
(Continued from Page 1A)

According to the probation revocation petition, Cappellini:
- ■ Failed to report to the probation/parole office for appropriate supervision.
- ■ Admitted drug use during his probation.
- ■ Intentionally and knowingly failed to complete court-mandated treatment for drug use at the Clear Brook treatment center.
- ■ Admitted to two probation officers he used cocaine once or twice a week since ending outpatient treatment.

The hearing is scheduled for 2 p.m. today before Court of Common Pleas Judge Michael Conahan. The judge is expected to determine if the violations occurred and if there are sufficient grounds to revoke Cappellini's probation. The judge then can resentence Cappellini, reinstate his probation or impose a prison term.

If Cappellini had successfully completed his probation, the charges against him could have been dismissed and his record expunged.

Luzerne County District Attorney Peter Paul Olszewski Jr. said Wednesday the probation department notified him Friday of Cappellini's alleged violations.

Olszewski then contacted Kershaw, an assistant district attorney in Philadelphia. Kershaw was appointed to prosecute Cappellini's case after Olszewski asked to be removed because of his office's relationship with Cappellini's father.

Cappellini alternately admits and denies having a drug problem and tries to tailor his outpatient treatment to his benefit.

Probation/parole officer Eugene Duffy
Excerpt from character report

Kershaw could not be reached Wednesday for comment.

Olszewski began investigating allegations about "possible significant improprieties" in the county probation office and assigned a detective to conduct interviews.

In a Feb. 14 report to Olszewski, probation/parole officer Eugene Duffy wrote: "It is apparent the defendant has a drug problem." Duffy characterized Cappellini's behavior as erratic and inconsistent.

Cappellini alternately admits and denies having a drug problem and tries to tailor his outpatient treatment to his benefit, Duffy wrote.

"He is constantly trying to make deals and bargains," Duffy wrote.

In his report to Olszewski, Wolinsky recounted the following:

Assistant Probation Chief

James Marinello told Wolinsky Feb. 7 that Cappellini might be doing illicit drugs. Wolinsky said he called Cappellini and asked him to report to the office, but the attorney told him he had to be in court.

Wolinsky waited until 5 p.m., but Cappellini never showed. He later told Wolinsky he had checked into the hospital.

Wolinsky and probation officer Richard Heffron went to Cappellini's house and tested his urine. Later, Cappellini told Wolinsky he wasn't coherent at the time of the test and denied using drugs. He said medicine he takes caused the positive test.

Attorneys Joseph Sklarosky and Ferris Webby represented Cappellini at his sentencing. Neither attorney could be reached Wednesday for comment.

A routine probation stipulation is that defendants avoid people who use drugs or alcohol. Cappellini, a former assistant public defender, was allowed to handle drug cases, Conahan ruled.

Luzerne County President Judge Patrick J. Toole refused to acknowledge or comment on either the Cappellini case or the investigation into the probation department. He said the probation department routinely sets testing guidelines.

After the charges were filed, Cappellini told a newspaper reporter he had been "set up."

Times Leader reporter Jerry Lynott contributed to this report.

Wife blames system for husband's setback

■ *Deborah Cappellini says the county parole office failed to check whether her husband was being treated for his drug addiction.*

By DAWN SHURMAITIS and MITCH MORRISON
Times Leader Staff Writers

The Luzerne County criminal justice system failed admitted drug user Gifford R. Cappellini, his wife claimed this week during an emotional interview.

When Cappellini pleaded guilty last fall to possessing cocaine valued at $190, his wife Deborah hoped the veteran defense attorney would stay clean.

But, she says, the Luzerne County Adult Probation/Parole Office failed to monitor whether Cappellini was going for treatment.

He wasn't.

The county probation office also failed for five months to test Cappellini to see if he was using

■ See WIFE, Page 10A

TIMES LEADER/CLARK VAN ORDEN
Deborah Cappellini says the Luzerne County Probation/Parole Office failed to monitor whether her husband, Gifford R. Cappellini, was going for treatment.

Wife

(Continued from Page 1A)

drugs.

He was, according to a report filed Wednesday by the probation department.

Cappellini's urine tested positive for heroin and cocaine on Feb. 8. Random testing was a stipulation of his probation.

Experts in drug rehabilitation expressed surprise by the time between the sentencing and the only drug test.

"I'm not sure you could find a guy on a drug offense who's gone six months without a drug test," said Joe Mecca, assistant director of the Lackawanna County Probation office. "The average is once a month for drug offenders."

Family connection also played a part, his wife alleges. Gifford is the son of Luzerne County Court of Common Pleas Judge Gifford S. Cappellini.

"I believe my husband thought he could do anything because he was the judge's son," said Deborah Cappellini, who plans to divorce her husband. "They failed Gifford. Cocaine is not a drug you get over in 28 days at Clear Brook."

Clear Brook Inc. is a drug treatment center Cappellini entered the day after his arrest in March 1995. He stopped attending court-ordered out-patient counseling, the probation department reported.

Lackawanna County's probation office averages 50 to 75 random drug tests a month. Its annual case load is between 800 and 1,000 convicts. Mecca could not say what percentage are drug-related.

Mecca, who would not comment specifically about the Cappellini case, questioned the monitoring process. A probation officer is expected to work out a detail treatment plan and ensure the offender follows through, Mecca said.

Treatment varies from client to client, said Doris Shappell, spokeswoman for the state Probation and Parole Board. Despite the wide latitude, drug and alcohol experts say a rigid treatment plan and constant supervision are vital toward a client's recovery.

"An addict early on in treatment needs to be monitored," said Carmen Ambrosino, chief executive officer of the Wyoming Valley Drug and Alcohol Services.

A 23-year veteran of the drug and alcohol field, Ambrosino said drug users trying to break their addiction are routinely advised to "change their playmates, change their playpen and change their playthings."

After sentencing, Cappellini, a former assistant public defender, continued representing alleged drug users.

Cappellini's wife likened that to "allowing an alcoholic to work in a bar."

Deborah Cappellini, 44, said she will try to get custody of the couple's three children, ages 9, 12 and 16. She has been staying at a hotel since Sunday, after Dallas Township police escorted her from the couple's home on Westminster Drive.

Gifford Cappellini received an emergency relief from abuse order from District Justice Paul Robert. Cappellini said in the affidavit his wife threatened him and smashed a kitchen plate against a wall in their home during an argument.

When police arrived, Deborah Cappellini told them her husband violated his probation by using illegal drugs again. The emergency abuse order expired at 4:30 p.m. Monday.

TIMES LEADER/CLARK VAN ORDEN

Deborah Cappellini, wife of Gifford R. Cappellini, has been staying at a hotel since Sunday, after Dallas Township police escorted her from the couple's home on Westminster Drive. She told police her husband violated his probation by using illegal drugs again.

So, here we are. It is a lot to digest but it is an important foundation for this story. Remember back when Debbie and I first talked. She told me the story about her children and their custody. Take a good look at the previous picture. There she is living in a hotel room because she smashed one of her own plates against one of her walls in her own house. She hadn't been the one who tested "Hot" for cocaine and heroin while on probation, yet she was the one removed. She was the one displaced from her own home by a self admitted drug addict who had just violated his probation but was the son of a Luzerne County Judge. It simply makes my blood boil.

A little bit of history here and then we shall move forward: One of the most mystifying experiences of my life occurred during my trial. At one point Attorney Piccone held up the most damning (to his case) piece of evidence that existed in the entire case. It was evidence that I was going to use to, "blow them out of the water" when it was my turn to defend myself. He held the evidence high, shook it like a Schnauzer would shake a rat and declared that he had proof positive his client would prevail. He then presented the document into evidence as one of his own exhibits. It was evidence that sank his entire case. I remember sitting there in shock. My attorney and I looked at each other as I wrote down on my yellow pad, "What the hell is he doing?"

My attorney looked at me, shrugged his shoulders and whispered, "I'll be damned if I know"? The reason I am bringing up this matter at this point is to better explain the following newspaper articles. Spend some time reviewing the highlighted article on page 181. It looks like a mess but has a ton of very relevant information in it. It also lays a good foundation for the story going forward. It was written by Carol Crane, one of the finest reporters I have ever met.

CHAPTER THIRTY-FOUR

Judge Gifford Cappellini, "The Man"

---

*I*t has been said that, "You can judge a man's character by what he does when no one is looking." My question to you is, what can we deduce about a man's character from observing his actions "When everyone is watching?"

Probation office under scrutiny

County whistleblower said to be cooperating with state investigators

By CAROL CRANE
Citizens' Voice Staff Writer

There were some empty desks in the Luzerne County Adult Probation office on Thursday.

Absent yesterday, according to several sources, were department heads Stephen Wolinsky Jr. and Ann Marie Braskey. Meanvhile, Jamie Marinello, who is second in command under Wolinsky, was not at his desk because he was meeting with agents from the state Attorney General's office.

The absenteeism and meeting come on the heels of a revelation that the state attorney general's office had launched a criminal investigation into alleged mishandling of the probation of Attorney Gifford R. Cappellini. Records show that two weeks ago, Cappellini tested positive for cocaine and heroin use.

But Cappellini's Feb. 8 drug test was the first time he had been tested since pleading guilty on Sept. 11 for trying to buy cocaine. As a term of his one-year probation, Cappellini was ordered to submit to routine drug tests which, in most cases, are administered to drug offenders once a month.

But, numerous allegations have surfaced that Cappellini was not made to report for routine drug testing because his father is a Luzerne County senior judge and his sister, Dotie Cappellini, works in the Adult Probation office. Eugene Duffy Jr., Cappellini's probation officer, is the son of Luzerne County Prothonotary Eugene Duffy. The elder Duffy also practices law in Luzerne County.

Senior Judge Gifford Cappellini, however, denied he ever attempted to influence the Probation Office to give preferential treatment to his son. "How would I ever get involved in something like this?" the Judge remarked. "I had nothing to do with this case. Nothing, whatsoever. I know he's my son and all, but I can't help that."

Referring to comments that alleged political connections delayed his son's drug testing by almost six months, the judge responded that persons who would make such accusations are "sick people."

Sources close to the elder Cappellini say he and other family members are devastated by the latest evidence of his son's drug abuse. Another source said Attorney Cappellini's brother Jeffrey, who also is a lawyer, has not spoken to his brother for some time.

On Tuesday, Duffy Jr. refused to talk to reporters. At least, two sources said Duffy Jr. appeared to be unfazed yesterday over the disclosure that he failed to try to enforce the provisions of Attorney Cappellini's probation. Instead, Duffy Jr., the sources indicated, vowed out loud to find out who "leaked" the information about Attorney Cappellini to the media.

The same sources said several office workers are "upset" that Marinello is cooperating fully with state investigators who are looking into the allegations. Marinello, a 22-year-veteran employee of the Probation office, declined to comment. However, a source close to him said it is Marinello's intent to "do the right thing." The source said because they perceive him as "a whistle blower."

When asked to comment on the Cappellini case and the criminal investigation of the Adult Probation office, Wolinsky said, "I have absolutely nothing to say." Asked if any one in his office could comment on allegations that Cappellini got special treatment, Wolinsky replied with a terse "no comment."

Dotie Cappellini did not return a phone message left on her answering machine. Brasky has an unlisted phone number.

Attorney Cappellini's wife, Deborah, on Thursday morning alleged on a local radio talk show that she was mentally and physically abused throughout her 22-year marriage to the once prominent defense attorney. Sources associated with Deborah Cappellini indicated that last year, she approached not only the Judicial Inquiry Review Board but the FBI about her husband's drug use. The sources said Deborah Cappellini "go nowhere" with her complaints.

After he pleaded guilty last September to drug charges, he entered into substance abuse counseling at Clear Brook Lodge but did not continue on with treatment.

According to sources, the Adult Probation office did not demand that Attorney Cappellini submit to a drug test until after someone called the state attorney general's office to complain. As a result, the state attorney general's office contacted Luzerne County District Attorney Peter Paul Olszewski, who, upon learning that the complaint was legitimate, turned the matter over to the attorney general's office for a criminal investigation.

Deborah Cappellini said during her radio interview that her husband obtained an order a few days ago removing her from their Back Mountain home. She said she plans to divorce her husband and vowed to wage an intense legal battle to obtain custody of the couple's three young sons.

(Staff writer Harry Yanoshak contributed to this report.)

Friday, February 23, 1996

SATURDAY FEBRUARY 24, 1996

Judge denies exerting influence

State investigators want to know why a county office didn't make a judge's son submit to drug tests or continue counseling.

By ANTHONY COLAROSSI
Times Leader Staff Writer

WILKES-BARRE — Judge Gifford S. Cappellini was questioning and debating with the tone and ferocity of a young prosecutor Friday.

But he wasn't in the courtroom. And he wasn't arguing a legal position.

Gifford S. Cappellini

Sitting in his office, angry and passionate, Cappellini vented his annoyance with the media.

"With the stroke of a pen or a bite on TV, people in the media can destroy people faster than any force I've heard of," Cappellini said. "I don't think any accusation, unfounded, should be put into print."

Cappellini is referring to the public associations drawn between his position as Luzerne County Court of Common Pleas

■ See CAPPELLINI, Page 8A

Cappellini —
(Continued from Page 1A)

part-time senior judge and the office of the Luzerne County Adult Probation/Parole Department.

The judge's son, Clifford R. Cappellini, tested positive for cocaine and heroin Feb. 8. Drug use violates the terms of his probation for misdemeanor drug charges.

But the probation/parole department is under investigation by the state Office of Attorney General. Investigators are asking why the younger Cappellini was not initially ordered to submit to drug tests and to continue drug counseling.

Dotte Cappellini, his sister, works in the probation/parole department. And Judge Cappellini openly states he is friendly with many workers in that department.

But those associations do not mean the judge influenced that office on his son's behalf or that workers in the office gave the younger Cappellini preferential treatment because of his father, Judge Cappellini said.

"For that to appear that I had influence on that office is outrageous and untrue," Judge Cappellini said. "They have no reason to fear me. I don't have anything to do with their jobs."

Judge Cappellini said the professionalism of both his office and his daughter's prevents personal relationships from influencing responsibilities.

The judge said he and his daughter should be graded on their competence and not their familial relationship.

"Everybody's being made an example of because he happens to be my son," Judge Cappellini said. "What disturbs me is that there are too many innuendoes here that have formulated in people's minds."

Earlier this week, a special prosecutor planned to revoke the younger Cappellini's one-year probation. But Luzerne County Court of Common Pleas Judge Michael Conahan granted him a continuance on his alleged parole violations.

Conahan has the full range of sentencing options he had at the initial sentencing, if he revokes Cappellini's probation.

If his probation is revoked, Cappellini may be resentenced and could face one year in prison or a $5,000 fine, a maximum penalty, according to state sentencing guidelines.

The judge refused to speak about his son's case. But he said his son needs continued drug treatment and that he hopes he is getting it.

As for himself, Judge Cappellini says the questioning and the assumptions do not affect his work as a part-time senior judge.

"Is the pressure too much for me to continue? No," Cappellini said. "I will not let personal matters affect what I'm doing in this.

To truly understand the hidden threat in the prior interview, one only needs to know the following fact: Probation Officers in Luzerne County get their jobs because a Luzerne County Judge appoints them. There is no test or pre-qualification process. When the positions become available, the county does not even run a "Help Wanted" ad in the local papers. One hundred percent of the entire Probation office is staffed by the Judge's of the county. Judge Cappellini is implying that once a PO Officer is hired judges no longer have any control over their employment.

The Probation Office is completely and directly controlled by the judges. Judge Cappellini went so far as to appoint his own daughter to her position as a Probation Officer. He has publicly denied doing so, but his denial is a lie. Oh my, I just called Judge Cappellini a liar! He is.

Please take a look at the highlighted areas on page 186. I especially like the fact that Judge Cappellini lies about the appointment of his daughter by him and then admits that he would do it anyway. Great Judge!

The Sunday Times Leader

LUZERNE COUNTY'S LARGEST CIRCULATION NEWSPAPER • 7 DAYS A WEEK

SUNDAY, JUNE 2, 1996

http://www.leader.net/ — $1.50

SAVE $$$ WITH COUPONS NOT AVAILABLE IN ALL AREAS

OPINION
Corbett says no offense meant.
The columnist comments on the situation in Hazleton.
Page 3A

SPORTS
Seminary falls in first round of states
Hemfield ends Blue Knights' title hopes quickly.
Page 1C

FEATURES
Technology goes to the dogs
The benefits of putting a microchip on a pooch are many.

Judges dole out own 'friends and family' deals

■ Luzerne County Court of Common Pleas judges' influence in hirings goes beyond county's Adult Probation/Parole Office.

By MITCH MORRISON and TIMOTHY J. GIBBONS
Times Leader Staff Writers

Luzerne County Judge Gifford Cappellini hired his son, Jeffrey, as his law clerk in 1988.

But the hiring wasn't nepotism by Cappellini's definition.

"If you want to appoint someone who doesn't know his job (just) because he's related to you, that's wrong," says Cappellini, 70, a senior judge on the Court of Common Pleas bench.

But if the person is qualified, it's not nepotism, even if there is a family relationship, says Cappellini. Jeffrey Cappellini earned $24,100 before relocating to Arizona two months ago.

When it comes to hiring, the county's eight judges wield substantial power.

In all, they oversee eight offices staffed by 280 workers who earn $7.2 million in salaries and benefits. The judges are responsible for hiring for all of the offices but leave the decision-making in the magistrates' offices up to the magistrates.

One of those offices, the Adult Probation/Parole Department, is being investigated by the state amid allegations of favoritism toward another of Cappellini's sons, Gifford R., who was on probation on drug charges.

Probation officer Gene Duffy Jr. never tested Cappellini in five months because he said he feared repercussions from Judge Cappellini and the judge's daughter, Dodie Cappellini, who works with Duffy in the pa-

■ See NEPOTISM, Page 16A

More/Inside
■ **Enough!** Courthouse nepotism has gone on for too long, News Talk callers say. **16A**
■ **Starting off:** If you want a court-related job, don't rely on the classifieds. Instead, take a walk to the courthouse and head to the basement. **16A**
■ **Naming names:** List of judges' hirings. **16A**

Nepotism

(Continued from Page 1A)

role/probation office.

Since then, county workers have sarcastically called the parole/probation office, "All in the Family."

But nepotism and patronage permeate more than just the walls of the parole/probation office. It can be found in many of the other seven offices: Domestic Relations, court administration, stenographers, juvenile detention, juvenile probation, orphans court.

A Sunday's Times Leader investigation last week showed the practice of county judges hiring family and friends to court-related jobs is common.

Since then, more than two-dozen callers telephoned the newspaper to report cases of judges hiring friends and family.

Most of the callers focused on appointments made by Cappellini, President Judge Patrick J. Toole and Joseph Augello.

■ **Cappellini**: Cappellini's daughter, **Dodie**, works as a parole/probation officer and makes $27,674 a year. County records show Cappellini appointed her to her current position in May 1992.

The judge, however, emphatically denied making the appointment and said court records must be wrong.

"No way, I absolutely did not appoint her," Cappellini said, adding that it was Orphans Judge Chester Muroski who hired Dodie Cappellini to the parole/probation office. Muroski said he could not remember if he hired Dodie.

"It's possible," said Muroski. "I don't have records on who I appointed."

But, Cappellini added, "I would appoint her if I had the opportunity."

Cappellini also appointed **Carol Anstett**, an administrative aide in the parole/probation office and wife of former county assessor John Anstett. Carol Anstett earns $18,950.

■ **President Judge Patrick J. Toole Jr.**: Appointed his son, **Michael**, as law clerk in 1985. He earns $26,300. Toole's oldest son, **Patrick III**, is paid almost $33,800 as a support officer in the county domestic relations. Court records do not show which judge appointed him.

Friends appointed include: Brian Leighton, parole/probation officer, $33,775; his brother, John Leighton, Domestic Relations support officer, $33,775; Brian Bufalino, a law clerk for Judge Mark Ciavarella, $10,501; and Sam Arnone, a parole/probation surveillance officer, $19,100.

■ **Joseph Augello**: Friends appointed by Augello include: **Tom Paratore**, a parole/probation surveillance officer and son of Fraternal Order of Police Lodge 46 President Joe Paratore, $20,200; **Phyllis Mantione**, office manager at parole/probation, $20,475; and **Peter Adonizio**, parole/probation officer and a former part-time worker of Gramercy Ballroom & Restaurant in Pittston, which is owned by members of the Augello family, $26,650.

He also appointed **Christopher Patte**, a parole/probation officer and son of restaurateur/Democratic politico Pat Patte, $25,650, and **Marita Morreale**, a parole/probation surveillance officer and wife of county Treasurer Mike Morreale, $19,100.

■ **Orphans Court Judge Chester Muroski**: his wife, **Cynthia**, works as his law clerk, earning $25,300.

Also appointed: **Gene Duffy Jr.**, a parole/probation officer and son of county prothonotary Gene Duffy, $33,775.

■ **Ann Lokuta**: Appointed friend **Beth Boris**, law clerk and daughter of Wilkes-Barre councilman Al Boris, $25,306.

■ **Senior Judge Bernard Brominski**: Appointed friend **Michael Vecchio**, a parole/probation officer, $33,775.

■ **Late President Judge) Robert Hourigan**: Appointed his son-in-law, **Stephen Wolinsky Jr.**,

FRIDAY, APRIL 26, 1996 — WILKES-BARRE, PA

Probation case weaves family web

■ A county judge denies any influence was brought to bear in his son's drug case.

By DAWN SHURMAITIS
Times Leader Staff Writer

WILKES-BARRE — Reading Eugene Duffy's arrest affidavit is akin to playing a game of connect the dots.

Only this game involves employees of the Luzerne County Courthouse, their relatives and co-workers.

First, there is convicted drug user attorney Gifford R. Cappellini, whom probation officer Duffy was supposed to supervise. Cappellini, a former public defender, is the son of a senior Luzerne County judge. His sister, Dodie Cappellini — the judge's daughter — works alongside Duffy in the county probation department.

Thursday, all the dots came together in a 24-page arrest affidavit that alleged Duffy falsified Cappellini's probation case file. The affidavit details the evidence while naming plenty of names and suggesting members of the Cappellini family tried to influence Duffy's handling of the lawyer's probation on drug charges.

Senior Judge Gifford S. Cappellini continues to deny vigorously ever influencing his daughter or her co-worker, Duffy.

■ See FAMILY, Page 18A

Probation officer free on bail admitted making up dates

By JERRY LYNOTT
Times Leader Staff Writer

WILKES-BARRE — A Luzerne County probation officer is free on bail, accused of fabricating dates to hide his mishandling of a case that attracted the attention of state Office of Attorney General Investigators.

Eugene Duffy admitted making up dates for monthly supervision reports attorney Gifford R. Cappellini sent him as part of his probation for a drug charge, according to the attorney general's office. Paperwork accompanying Duffy's arrest warrant quote him telling investigators, "I panicked. I knew there was going to be an investigation. I made the shit up and placed it in the (Cappellini's) file."

Duffy's attorney, John Moses, called his client's arrest "a stab in the dark." Moses acknowledged Duffy wrote dates on a sheet of paper. But he contended the paper was not an official document. Moses said Duffy intended to use the paper to help him testify at Cappellini's probation revocation

■ See DUFFY, Page 18A

Luzerne County Adult Probation Officer Eugene Duffy, left, arrives for his arraignment Thursday in Wilkes-Barre. Accompanying Duffy is his attorney, John Moses.

Family

(Continued from Page 1A)

"Whoever put that in the affidavit better be prepared. They made a big mistake. I think (the attorney general's office) messed up," the judge said from his home Thursday, two hours after state agents charged Duffy, 33, of West Hazleton, with four misdemeanors.

The allegations stem from probation department assistant chief James Marinello, who told state investigators Duffy avoided testifying Cappellini for drugs because he feared the power of the Cappellini family.

Marinello's boss, probation chief Stephen Wolinsky, told investigators "that on February 8, 1996 Gene Duffy and Dodie Cappellini jointly advised him that retired Luzerne County Judge Gifford Cappellini wanted a report on this entire matter."

The Judge denies the allegations.

"Absolutely not. Without any question. No. The answer is no," he said.

"I didn't ask for any report. Ever. I never had anything to do with this case."

The judge said he spoke to Wolinsky only once, recently, when the probation chief was smoking a cigarette outside the courthouse. He said he told Wolinsky he couldn't understand "this whole mess." He said he still does not believe Duffy did anything wrong.

"Duffy is a friend," the judge said. "His father is a friend."

Duffy's father, Eugene Duffy Sr., is the county prothonotary.

The judge said he spoke to Duffy once, after his daughter called him from a local bar, where she was with a "very upset" Duffy. The phone call was placed after the investigation opened.

"I told him to calm down," the judge said of his conversation with Duffy. "I was disturbed at what was happening to him."

Marinello, according to the affidavit, said Duffy told him he had been approached by Dodie Cappellini, "who stated that if tested, the Defendant (attorney Cappellini) would come up 'hot'."

Marinello, who once described himself as Serpico — after the New York City police officer who blew the whistle on police corruption — said he was satisfied with the attorney general's investigation. But he refused to comment specifically Thursday.

"I expected nothing less than a non-political, quality investigation," Marinello said. "It's not over yet."

Marinello, who once expressed concern that his discussions with the attorney general investigators might get him fired, said Thursday "I'm not worried about my family.

Cappellini's mother serves on the Clear Brook Inc. board of directors.

The two-month investigation that resulted in Duffy's arrest was sparked by Luzerne County District Attorney Peter Paul Olszewski Jr.

In a rare move, Olszewski contacted the state attorney general's office about possible criminal improprieties in the probation department. Olszewski acted after receiving a memo from President Judge Patrick J. Toole outlining allegations made by another probation department employee.

According to the affidavit, Olszewski cited a potential or actual conflict of interest and asked the attorney general to intervene "due to the involvement of Judge Cappellini; his son, Gifford Cappellini, esquire; probation officer Dodie Cappellini; and Eugene Duffy, son of Luzerne County Prothonotary, Eugene Duffy Sr."

"Obviously, an investigation needed to be done," Olszewski said Thursday. "The judge's daughter was mentioned. The son was mentioned. Whether an arrest was made today or not, I did what was right."

Based on the allegations raised in the affidavit, Olszewski said he has some concerns about the operation of the probation department, which supervises the criminals Olszewski prosecutes. But he said he was not prepared at this time to detail those concerns.

Because Duffy has no criminal record and the charges against him are misdemeanors, Olszewski said it is unlikely he would serve any jail time if convicted.

Olszewski said probation is likely, but Duffy's case would have to be handled by an office other than the county probation department.

The Luzerne County Railroad

Court-related job search starts in basement

If you want a court-related job in Luzerne County, don't rely on the classifieds.

You won't find it there.

Instead, take a walk to the county courthouse on North River Street. Then, head to the basement.

"Go to (Chief Clerk/Administrator) Gene Klein and get an application," said Court Administrator Wilbert Thomas.

When you complete the application, bring it to the court-related department.

Each court-related department makes up its own list of open positions and distributes it itself, Thomas said. Some departments post job openings on bulletin boards at the courthouse.

But, ultimately, the jobs in the eight court offices are handed out by the Court of Common Pleas judges.

President Judge Patrick Toole has the first choice of making the appointment. When he doesn't want to make the appointment, another judge is given the opportunity.

Court-related jobs filled by judges' hiring

- **Juvenile Court**
- **Toole: 5**
  - Holly Croop
  - Betty Jean Fenimore
  - Maridee Kelly
  - Jerome Prawdzik
  - Joseph Farinella
- **Hourigan: 4**
  - John Boyle
  - Sadie Cole
  - Margaret Harvey
  - Theresa Kline
- **Muroski: 4**
  - Mary Jo Alberola
  - George Scutch
  - Maureen Yankovich
  - Nora Gill
- **Brominski: 3**
  - Peter Namyowicz
  - Anthony Piazza
  - Walter Symons
- **Podcasy: 2**
  - Elaine Yozviak
  - Jeff Bozek
- **Cappellini: 1**
  - Thomas Lavin

- **Conahan: 1**
  - Matthew Skrepenak
- **Lokuta: 1**
  - Ronald Palermo
- **Mundy: 1**
  - Denise Mehal
- **Olszewski: 1**
  - Norman Magyar
- **Miscellaneous: 15**
  - Records do not indicate who appointed 15 current juvenile court employees.

- **Orphans Court**
- **Muroski: 5**
  - Marion Babcock
  - Sean Duesler
  - John Eichom
  - Cynthia Muroski
  - Richard Wojtowicz
- **Hourigan: 1**
  - Sharon Bitzel
- **Toole: 1**
  - Gerald Wassil
- **Miscellaneous: 2**
  - Records do not indicate who appointed 2 current orphans court employees.

the parole/probation officer, that's in twenty-level with the work $53,251.

Several of the judges' friends and relatives contacted for this story refused comment or did not return phone messages.

Two did comment about their appointments.

Brian Bufalino, 27, and son of prominent GOP attorney Charles Bufalino, said he applied to be Judge Ciavarella's law clerk shortly after the judge's election victory last fall.

"I was surprised to get it," said Bufalino, a Boston College law school graduate who was appointed by Toole.

He acknowledged that his family's name gave him an edge in the process but said he did not ask his father to lobby on his behalf.

"People know my father and my brother, C.J. They know the family name, and family.. They know the family's reputation.

"There's a level of trust," he said. "But it's not like anybody's pulling strings."

John Leighton, a close friend of Judge Toole's three sons, said connections probably helped him secure a job in 1978 a few months after he graduated college.

"There's no question it doesn't hurt to know somebody in this day and age," Leighton said. "And

State has bad reputation

The American Bar Association might say "someone off the streets."

In 1990, the bar association updated the Model Code of Judicial Conduct, listing principles each judge should follow.

On appointments, the 1990 code states: "A judge shall avoid nepotism and favoritism."

The Pennsylvania Supreme Court updated its judicial code in 1990, but did not include the bar association's hiring restrictions.

Instead, the state discourages hiring based on favoritism. It does not address nepotism.

Jim Alfini, dean at Northern Illinois University's Law School, said the practice of judges making appointments varies from state to state.

Pennsylvania, he said, is among the most liberal — giving local judges broad hiring powers.

He calls the state's policy dangerous.

"We generally refer to executive and legislative branches as politi-

... Would you rather hire someone you know or someone off the streets?"

cal," he said. "The judicial branch is not supposed to be political.

"We expect judges to be independent. If they're making what looks like patronage appointments, then it makes a difference for those positions to be seen free from influence."

Alfini said he was not surprised that Pennsylvania does not include nepotism in the judicial conduct code.

He said the state has one of the worst reputations for judicial conduct, from nepotism in common pleas courts to ethics and criminal probes against state Supreme Court justices, including the impeachment of Rolf Larsen in 1994 for using court employees to obtain prescription medication for him.

"Some of the most egregious disciplinary cases have come out of Pennsylvania," Alfini said. "There is a history of protectionism of judges."

Please read the following article in its entirety.

Steve Corbett

System is sick and sickening

Lawyer Gerry Deady faced witness Gene Duffy.

The attorney asked the Luzerne County probation officer about the day when Duffy visited Gifford R. Cappellini and asked him to pee in a bottle.

Duffy said he had to wait about 40 minutes for Cappellini to give him the sample.

"He was having difficulty urinating," Deady said Monday.

"Correct," said Duffy.

As of early Monday afternoon, this was the main documented evidence of Cappellini's difficulty with the penal system.

Unlike most defendants, legal difficulty is not something to which the well-known lawyer and son of a county judge is accustomed.

On Monday, a courtroom jammed with spectators, including at least two county judges, gathered to watch the unfolding saga of this sad and terribly pampered drug addict.

The 43-year-old son of senior Judge Gifford S. Cappellini was in court for a hearing to decide if his probation would be revoked.

By late Monday, a judge decided that Gifford goes to jail next week.

Almost nobody expected that to happen.

Most people expected Cappellini to be reassigned to probation and drug testing.

Now he'll pee in a prison bottle. Maybe they'll let Duffy come by to visit the sample.

Debauchery sent this judge's son into the gutters looking for a fix. Let's hope he finally straightens out because he's far from healed.

Neither is the system.

Most non-judges' sons rarely receive the attention reserved for Cappellini.

Even now, numerous inmates at the Luzerne County Correctional Facility should be dragging their cups against the bars of their cells in protest.

Because although a coddled Cappellini is going to the can, he got away with too much for too long.

The system needs therapy, too.

After reading the papers, at least one county prisoner is screaming about how officials revoked his probation and locked him up in June for having a beer in a bar.

As for the judge's son, it took the threat of adverse publicity to rattle probation officials.

Even after testing positive for cocaine and heroin, Cappellini stayed on the street working as a lawyer and functioning as the father of three impressionable children.

I've talked to at least one attorney who says he's had clients serving probation who have lost the right to any contact with their kids after a simple allegation of drug use, let alone a positive urine test for hard drugs.

But not Cappellini.

Back in September, though, police busted Cappellini trying to buy coke from a police informant. The nice judge sentenced him to one-year probation with the stipulation that he not snort dope anywhere, including the courthouse steps at rush hour, and that he pee in a bottle whenever he was asked.

Cappellini's lawyers argued that he complied.

Duffy testified Monday, however, that Cappellini told them he was doing coke once or twice a week since he dishonorably left the treatment program at Clear Brook.

Unlike the day when Duffy stopped by and Cappellini almost could not pee, at Clear Brook he allegedly would not pee.

Duffy testified that Clear Brook officials relayed this information to him in a letter.

Cappellini's discharge occurred in November, Duffy said.

Yet, nobody asked Cappellini for a drug sample until February, and that happened only because somebody called state investigators to dime out Cappellini as well as the probation office.

Now that the state attorney general's office is investigating probation practices and other charges, maybe this disorder will change.

But I doubt it.

Looks like it's getting worse instead of better.

Deady said in court Monday that the state Department of Health is investigating Clear Brook's handling of the Cappellini case.

Cappellini's mother, Dorothy, is a board member there.

Talk about difficulty.

Steve Corbett's column appears Tuesday, Thursday and Sunday.

The following headline is one of my favorites of all time. It is equivalent to the famous "Dewey Wins, Beats Truman" headline from back in 1948. When I read the article I simply could not believe what I was reading. According to the newspaper, it was a done deal. Attorney Cappellini was required to report to prison the following Monday at 9am on March 11, 1996. I thought to myself how wrong I had been with my public prediction that the judge's son would never see the inside of a jail cell as a prisoner. I never thought, going forward, that it would feel so bad to be proven so right.

5 March, 1996

Cappellini sent to jail

The lawyer will spend 45 days to one year in jail for breaking his probation on drug charges.

By JEFF WALSH
Times Leader Staff Writer

WILKES-BARRE — Jail was the only option left for admitted drug user attorney Gifford Cappellini, a prosecutor said Monday.

After a six-hour hearing, Cappellini was found in violation of his probation after he tested positive for cocaine and heroin in a random drug test Feb. 8.

Gifford Cappellini

He must now spend 45 days to one year in the Luzerne County Correctional Facility — three blocks away from the building where his father serves as a senior judge.

According to the sentence delivered by Luzerne County Court of Common Pleas Judge Michael Conahan, Cappellini may apply immediately for work release. Cappellini, 43, must also submit to weekly and random drug tests, and have no contact with people associated with drugs or alcohol — including his clients, the judge ruled.

Cappellini, of Dallas Township, pleaded guilty Sept. 11 to trying to buy cocaine from a client. He must report 9 a.m. Monday to begin serving his sentence at the prison.

Deputy Attorney General Michael Kershaw said jail was necessary because Cappellini already had gone through inpatient treatment for his addiction.

"He was given the chance to straighten out — he failed," Kershaw said. "He's a very disingenuous individual."

Cappellini's lawyers, Gerald Deady and Thomas Marsilio, said

AA sponsor: Lawyer is misunderstood

By DAWN SHURMAITIS
Times Leader Staff Writer

Charlie Yetter proudly shows off gold-plated proof of his sobriety.

The round chip is marked with the number of years he has stayed off the bottle and on the wagon: 21.

Yetter carries the chip everywhere. On Monday, he took it with him to court, where he testified under oath that attorney Gifford R. Cappellini is drug-free.

"I'm not a chemist, but I believe him," said Yetter after Cappellini's hearing. The 50-year-old Wilkes-Barre man acts as a sponsor — a kind of rehabilitation coach — to Cappellini, who is heading to jail for violating his one-year probation on misdemeanor drug charges.

Monday, Yetter offered an entirely different picture of the well-known defense lawyer and son of a senior Luzerne County judge, painting Cappellini as a victim of a "bungling democracy."

Yetter sponsors between 12-15 drug and alcohol addicts but estimates he has helped hundreds during the years. He said he would know "within 48 hours" if Cappellini used cocaine.

He would know by his attitude and his eyes.

■ See SPONSOR, Page 8A

they might have issues to raise on appeal but wouldn't elaborate.

Most of Cappellini's defense on Monday attacked the scientific validity of the drug tests performed and how many people had access to Cappellini's urine sample prior to it being sent to a lab for testing.

Deady traced the path of Cappellini's urine from the time it left

■ See JAIL, Page 8A

Jail

(Continued from Page 1A)

his body Feb. 8 until it was retested at an independent drug lab Feb. 13. Both times, the urine tested positive for cocaine and heroin — although a prescription drug Cappellini was taking at the time could have accounted for the false positive for heroin, experts on both sides agreed.

Cappellini testified he has "absolutely not" used any illegal drugs while on probation. Most of his testimony was about what prescription drugs he was taking at the time of the drug test, but he did manage to cast some doubt on the practices at the county probation department.

State investigators have previously confirmed they are probing possible criminal improprieties regarding the department's handling of Cappellini's probation.

Cappellini said that after probation officer Eugene Duffy Jr. administered the drug test, the results were "breaking up" regarding cocaine or heroin, although he didn't elaborate on what that meant. He said Duffy told him: "Why don't you just admit to it? We'll work it out in-house. We won't have to go to a judge."

Testimony revealed that on Feb. 8, Duffy and probation officer Richard Heffron got directions to Cappellini's house from his sister, who also works in probation, and drove to his home.

Cappellini was in bed with the flu when they arrived. It took him nearly 40 minutes to urinate into the bottle, the probation officers said.

"He admitted to myself and agent Heffron he's been using cocaine once to twice a week since his discharge from Clear Brook," Duffy testified. "I think the defendant has a serious drug problem and needs intensive drug counseling."

Duffy testified he has conducted between 75-100 drug tests during his 10-year career and none tested false-positive.

Heffron admitted during Deady's cross-examination he did not write down the names of the two prescription drugs Cappellini said he was taking for back problems.

Prosecution witness Dr. Leo DeAngelo testified that Toxicon laboratories retested Cappellini's urine for nine different classes of drugs, including opiates and cocaine. Defense witness Dr. Fred Sauls said the handling of Cappellini's urine was "sloppy," and he wouldn't even consider using the sample, with which he had "very little faith."

He said Duffy's lack of precision in administering the test — such as the temperature of the chemicals, the angle of the dropper used and how the samples were mixed — made the test invalid.

Before the start of the hearing, Deady made a motion to dismiss the case due to prosecutorial misconduct. He said Kershaw violated the rules of professional conduct when he previously told a reporter he hoped everyone would do the "right thing" with regard to Cappellini's case.

"That is absolutely improper because that statement violates all rules of professional conduct," Deady said.

Conahan dismissed the motion. When asked if he would report Kershaw to the state Disciplinary Board, Deady said such actions are confidential.

"I cannot comment on anything I might do along those lines," he said.

Staff writer Dawn Shurmaitis contributed to this story.

TIMES LEADER/RICHARD SABATURA

Attorney Gifford Cappellini, right, leaves the Luzerne County Courthouse on Monday with his attorneys Gerald Deady, center, and Thomas Marsilio. Cappellini was found in violation of his probation and sentenced to 45 days to one year in the Luzerne County Correctional Facility.

After the news hit that a Luzerne County Judge's son was going to jail, there was almost spontaneous dancing in the streets. The entire psyche of the county almost seemed to change overnight. So much so, that the following editorial was published the very next day. Please take your time while you read this article. Try to feel the hope and passion of the writer. Little did he know that the darkest days for Luzerne County lay ahead. That light at the end of the tunnel was not daylight nor was there fresh clean air. It was the Luzerne County Railroad's Express Train to Hell coming towards the entire county at full speed.

6 March, 1996

The Times Leader
A Capital Cities/ABC, Inc. Newspaper

The region-wide promise of a local court action

Now, maybe it's a stretch to find hope for downtown Wilkes-Barre in the jail sentence of Gifford Cappellini.

But maybe not. Because as the sentence confirmed, Luzerne County has indeed changed. The nepotism, favoritism and patronage that crippled local government for 100 years still may be in place. But they're weaker than ever before.

And that's exactly the kind of trend that could lead to great things ahead for Wilkes-Barre.

Gifford R. Cappellini, son of a prominent and respected local judge, got sentenced to 45 days to a year in jail Monday for violating his probation. Cappellini had tested positive for cocaine and heroin in a random drug test on Feb. 8.

For a moment, put aside the suspicion that Cappellini is getting off with a light sentence. The fact remains a judge's son is going to jail. Once upon a time, not only would a judge's son have avoided going to jail at all, he likely would have avoided being put on probation in the first place.

Pennsylvania politics in 1980 were sadly but notoriously corrupt, say the authors of that year's reference guide to the states, *The Book of America*. The corruption had existed for generations. And one of the ways corruption shows up is in favored treatment for families of the powerful.

But on Monday, Gifford R. Cappellini got sentenced to jail.

Since 1980, something seems to have changed. What?

The answer could be "anger," an unusually healthy emotion where politics and government are concerned.

Nepotism, corruption and favoritism these days make headlines. They make the lead story on the evening TV news. They make Steve Corbett's column, the letters-to-the-editor, and local radio talk shows, too.

Which is a long way of saying they make the public mad. That's new. People in Northeastern Pennsylvania used to be a lot more accepting of the way politics worked, and a lot less willing to get angry or upset.

The media — including this newspaper — had a hand in the complacency. In journalism circles, The Times Leader of the 1960s and earlier would not have been called an aggressive newspaper. Instead it fit the tenor of the times — which, in Wilkes-Barre and many other small cities, meant caution rather than crusades.

But the paper (and other media outlets) changed. The definition of news expanded. Today that definition includes school-board members hiring their relatives, the patronage jobs doled out by county commissioners and the comings and goings in court of a judge's son.

Headlines and news broadcasts about such items both reflect and inspire public opinion. But in the end, local leaders hear an unmistakable message, and once-common practices become a bit less common every year.

That's the change that augers well for Wilkes-Barre. The more local governments turn away from patronage and nepotism and toward more modern, progressive practices, the better for every community in the region. Twenty-first century cities need 21st century governments, rather than governments hobbled by practices as creaky and outdated as our Depression-era voting machines.

And maybe, just maybe, progressive and modern governments may slowly be on their way.

Cappellini admits drug use in records

handwritten: 8 March 1996

■ *Three days after their client said he didn't use drugs on probation, his lawyers filed papers that say he did.*

By JEFF WALSH
Times Leader Staff Writer

WILKES-BARRE — When asked by his own lawyer Monday if he had used drugs while on probation, attorney Gifford R. Cappellini answered clearly.

"I have absolutely not," Cappellini told Gerald Deady.

Luzerne County Court of Common Pleas Judge Michael Conahan believed Cappellini was using drugs, revoked his probation, and sentenced him to jail time.

Three days after the revocation hearing, Cappellini's lawyers filed paperwork that contradicts their client's testimony.

In post-sentence motions asking to modify or vacate Conahan's sentence, attorney Al Flora Jr. wrote that during Cappellini's probation, he "continued to be drug dependent and was unable to cope with and recognize the full severity of his condition."

Cappellini "admits that, due to his drug dependency, he is in need of intensive treatment and monitoring," Flora wrote.

This is Flora's first appearance in the Cappellini case. The revocation hearing was handled by Deady and Tom Marsilio, who replaced Cappellini's two previous lawyers.

Cappellini, 43, of Dallas Township, pleaded guilty Sept. 11 to trying to buy cocaine from a client. Cocaine was found in the lawyer's urine after a random drug test was performed Feb. 8. He was found in violation of his probation Monday, and he must spend 45 days to one year in the county jail. He is scheduled to report Monday, March 11.

Both Flora, who wrote the motion, and Marsilio would not comment Thursday on the discrepancies between the motion and prior testimony. Cappellini was out of his office Thursday afternoon and could not be reached for comment.

Deputy Attorney General Michael Kershaw, who is prosecuting the case, was also unable to comment on the case.

The motions also charge that the county adult probation department failed, due to staffing and the lack of an approved punishment plan, to adequately monitor Cappellini's rehabilitation. His sister works in the county probation office. His father is county Senior Judge Gifford S. Cappellini.

In his motion, Flora charges Conahan:

■ Refused to apply the state sentencing guidelines.
■ Acknowledged alternative treatment plans, but did not state why he went outside the state guidelines and chose incarceration.
■ Cannot put restrictions on Cappellini's law practice.
■ Should grant any other relief deemed appropriate in the "interest of justice."

A hearing on the post-sentence motion will be scheduled by Conahan 9 a.m. Monday, the same time he will rule whether Cappellini can remain on bail until any post-sentence motions and possible appeals to the state Superior Court are resolved.

The bail motion notes Cappellini is:

■ Disabled at present, due to "the disease of alcoholism" and his recent automobile accident.
■ Receiving threatening phone calls from the county prison, and feels that if he were to be incarcerated there, he might suffer bodily injury or death.
■ The sole custodian of his three minor children.

Attorney Cappellini was ordered to report to jail by Judge Conahan to begin a forty-five day to one year sentence. The day he was ordered to report to jail Cappellini simply didn't show up. The best part is that no one went to get him. I thought to myself, "Let's see him get out of this one." At 9 am on Monday, 11 March 1996, Attorney Gifford Cappellini was a no show. At this point a warrant for his arrest should have been issued. Instead, a few hours later a mysterious, unscheduled hearing took place in Judge Conahan's Courtroom. The next day we all got to read about it via the following newspaper article My question is an obvious one Just how does someone, anyone, not show up for jail when ordered to do so by the court and have nothing bad happen to them?

I keep going back to that headline on the front page of the Citizens' Voice (page 180) where Judge Cappellini angrily states that his son has received no special treatment. Once again, Judge Cappellini, it is my opinion that you are a liar. Not only was your son receiving special treatment, but it was "in your face" special treatment.

I will go one step further. I believe that you were the one orchestrating the special treatment and I honestly believe the influence you were exerting over Judge Conahan was downright sinister.

LOCAL

Cappellini to remain free on bail

■ *Attorney was scheduled to report to jail Monday to serve 45 days to one year for violating his probation-related to drug charges.*

By JEFF WALSH
Times Leader Staff Writer

WILKES-BARRE — Attorney Gifford Cappellini will remain free through his appeal process, after a ruling Monday by a county judge.

"He was entitled to bail and the judge made the right decision," said Al Flora Jr., one of Cappellini's lawyers.

As part of the conditions of his bail, Cappellini, 43, of Dallas Township must submit to weekly and random drug testing and enroll in an outpatient treatment program.

Cappellini was scheduled to report to the county jail Monday to serve 45 days to one year for violating his probation. Cappellini, the son of a county senior judge, pleaded guilty Sept. 11 to attempting to buy cocaine from a client. Cocaine was found in his urine after a random drug test was performed Feb. 8.

Deputy Attorney General Michael Kershaw, who is prosecuting the case, said that not only was bail improper in this case, "but even if it were proper, this man's a danger to himself and society."

Cappellini's lawyers — Tom Marsilio, Gerald Deady and Flora — presented case law attempting to show Cappellini does not have to be incarcerated while his post-sentence motions and possible state Superior Court appeals are filed.

After Luzerne County, Court of Common Pleas Judge Michael Conahan granted the $7,500 recognizance bail, Kershaw said he was "disappointed," but declined to discuss the case further.

Conahan, after a six-hour probation revocation hearing Feb. 4, found Cappellini guilty of violating the conditions of his probation and ordered the jail time.

Conahan plans to rule on Cappellini's post-sentence motions at 1 p.m. March 19. The motions seek to reduce or vacate Conahan's sentence. At that time, Conahan may also hear testimony about another instance where Cappellini possibly violated probation.

After Conahan ruled on the bail issue, Kershaw showed the judge a letter he received alleging another probation violation. Kershaw said he received the letter from county Assistant Chief Probation Officer James Marinello.

Conahan returned the letter to Kershaw and told him there were proper procedures to introduce such allegations. Flora said they were unaware of the content of the letter.

"He said the letter itself would indicate a probation violation," Flora said. "We have no knowledge that would indicate that."

Flora said the way Kershaw and Marinello presented the letter to the court was "absurd."

"Mr. Marinello knew it was not being brought before the court in a normal manner," Flora said.

Marinello refused to comment, aside from saying he was working with the state attorney general's office regarding the letter.

Conahan said he might have to rule on any claims made in the letter before the scheduled hearing March 19.

TIMES LEADER/RICHARD SABATURA
Attorney Gifford Cappellini stands outside the courtroom of Luzerne County Court of Common Pleas Judge Michael Conahan on Monday before a hearing at which Conahan ruled the lawyer may remain free on bail.

Cappellini hearing surprises lawyers

■ *Duration and parade of witnesses regarded as unusual in this type of case.*

By DAWN SHURMAITIS
Times Leader Staff Writer

WILKES-BARRE — If there's one thing area lawyers can agree upon about fellow attorney Gifford R. Cappellini's probation hearing, it's that the judge was in an unenviable position.

"On the one hand, you can say that because he's a lawyer you give him a break because he can make a contribution to society," said Wilkes-Barre attorney John Moses, reacting Tuesday to the outcome of Cappellini's hearing on Monday. "On the other hand, you can say that because he held a position of influence he should be held to a higher standard."

Luzerne County Court of Common Pleas Judge Michael Conahan ruled Cappellini violated his probation by failing a drug test and, as punishment, must serve a 45-day to one-year sentence.

Gifford R. Cappellini

No special treatment planned
Page 8A

Moses says that nine times out of 10 a first-time offender such as Cappellini — charged with the lowest level misdemeanor for trying to buy cocaine from a client — would get a break, not a jail sentence.

That's why Moses was disturbed by the results of a non-scientific WBRE-TV, Channel 28 phone poll Monday night that showed 96 percent of the callers believed Cappellini was given preferential treatment because his father is senior Judge Gifford S. Cappellini.

"I feel very strongly that is not the case," Moses said. "You can always imagine the tentacles reaching in. But in this case, that is such baloney."

Defense attorney Charles Gelso said he expected Conahan to order Cappellini back into drug treatment.

"But obviously, Michael Conahan did what he thought was best, not only for Cappellini, but for the system," Gelso said.

Other uncharacteristic features of Monday's hearing were:

■ Most revocation hearings last about 10 minutes. Cappellini's lasted six hours, the attorney said.

■ It is highly unusual for the state to call witnesses to testify to the validity of a drug test. In most hearings, a judge would simply accept the report. Monday, the defense and the prosecution each

■ See **CAPPELLINI**, Page 8A

8A The Times Leader, Wilkes-Barre, PA, Wednesday, March 6, 1996

Cappellini

(Continued from Page 1A)

called an expert in drug testing to the stand to face aggressive questioning.

Cappellini could face additional action by the Disciplinary Board of the Supreme Court of Pennsylvania, which polices lawyers. But even if he temporarily loses his law license, he could get it back.

West Pittston attorney Joe Castellino served four months in a federal prison and lost his right to practice law after he admitted to selling cocaine in the mid-1980s. The state Supreme Court restored his right to practice law in September 1994, more than six years after he was disbarred. In January, his father, Luzerne County Recorder of Deeds Frank Castellino, rehired him to a $6,400-a-year office solicitor job.

Former Luzerne County Court of Common Pleas Judge Arthur Dalessandro served nine months in federal prison after pleading guilty to tax evasion in 1990. Dalessandro was readmitted to the bar in November 1992, after the state Supreme Court ruled that he be allowed to resume practicing law because income tax evasion couldn't be classified as official misbehavior.

"I don't see any reason why someone couldn't come back and engage in law," said attorney Joseph Persico, president of the Luzerne County Bar Association. "Fortunately, in our country we have the opportunity to try again. We're all human. We all make mistakes."

Cappellini, 43, of Dallas Township, was originally sentenced Sept. 11 and ordered to submit to random drug tests.

But five months passed before the county probation department conducted the first test. That failure prompted a still ongoing state attorney general's office investigation into employee conduct at the probation department.

Monday, Judge Conahan said the state, and not the county, will supervise Cappellini's parole after he completes his sentence.

Department chief Stephen Wolinsky refused to comment Tuesday.

TIMES LEADER/BOB ESPOSITO
Defense attorney Gerald Deady, left, confers with his client, attorney Gifford Cappellini on Monday at the lawyer's probation revocation hearing.

To jail, lawyer is just another inmate

By DAWN SHURMAITIS
Times Leader Staff Writer

When attorney Gifford R. Cappellini reports to the Luzerne County Correctional Facility next week he will be treated like any of the other 444 inmates: roast beef and mashed potatoes for supper, a single cell or maybe a cell mate and occasional visits to the prison law library.

And though at least two of Cappellini's current female clients are serving time in the same jail, he won't be able to consult with them there. There is no fraternizing between the sexes, said Deputy Warden Rowland Roberts.

Monday, Judge Michael Conahan ruled Cappellini violated his probation by failing a drug test and, as punishment, must serve a 45-day to one-year sentence.

But much of that time could be served outside prison walls. According to Conahan's ruling, Cappellini may apply for immediate work release, which means he can be a moneymaking lawyer by day and a locked-up inmate by night.

As sentencing judge, Conahan sets the terms. The judge can make the inmate wait until he or she serves half of a minimum sentence without incident before applying to the sentencing judge for the work release program. Or a judge may send the offender immediately to the work release program.

Roberts said about 70 of the county's inmates are participating in the work release and driving-under-the-influence programs. The work release program is for minimal risk offenders, who return after each shift to a separate facility outside the main prison building. That building is locked, but there are no bars on the windows.

Laying into the law

■ In 1992, the Disciplinary Board of the Supreme Court of Pennsylvania disposed of 4,512 complaints against lawyers.
■ Two hundred lawyers were disciplined. Disciplinary action ranges from the lowest form — informal admonition — to disbarment.
■ In 1995, the board disposed of 4,963 complaints. All told, 236 lawyers were disciplined.
■ There are 585 active attorneys in Luzerne County. From 1992 to 1995 the board disciplined a total of 19 county lawyers — five were disbarred.

All inmates, whether housed at the jail or participating in the work release program, are treated the same, Roberts said.

Despite probation violation report, Judge Conahan grants Cappellini bail

Citizens' Voice, Wilkes-Barre, Pa.   Tuesday, March 12, 1996 — 6

Attorney Gifford R. Cappellini, who was scheduled to start a 45-day to one year jail term Monday for violation of probation without verdict on drug charges, is free on $7,500 own recognizance bail, pending appeal.

The bail was awarded despite a report made at a Monday hearing that Cappellini has twice violated his probation.

Deputy Attorney General Michael Kershaw said that since last Monday, he had learned that Cappellini had violated his probation a second time. Cappellini was charged with one probation violation and was ordered to jail last Monday by Judge Michael Conahan.

Neither Kershaw nor Cappellini's three defense lawyers would comment on the report, which was provided to Kershaw by Assistant Chief Probation Officer James Marinello. Judge Conahan awarded bail despite the report that Cappellini violated his probation a second time. Conahan said that Marinello did not follow proper procedures in filing his statement.

A source close to the proceedings said that Cappellini's violation has nothing to do with drug use. The defense motion for modifying or vacating the sentence.

Cappellini, 42, of Dallas Township, was arrested March 29, 1995, by the Wilkes-Barre Drug Task Force and state attorney general, including Deputy Attorney General Michael Kershaw of Philadelphia, and charged with solicitation to possess a controlled substance, and criminal attempt to possess a controlled substance.

Cappellini appeared before Judge Conahan last Sept. 11 and entered a plea of no contest to the charges. He was placed on probation without verdict for one year with special conditions, including drug testing.

It was alleged by the Luzerne County Department of Probation and Parole that Cappellini was in violation of his probation and a drug test in January proved positive the defendant was using drugs. It was alleged he admitted using drugs once or twice a week.

Judge Conahan conducted a lengthy court hearing March 4 and revoked Cappellini's probation. The judge sentenced the defendant to a jail term of 45 days to one year. The court ordered weekly random drug testing and the defendant was to refrain from alcohol and drugs and have no contact with persons connected with drugs, including present or potential clients in his law practice. It was stated the defendant could participate in the work release program at the prison.

Attorneys Gerald Deady and Thomas Marsilio (succeeding prior counsel, attorneys Ferris Webby and Joseph Sklarosky, Sr.) filed a petition for bail, pending appeal.

Meanwhile, Attorney Al Flora, Jr., serving as special appeal counsel for the defendant, filed a motion to vacate or modify the sentence.

The court was asked to impose sentence in accordance with the sentencing code. Among other things, the court was asked to eliminate the restrictions placed on the defendant in connection with his law practice.

Judge Conahan has set a hearing for March 19 on the petition for vacating or modifying the sentence.

Attorney Kershaw presented a letter to Judge Conahan Monday during the court hearing, stating that it was given to Kershaw by James Marinello, an assistant chief in the Luzerne County Adult Probation and Parole Office.

Judge Conahan immediately returned the letter to Attorney Kershaw.

It was revealed the letter claimed Cappellini has once again violated the conditions of his probation.

Attorney Kershaw refused comment on the letter when later questioned by members of the news media.

"Cappellini is a danger to himself as well as society." He cited a number of state court cases of a similar nature.

Cappellini's attorneys said that Marinello's report is a last-minute attempt to bolster the commonwealth's case.

Judge Conahan applied special conditions in connection with bail, including arrangements be made for outpatient rehabilitative counseling, and also drug testing "by whatever means."

Jurisdiction in the case of the defendant is transferred from the Luzerne County Adult Probation and Parole Department to the state Probation and Parole Department.

CHAPTER THIRTY-FIVE

The Wheels of Injustice

The wheels of "Injustice" spin faster in Luzerne County than the wheels of justice. Give me a break! Better yet, let's give Attorney Cappellini a break. After all, this is America and every drug abuser and probation violator should be given the same latitude to continue the behavior that got them into trouble in the first place. Instead of going back to the sentencing judge with his hat in his hand and begging for forgiveness, Attorney Cappellini and his attorneys attacked the sentencing judge. You read right-- they attacked Judge Conahan.

I have some pretty scary first-hand knowledge about judges and their egos. The metamorphosis that occurs when a lawyer/politician actually becomes a "God," I mean a judge, is not only frightening but almost always universal. Yes, there are a few exceptions, but not many. The sentencing judge in this case, Judge Conahan, years later would become one of two judges known worldwide as a "Kids for Cash" judge. This scandal would come to rock the Pennsylvania Judicial System to its very core. When you get a chance, Google "Kids for Cash." It will be the focus of my next book.

60 Minutes, 20/20, Time Magazine and countless other National and International media outlets have done major feature stories about Judge Conahan and his alleged co-conspirator, Judge Ciavarella. Judge Conahan was not only powerful but, according to the FBI, IRS, and the US Attorney's Office, this judge was one of the most, if not the most, corrupt judges in the history of the United States. That, my friend, is quite a statement.

Let's get back to pissing off the sentencing judge. Attorney Cappellini and his band of merry attorneys launched an all out assault on Judge Conahan's handling of this case. Basically, they claimed if it were not for the judge's complete disregard for the law and its procedures, Attorney Cappellini would be accepting the Nobel Peace Prize instead of looking at hard time in prison. I thought to myself, how much more fun can this get? A lawyer attacking a Luzerne County Judge was unprecedented. A Cappellini being that lawyer was better than my imagination could ever dream up. One of them was going to go down in flames. I became giddy with excitement. Either a Luzerne County Judge was going down or a Cappellini. Maybe that Disney guy was right after all……

How do you attack a powerful judge and win? The only way that I know of is if the judge allows you to win. And that, my friend, is a very rare instance indeed. After all, he not only was caught breaking the law, but after throwing himself at the mercy of the court, received a hand slap.

Attorney Cappellini then violated each condition of his probation, by his own admission, some dozens, if not hundreds, of times. Each and EVERY violation was a major violation that individually would have cost Joe six-pack his freedom. On top of violating all of the terms of his Probation, he was continuing to acquire cocaine and heroin. Acquiring cocaine was the very reason he was charged with a crime to begin with. Each time he acquired more drugs he was committing a new crime, though he was never charged.

He was sentenced to jail and simply didn't show up when ordered to report. As you have seen, it is all over the news. To top it off, he then publicly attacked the sentencing judge as incompetent.

Judge Conahan made numerous public statements in open court regarding these attacks and it was clear that he was not amused. I can't think of a single reason why Judge Conahan would not throw this clown into jail as he would normally be required to do--except for one.

If you guessed "cash" you would be guessing wrong. I believe that any amount of cash (under six figures) would never come close to scratching the surface. I believe it would have to be something much more substantial and evil. I believe that somebody had the "goods" on Judge Conahan.

Think about it. For all the reasons I have stated, there isn't a judge alive who would have allowed anyone to do and say what Attorney Cappellini did and said. To be made a fool of in such a fashion would have to go to Conahan's very core of existence. Who could hold such damaging information and also have the balls to use it against Conahan?

Probe is Underway to Determine How Judge's Son Avoided Drug Testing

by Mitch Grochowski

A probe is underway by the Pennsylvania Attorney General's office to determine why the son of a prominent judge did not have to submit to court-ordered drug testing for five months.

When Gifford Cappellini finally was tested, his urine was loaded with heroin and cocaine, according to officials.

As a result, Cappellini was given up to a year's prison sentence last Monday for violating his parole on a drug offense conviction.

Cappellini is the son of Luzerne County's most senior judge.

Although he was ordered by the court to submit to routine drug testing, it appears the only one that was ever administered to him was when probation department representatives appeared at his home on Feb. 8 and demanded a urine sample. It took them 45 minutes to do it.

Pennsylvania Attorney General's office to determine why the son of a prominent judge did not have to submit to court-ordered drug testing for five months. [repeated text omitted]

to submit to drug testing, the judge's son never even showed up at the probation office to file mandatory papers on a monthly basis. Instead, he sent his secretary to the probation department with the documents.

The Luzerne County Probation Department's sudden demand for a urine sample came in the wake of a leak that the Attorney General's office was investigating new drug allegations against Cappellini, the Metro has learned. The fact that Cappellini did test positive from the Feb. 8 urine sample is indicative that the offender had renewed access to controlled substances as the AG's office suspected.

Also fueling the Attorney General's probe, according to Metro sources, is that fact that Cappellini's sister, Dorie, is an employee of the Probation Department.

The thrust of the probe is reported to be whether Cappellini's sister and/or other members of the Probation Department deliberately tried to shield the defendant after he blatantly violated parole by using drugs again.

When Atty. Cappellini initially was convicted for trying to buy narcotics from one of his legal clients, he agreed to enter a drug rehabilitation program at Clearbrook where his mother happens to be a board member. Supporters of Cappellini are painting his probation revocation and the Attorney General's probe as nothing more than a vendetta against Senior Judge Cappellini by his political foes.

Nevertheless, some courthouse employees interviewed by the Metro expressed their opinion that an investigation is warranted given the power influence triangle of Cappellini's father as senior judge, his sister

mother as a director of the drug rehabilitation center where he enrolled.

The defendant's sentence for the parole violation is from 45 days to a year in jail. He is eligible to apply for work release.

> The distance is nothing; it is only the first step that is difficult.
> —Mme Du Deffand

Veteran's Post

A while ago, the brother of a Gulf War vet with a drinking problem wanted to know if getting him into A.A. would affect any chance of later treatment by the VA. I asked if any reader had an answer. The first letter I got was from Bob Shreve, a retired USAF First Sergeant who is now a State Probation Officer in Clarksville, Tenn. I've had to excerpt from his letter because of space, but the basic information remains as follows:

"Veterans with drug and alcohol abuse problems (can) contact the closest VA Hospital (for) both psychiatric and abuse problem assistance at no charge. Veterans and non-veterans alike can receive free treatment and assistance through local Union Resource Mission Agencies. In middle Tennessee, both Murfreesboro and Nashville VA hospitals treat veterans for these problems..." Thanks to Bob and everyone who said the same thing in their letters

It certainly wasn't Attorney Cappellini. He was too busy snorting white powder up his nose. It couldn't be Attorney Cappellini's sister, the probation officer. She had her own hands full just trying to keep herself out of jail for obstruction. No, it would have to be someone who not only had a dog in this fight, but someone with the reputation to back up a threat. Someone who wouldn't care what it looked like or how many bodies were thrown under the bus. All of my indicators pointed to only one person.

I dare anyone to come up with a better explanation. If I am accurate, the ramifications are huge. As of the date of this book, Judge Conahan has been indicted under the RICO Act by a Federal Grand Jury on a forty-eight count laundry list of charges. Prior to the Grand Jury, he had pled guilty and entered into a plea agreement that required him to spend eighty-seven months in a Federal Prison. A Federal Judge rejected his guilty plea as being too lenient, hence, the Grand Jury intervention. Eighty-seven months is what he agreed to. That fact alone is staggering.

Think about it and see if you come up with any other reason for Conahan's handling of this case in this fashion. I'm all ears.

Cappellini accused of defying court order

■ Attorney, on probation related to drug offenses, tried to lure drug user as client, documents say.

By DAWN SHURMAITIS and WILLIAM SPECHT
Times Leader Staff Writers

WILKES-BARRE — Attorney and admitted drug user Gifford R. Cappellini is going to court — again — to face allegations he violated a court order — again.

Cappellini is scheduled to face special prosecutor Michael Kershaw on Tuesday at 1 p.m. for calling a known drug user and trying to solicit him as a client, according to court papers filed Wednesday. Furthermore, papers say, Cappellini guaranteed the potential client an appearance before a different judge.

Cappellini, 43, of Dallas Township, did not return a phone call to his Kingston law office Wednesday. His defense attorneys could not be reached for comment.

Here is what happened March 6, according to court documents:

■ Cappellini called Luzerne County Correctional Facility Inmate Thomas Gale, who was in jail for violating probation on charges of resisting arrest and disorderly conduct.

■ Gale, 20, of Pittston, already had appeared before county Judge Michael Conahan three times and was afraid he would get

■ See CAPPELLINI, Page 16A

★16A The Times Leader, Wilkes-Barre, PA, Thursday, March 14, 1996

Cappellini—

(Continued from Page 1A)

a harsher sentence if he faced Conahan again- for testing "hot" for either drugs or alcohol.
■ Cappellini told Gale that if he represented Gale, the judge wouldn't be able to sentence Gale because of a conflict of interest.
The conflict? Cappellini is appearing before Conahan.

On Sept. 11, Conahan sentenced Cappellini to one-year probation on charges he tried to buy cocaine from a client. On March 4, Conahan found Cappellini guilty of violating his probation by testing positive for drugs, but allowed him to remain free on bail pending appeal. The judge ordered Cappellini to refrain from associating with people using drugs or alcohol, including clients or potential clients.

Kershaw wants the judge to revoke Cappellini's bail and impose a new, harsher sentence. Conahan will hear Kershaw's arguments and listen to his witnesses on Tuesday.

At the same hearing, Cappellini's defense team is expected to tackle double duty: arguing against bail revocation while pushing for a new, more lenient sentence for the probation violation.

Kershaw based his petition on a report written by James Marinello, assistant chief of the Luzerne County Adult Probation/Parole Department. In the report, Marinello said Gale contacted him and described his conversation with Cappellini.

Gale served his latest stint in county jail from Feb. 29 to March 7. According to court papers, Conahan sentenced Gale on Dec. 22, 1995 to one-year home confinement and ordered a 9 p.m. curfew, mandatory alcoholics anonymous meetings, a full time job, random drug and alcohol tests and no association with drugs or alcohol or anyone using drugs or alcohol.

Kershaw's petition does not specify how Gale tested "hot" but says "Cappellini intentionally and contemptuously communicated with a person known to him to be a drug user."

Gale could not be reached for comment Wednesday.

It is not known if Cappellini represented Gale previously. Cappellini is not listed in any of Gale's case files at the Luzerne County Courthouse.

If the most recent allegations against Cappellini are true, there also are professional conduct considerations, according to law professor Laurel Terry of the Dickinson School of Law in Carlisle.

The Pennsylvania Rule of Professional Conduct prohibits lawyers from soliciting a prospective client unless the parties had a prior professional relationship or the lawyer offers his services for free, Terry said.

A message left with the Luzerne County Bar Association on Wednesday was not returned.

Gifford P. Cappellini's trip through the other side of the legal system

■ **March 30, 1995:** Tries to buy $190 worth of cocaine from a client. Arrested for solicitation to possess a controlled substance and criminal attempt to possess a controlled substance.

■ **Sept. 11, 1995:** Cappellini pleads guilty and is sentenced to one-year probation without verdict. The court orders him to submit to random drug tests, counseling and treatment.

■ **Feb. 8, 1996:** A drug test administered by a probation officer finds traces of cocaine and heroin in Cappellini's urine.

■ **March 4, 1996:** Judge Michael Conahan finds Cappellini guilty of violating his probation. The judge revokes Cappellini's probation and orders him to report to county jail on March 11 to serve 45 days to one year. The judge also orders Cappellini to undergo weekly and random drug tests and to have no communication or contact with persons associated with drugs, including clients.

■ **March 6, 1996:** Cappellini allegedly violates his probation by intentionally communicating with a person known to be a drug user.

■ **March 6, 1996:** Cappellini's defense team files motions asking to modify or vacate Cappellini's March 4 sentence.

■ **March 11, 1996:** Conahan allows Cappellini to remain free on bail pending his appeal.

■ **March 13, 1996:** The prosecution files court papers asking Conahan to revoke Cappellini's bail, resentence him and sanction him for contemptuous conduct.

■ **March 19, 1996:** Hearing scheduled on defense motions, bail revocation and latest allegation of bail violation.

Cappellini petitions to avoid jail

By MELISSA DONOVAN
Times Leader Staff Writer

WILKES-BARRE — All of his appeals are exhausted, but former county defender Gifford R. Cappellini is taking another shot at escaping a jail term for a drug conviction.

On Tuesday, his lawyer filed a petition arguing that the 45-day to one-year jail term would be a "manifest injustice" that would force his children into foster care.

Cappellini Jr., the son of a Luzerne County senior judge and brother of a probation department employee, was sentenced to jail after failing drug tests last March, six months after pleading guilty to attempting to purchase cocaine from a client.

Reached at his parents' Wilkes-Barre home Tuesday, Cappellini said the youngest of his three sons, age 10, lives with him. The boy could end up in foster care if he goes to jail, Cappellini said. His other two sons, age 14 and 17, live with their mother, he said.

"It's in the hands of my higher power now, so I have nothing more to say," he said.

The Superior Court of Pennsylvania rejected his appeal last month and all other appeal periods have expired, according to a petition filed by his attorney, Al Flora.

But the petition argues that Cappellini should be allowed to stay out of jail because he has been able to stay drug-free as a result of court-ordered monitoring and counseling.

The jail sentence "was designed to forcibly impress upon the defendant the need for treatment which at that time the court believed could only be obtained in an institutionalized setting such as county prison," Flora wrote.

The petition was submitted to Luzerne County Court of Common Pleas Judge Michael Conahan.

Flora declined to comment.

The two following documents are copies of actual criminal court dockets in the Cappellini drug case. The first is the March 4, 1996 order signed by Judge Conahan sentencing Attorney Cappellini to jail. It is easy to read and very straight forward.

M. Kershaw, District Attorney
C. Rachilla, Court Stenographer
G. Deady, Atty. for Defendant

COURT OF COMMON PLEAS - CRIMINAL DIVISION
COUNTY OF LUZERNE
THE COMMONWEALTH OF PENNSYLVANIA
vs.
Gifford Cappellini Jr.

No. 12622

CHARGE: Possession
No. 1305   19 95
DATE: March 4, 1996

Revocation of Probation without Verdict

Deft found in Violation of Probation w/o Verdict by the Court

Probation w/o Verdict Revoked

Deft found guilty of solicitation by the court to possession of a contrl substance and also to criminal attempt to possess a contrl substance.

Deft sentenced to L.C.C.F. Min. 45 days to Max. 1 year.

During Parole deft to be with Electric Monitoring-Parole to be transferred to the State.

Deft to report to Sheriff's Office March 11, 1996 at 9:00AM

Submit testing weekly and random

No communication of contact with persons assoc with drugs including Law Practice

May apply for Immed Work Release

Deft advised of Appeal Rights

CLERK: John Hyder
Judge Michael Conahan

The Luzerne County Railroad

Now take a look at the following document that is dated May 2, 1997, over one year later. I will help with the bad hand writing. I will spell out what the abbreviations mean. The first line reads: Defendant petition for immediate parole and request for time served was denied by the court.

Very curious as Attorney Cappellini had no time served other than Probation which he violated. The next line is the kicker!

Defendant to serve his 45 days at Luzerne County Correctional Facility-this will be served under Department of Probation and Parole starting today.

Next line: Immediate parole AFTER minimum county sentence with state supervision.

I have contacted a number of people in the know, and nobody but nobody remembers any such hearing, any such sentencing, or any such jail time being served.

| M. KERSHAW Phil A. | M. COLLERAN | A. FLORA |
| District Attorney D.A. | Court Stenographer | Atty. for Defendant |

No. 19296

COURT OF COMMON PLEAS – CRIMINAL DIVISION
COUNTY OF LUZERNE
THE COMMONWEALTH OF PENNSYLVANIA
vs.
1. GIFFORD R. CAPPELLINI JR.
2.
3.

Indictments ☐ Yes ☐ No	Transcripts ☐ Yes ☐ No	Commitment Issued ☐ Yes ☐ No
CHARGE POSSESSION (acts)		No. 1305 1995
PLEA	DISPOSITION	DATE MAY 2, 1997
Pay Costs of Prosecution ☐ Yes ☐ No		Pre-Sentence Investigation Requested ☐ Yes ☐ No

Deft. petition for Immediate Parole and Request for Credit for time served was DENIED by the court

Deft. to Serve His 45 DAYS at L.C.C.F. – this will be served under I.P.P starting today Immediate Parole AFTER minimum (County sentence with State supervision)

All Terms & Conditions previously Imposed will Remain Must follow all aftercare treatments.

Refrain from use of D/A
Do not frequent places serving D/A
Do not associate with persons using D/A
Random testing at least once per month
No contact or communication with persons using drugs

Case is still under Bail Agency terms & conditions

Deft advised of appeal rights

CLERK: John Hyder   JUDGE: Conahan J.

Well now, isn't that interesting? I'll say. The dynamics of what you just read about are staggering. First off, this hearing was apparently a secret hearing. A lot of people in Luzerne County would have circled the day on their calendar and taken it off of work to attend this hearing. I would have. Secondly, Attorney Cappellini was sentenced to jail immediately. That means he couldn't leave the courthouse to get his toothbrush and pajamas. He would get his ass shackled up and be physically taken to the Big House straight from the Courtroom. Apparently Judge Conahan had enough of Cappellini's "in your face" bad behavior as well as his bad mouthing. So Attorney Cappellini served his 45 days in jail as well as his entire probation without a hitch and became a model citizen and has focused his life on God and the drug addiction of Luzerne County youth................ Nope.

Somehow, between the courtroom and the one block transportation of his shackled ass to the jail, something happened because he never made it. Now I could speculate as to who may have stepped in and stopped the prisoner transfer, but I would only be speculating..........mind you.

What I find mildly amusing is that Judge Conahan, who would later become vilified as one of the most corrupt judges in the history of the United States left this docket page in the official record probably to cover his own ass.

To my knowledge, nobody from the court system, Sheriff's Office, Dept. of Corrections or even the State Attorney General's office ever leaked a word about the above events. How is that for frightening?

Please take a look at the following document. Read it carefully and then I will comment.

PALISSERY AND BROWN
ATTORNEYS AT LAW

N.K. PALISSERY
GLENN J. BROWN

33 WEST SOUTH STREET
WILKES-BARRE, PA 18701
PHONE: (717) 223-8082
FAX: (717) 225-0609

12 January 1997

246 WEST BROAD STREET
QUAKERTOWN, PA 18951
PHONE: (215) 529-0920
(215) 529-0921

PLEASE REPLY TO:
Wilkes-Barre

The Honorable Michael T. Conahan
Luzerne County Courthouse
200 North River Street
Wilkes-Barre, PA 18711

Re: Attorney Gifford Cappellini — 1305 of 1995

Dear Judge Conahan:

I was contacted by Attorney Gifford Cappellini today and was informed that he is seeking permission from this Honorable Court to leave Luzerne County for a single day this weekend to go to Atlantic City, New Jersey, with his father, Judge Cappellini.

As you are aware, Attorney Al Flora represents Mr. Cappellini and I write this letter in Attorney Flora's absence as he is on vacation until some time next week.

Please contact me with any objections that the Court has to Mr. Cappellini's plan for this weekend, if any. I look forward to hearing from you. Thank you.

Sincerely yours,

N. K Palissery, Esquire

NKP/dmp

Approved the 12th Day of Feb. 1997

What do you think Attorney Cappellini would do if he went to Atlantic City while on probation and did so without permission?

Let's add to the equation the fact that he may have believed that someone was about to squeal on him after the fact. We all know they have cameras all over the place down there. Well, the correct answer would be: He would try to cover his ass with the biggest blanket he could find. His father, the Judge, appears to have been doing an admirable job "not intervening" in his son's matters so far, so why not use him?

Well, there is a problem when Attorney Cappellini's attorney (to his credit) would not participate in the cover-up. My guess is that he didn't even know about the cover-up. Not a problem, let's just say Cappellini's attorney is on a ski trip. Wait, maybe Hawaii would sound better. It is winter you know.

Wait, maybe that's too many lies and Judge Conahan may ask about the slope conditions or the color of the sand in Hawaii, or why nobody, including his law partners, knew when he will return. Stick to generic "Vacation." Next, let's assume that Judge Conahan will have a problem with the out of state gambling junket so it is important to include Daddy's name in the letter. Wait! Let's make it sound like Daddy is the one actually requesting the permission. Better yet, since its Daddy asking, we can assume the answer will be yes and that Judge Conahan should only get back to him if there is a problem with the plans.

Now since the unauthorized trip occurred during the weekend of January 17th, date the letter January 12th and hope nobody will notice that it is now February 12th. Certainly no one will check and see that this letter was written on a Sunday. If somebody says anything, just tell them it is a typo.

What if none of the above happened?

What if this stationary from the Palissery and Brown Law Firm was stolen and Attorney Palissery doesn't even know this letter exists? One more kicker! What if Judge Cappellini doesn't know this letter exists either?

There is one more piece of housekeeping before we move on. Apparently, Judge Conahan had enough of the entire Cappellini family and said enough is enough. Conahan was not going to be made a fool of any longer. About this time Attorney Cappellini decided that he liked the "Old West" lifestyle so much that he moved to Arizona. Guess what? No, he didn't move there with Cowboy Harvey. He was not disbarred in Arizona so he could still play lawyer between snorts. I am still checking, but I have not found anywhere in Arizona that Attorney Cappellini's probation records were transferred or any law enforcement agency that his Probation was transferred to. Don't worry, I am still checking.

I promised you that this was going to get interesting. If you thought it was fun up to this point or at least mildly entertaining, hang on to your seat.

The two principle characters going forward are Probation Officer Eugene Duffy, Jr., who is the son of the then Luzerne County Prothonotary Eugene Duffy, Sr. A Prothonotary is the elected official who maintains the counties civil records in the courthouse. The Prothonotary and Judge Cappellini are very close personal friends.

Our next passenger, I mean character, is second-in-command at the Luzerne County Probation Office, Assistant Chief James Marinello. Assistant Chief Marinello is the direct supervisor of Probation Officer Duffy and has twenty-two years of experience as a Luzerne County Probation Officer and over ten years as the Assistant Chief. Somehow (the luck of the draw, I'm sure) P.O. Duffy becomes Attorney Cappellini's Probation Officer.

CHAPTER THIRTY-SIX

*D*oing the Right Thing in Luzerne County

I contacted Assistant Chief Marinello early in 2010 and interview him extensively for this book. At first he was very reluctant and stand-offish. He did, however, recognize my name and stated that he had followed my case in the newspapers back when it was unfolding. Marinello repeated to me many times, "I really don't want to relive that nightmare." Only after extensive prodding on my part did he open up. The more old newspaper articles and court documents he dug out for me to review, the angrier he got. Each conversation I had with him seemed to raise his adrenaline level another notch.

Assistant Chief Marinello recounted the following sequence of events:

After approximately five months of not being drug tested as required by court order, Attorney Cappellini was finally tested. As you have already read, his test comes back hot for not only cocaine but also heroin. Assistant Chief Marinello took it upon himself as P.O. Duffy's direct supervisor to review the Cappellini probation records. He discovered major discrepancies in the file.

Assistant Chief Marinello now found himself at a crossroads. After twenty-two years in the probation office he felt that he knew exactly what would happen if he took the information he had discovered to his boss, Chief Wolinsky. Nothing, absolutely nothing would happen. Marinello was confident that everything would be brushed under the carpet. At that point he decided to contact the Pennsylvania State Attorney General's Office and pass his information onto them. Assistant Chief Marinello stated, "I had at least two Probation Officers that appeared to have conspired to break the law and a sitting Judge that was exerting his influence into the whole matter. One of the Probation Officers was the daughter of that powerful judge and the other was the son of a powerful politician. I had no confidence that my boss could or would overcome the pressure that would be exerted if this matter were to be handled internally. I did what I felt and still feel was the right thing."

The State Attorney General's Office agreed with Assistant Chief Marinello and, rather than kicking the matter back to the county, launched their own investigation. It was at this exact point in time that Assistant Chief Marinello climbed aboard, "The Luzerne County Railroad." Just like I did on the fateful day that I deposited my million dollar check in the bank, he hadn't a clue that he was leaving on the trip of his lifetime.

When confronted with the evidence by Special Agents from the Attorney General's office, P.O. Duffy buckled. He provided a full written confession of his actions as well as the actions of P.O. Dodie Cappellini and Judge Gifford Cappellini.

Shortly after all of this transpired, P.O. Duffy and P.O. Cappellini met at Pattie's Sports Bar for drinks, a few blocks from the courthouse. Pattie's was a popular hangout for many of Luzerne County's finest judges and upper management at the Luzerne County Courthouse. That was until the owner was charged by the FBI in 2010 with running an extensive internet gambling ring out of the restaurant. As of this writing, a "forfeiture action" of the property has also been instituted by the Feds.

As a curious side bar, the owner was not only released on his own recognizance after his arrest, but was also allowed to leave the country by a Federal Judge in order to lead a gambling junket to Atlantis, in the Bahamas. Pretty amusing! I can't make this stuff up. I'm not that clever.

Published reports indicate that P.O. Duffy was in full panic mode at this meeting with P.O. Dodie Cappellini. One can only speculate as to exactly what was said, but it appears that P.O. Duffy felt he was the lone participant who was "going down" or was probably close to the top of his list as far as subjects broached that evening. As the drinks flowed and the anxiety increased, P.O. Cappellini did the unthinkable. She called her father, the judge, on her cell phone. After she briefed her father as to what was going down, he too, did the unthinkable. He spoke directly to P.O. Duffy via his daughter's phone.

Judge Cappellini does not deny any of this. He publicly acknowledges that he spoke to P.O. Duffy at this time, but not as a judge. He spoke to him as a friend. Since P.O. Duffy's father and the judge were such close friends, he felt it was important that he console his friend's son. Judge Cappellini apparently has an ability that no other judge in the world has. When he decides to, he can stop being a judge on command. It is just like when he can stop being Attorney Piccone's best friend while in the courtroom and then switch back to best friend mode at the end of the day. Same thing.

What advice did Judge Cappellini give to P.O. Duffy? I simply don't know and the judge isn't telling. What I do know is that he told P.O. Duffy to stop panicking and that everything was going to work out and be just fine when all was said and done. My question to you is, was that just generic well wishing or something much more sinister? I think that it would not be a stretch to say that P.O. Duffy made it clear that it was not his desire to take the fall all by himself. After all, he only did (or did not do) what was requested by the judge via the judge's daughter. Please read the following newspaper report very carefully. Take special note of the quotes in the article from the original arrest affidavit regarding P.O. Cappellini and Judge Cappellini.

Eugene Duffy Jr. arraigned — Citizens' Voice/Jack Kelley

Probation officer Duffy faces tampering charges

By CAROL CRANE
Citizens' Voice Staff Writer

Luzerne County Adult Probation Officer Eugene Duffy Jr. allegedly admitted to state agents that he placed falsified information into a file of a prominent local defense attorney who was on probation for drug offenses.

Duffy, according to the state attorney general's office, put the fabricated document into the attorney's probation file only after learning an investigation had been launched.

Duffy, 33, of West Hazleton, turned himself in on Thursday to face charges of unsworn falsification to authorities, tampering with or fabricating physical evidence, tampering with public records or information, and obstructing the administration of law or other governmental function.

Each charge is a misdemeanor of the second-degree. Each is punishable by up to two years in prison and a $5,000 fine.

Duffy who appeared before District Justice Martin Kane in Wilkes-Barre was released on his own recognizance. He was accompanied by his father, Luzerne County Prothonotary Eugene Duffy, and John Moses, his lawyer.

Appearing on behalf of the state attorney general's office were special agents Barry J. Moran and Kevin Cogan who are heading up the investigation.

While the elder Duffy appeared stoic during the brief arraignment, his son, dressed neatly in a tan suit, seemed confident and responded without hesitation to all questions asked by Kane. After the proceeding was over, the younger Duffy exited the building through a rear door to avoid a second onslaught of television and newspaper cameras which greeted him upon his arrival at the magistrate's office around 11:30 a.m.

Moses characterized the charges against Duffy as "an absolute joke" and a "stab in the dark." The attorney said the attorney general's entire case against his client centers on a single hand-written document which allegedly was Duffy's private jottings about the probation of Attorney Gifford Cappellini prepared in anticipation of a court proceeding. The document, Moses argued, was not meant to be a matter of public record or part of the main probation file.

"I'm telling you, (the attorney general's office) is grasping at straws," Moses remarked. "This case is going to be vigorously defended."

However, Moses' statements about the hand-written document stand in stark contrast to admissions contained in the 24-page affidavit of probable cause filed with Kane's office upon Duffy's arrest yesterday.

On Sept. 11, 1995, Attorney Cappellini was sentenced to one year probation without verdict following a pleading of no contest to charges of attempt to possess a controlled substance and solicitation to possess a controlled substance. Judge Michael Conahan also ordered Cappellini to undergo counseling and routine drug testing.

Eugene Duffy Jr., was assigned as Cappellini's probation officer. Cappellini's sister, Dodie Cappellini, is an officer in the adult probation office and his father, Judge Gifford Cappellini, serves as a senior judge on the county bench.

According to the affidavit of probable cause, problems arose on Feb. 14 when Luzerne County District Attorney Peter Paul Olszewski got a written note from
(See ARREST, page 52)

Arrest
from page 3

President Judge Patrick J. Toole Jr. which indicated there might be "certain irregularities," some potentially criminal in nature," connected with the probation office's handling of Attorney Cappellini.

Olszewski checked into the matter and found out an informant had notified Wilkes-Barre police and the state attorney general's office that Attorney Cappellini was using drugs. The unidentified informant insisted Cappellini was not being tested for drugs as per the terms of his probation. "Because of the influence of his family," The informant also told agents that Dodie Cappellini asked Duffy not to run a drug screen on her brother to save her family from any embarrassment. The information was related to probation Chief Steve Wolinsky on Feb. 8 via a hand-written memo from Assistant Chief James Marinello.

Marinello's memo recounts that he confronted Duffy with the information and that Duffy acknowledged he was approached by Dodie Cappellini who allegedly stated if her brother was tested for drugs, he would come up "hot." However, Duffy later denied he ever made such statements to Marinello.

A copy of Marinello's Feb. 9 memo was handed over to investigators. It begins by asking Wolinsky to conduct an internal investigation into the conduct of Dodie Cappellini and Duffy.

Agents from the attorney general's office confiscated the main probation file on Attorney Cappellini and found it to contain a hand-written sheet bearing six entries which indicates Cappellini reported in to his probation officer by mail. Duffy later admitted under questioning by agents from the attorney general's office that he drafted the sheet after the "(s—hit the fan" and to make himself "look good." He also admitted, the affidavit states, that he never physically saw Cappellini drop off any forms nor had he actually spoken to Attorney Cappellini since September 1995 except one time when he bumped into him in the courthouse.

The affidavit indicates Duffy told investigators, "I panicked. I knew there was going to be an investigation. I made up the sheet up and placed it in the file." Duffy also allegedly admitted to investigators, "I made up the form to make it look like I was doing my job" and added that he did it to "cover my ass."

Following Marinello's report to Wolinsky on Feb. 8, Duffy and another probation officer were sent to Cappellini's home in Dallas on Feb. 8 to obtain a urine sample. This action came after Cappellini failed to appear on Feb. 7 for the test which later came up positive for cocaine and heroin.

During an interview with investigators, Wolinsky reported that on Feb. 8, Duffy and Dodie Cappellini told him that Judge Gifford Cappellini was "mad and pissed" and that the judge wanted a full report on what was going on. Wolinsky said he refused to honor the judge's request. He also told investigators that although Duffy perhaps should have monitored Attorney Cappellini more closely, random drug testing is not done unless the office gets a complaint or has some evidence to suggest the defendant is using again. Wolinsky also told investigators that he did not believe Duffy had done anything wrong.

Duffy later told investigators that one week after the controversy surrounding Cappellini surfaced, a new policy was instituted within the probation office on random drug testing.

Duffy also submitted a hand-written statement to investigators in an apparent attempt to clarify a conversation between him and Judge Cappellini. Duffy wrote, "On Feb. 8, I spoke with Judge Cappellini on this case and he basically stated that I did my job correctly and not to worry about gossip in the courthouse. Dodie Cappellini placed the call to her father while we were at Patte's Sports Bar. She then said that her father wanted to speak to me. This call was basically a social call Dodie Cappellini advised me on Feb. 8 that her father was mad and pissed."

Noticeably absent from the affidavit was any interview with or statements from Dodie Cappellini.

Moran and Cogan declined to comment on whether more arrests were in the works but they were quick to emphasize the investigation was continuing.

Duffy is scheduled to appear for a preliminary hearing on May 28 at 10 a.m. before Magistrate Kane in Wilkes-Barre.

State files official charges against probation officer

By RICK ROGERS
Times Leader Staff Writer

WILKES-BARRE — The state's attorney general filed official charges against Eugene Duffy Jr. in Luzerne County Court of Common Pleas Friday in preparation for a pre-trial hearing Sept. 3.

The attorney general is charging Duffy, 33, a county probation officer, with charges of: unsworn falsification to authorities, tampering with or fabricating physical evidence, tampering with public records or information and obstructing administration of law or other governmental function.

Official charges had to be in place, a state attorney general spokesman said Friday, so that the judge could rule on them for the upcoming legal proceeding.

The charges are connected to Duffy's supervision of attorney Gifford R. Cappellini, who was sentenced by the county court to probation after being charged with criminal attempt and criminal solicitation to obtain cocaine.

The state is alleging that between Feb. 7 and Feb. 23, 1996, Duffy falsified probation records relating to Cappellini by inserting into his official file "a fraudulent, handwritten chronology of dates and other information concerning his supervision of ... Cappellini knowing that said dates and other information were false and incorrect."

John Moses, Duffy's lawyer, made a pre-trial motion July 15 to have the charges against his client dismissed. He claims mistakes in the state's case.

Judge Mark Ciavarella was scheduled to preside over the hearing on July 29, but recused himself citing Duffy's long-time ties to the county.

County President Judge Patrick Toole then asked the Pennsylvania Supreme Court to appoint an out-of-county judge to hear the pre-trial motion. Although a judge has not yet been assigned, the hearing has been set for 10:30 a.m. Sept. 3.

MIKE McGLYNN
The Cabbage Patch

Trust betrayed

When we talk about nepotism, it's generally from the perspective that the practice somehow should be banned because it provides family-connected flunkies seeking public jobs with an unfair advantage.

That's true, but current allegations of impropriety within the Luzerne County Adult Probation Office underscore another side of nepotism -- how it frequently provides malingering members of local VIP families with a layer of insulation from the chill of court orders which the rest of the general population is expected to follow, or do time. If the allegations leveled at two political legacies who repose in the Probation Office are valid, we can safely say the lid has blown off the courthouse in a big way.

With this one, there's more than enough blame to go around and it's reasonable to anticipate that the finger-pointing has only begun; it will take years before the dust settles this time around. And, while blame surely will be laid at the feet of the county's single-party political system, its blatant endorsement of nepotism as a way of life and the institutionalized tendency to cover for family and political cronies in cases such as that of Attorney Gifford R. Cappellini, if we can focus the blame through a single lens for only a moment, we might view things in just a slightly different light.

It is not unfair to say that rumors of Attorney Cappellini's drug addiction have been making the rounds at the courthouse and around town for years. Why his family was unable to persuade him to get the help he needed to right himself is strictly a family matter -- at least up to the point at which his family (allegedly) interferes in the probation process in order to protect him from possible jail time.

Family loyalty goes unrequited.

Eugene Duffy Jr., an adult probation officer assigned to monitor Cappellini's probation after he pleaded guilty to a couple of relatively minor drug charges, told the state attorney general's office he had not been as attentive as he should have been to Cappellini's activities.

At the behest of Cappellini's sister, also a probation officer, Duffy did not test Cappellini for drugs as he certainly should have done, Duffy allegedly told authorities. The sister, he said, had informed him that if her brother were to be tested for drugs he surely would set off bells and whistles.

Worse, Cappellini's sister, according to the attorney general's filing, suggested that she was acting in the place of her father, Judge Gifford S. Cappellini, in asking that Duffy lay off the kid.

A careful reading of the attorney general's complaint leaves loose ends, as Duffy at times seems to recant his accusations that the judge and his daughter pressured him to look the other way. He does, however, allow that he inserted a document into Cappellini's file to "cover my ass."

The complaint further indicates that the only reason the younger Cappellini's apparent violation of the terms of his probation regarding drugs came to light is because of the persistence of an in-house whistleblower at the courthouse. The whistleblower had the rumor mill churning at break-neck speed and it no longer was feasible to endeavor to keep the lid on, the complaint says. If any or all of the allegations are true, it's a sad commentary.

But, who among us honestly can claim to be surprised?

As far as blame goes, sure -- the system is inevitably corrupted when a courthouse at which the dispensation of justice should, both legally and morally, be a paramount concern is run like the family ice house.

The potential for corruption is compounded when the same courthouse is the feudal fiefdom of a single political party rarely placed in the position of having to answer at the polls for its mischief.

But, consider for a moment that our inevitable disgust at what seems to have happened in the probation office might overlook the festering guilt of a single man, a man who now has compromised the professional reputation of his sister and dragged his father's name into the dirt.

And that man is still toddling around on probation while his family pays the price of his sins.

Wilkes-Barre, PA, Sunday, April 28, 1996 3A

Steve Corbett

Judge is on the spot

As soon as "the s... hit the fan," to use Gene Duffy's words as quoted in his arrest warrant affidavit, I did my best to call Luzerne County Senior Judge Gifford S. Cappellini.

I wanted to ask if he needed to send his robe out to the cleaners.

But the justice refused to return my calls.

This surprises me because in the past Cappellini has always held court with me on a variety of topics. In those cases, I could count on the judge not only taking or returning my calls but counseling me ad infinitum on the finer points of the law.

Now maybe the judge needs his own counsel.

Based on the affidavit of probable cause filed by agents for the state attorney general against county probation officer Duffy, Cappellini's got a lot of explaining to do.

Authorities arrested Duffy Thursday on four criminal charges, including fabricating dates on official records to hide his alleged mishandling of a case involving the judge's son, Gifford R. Cappellini.

If you recall, a few months ago I wrote a column about my interview with Gifford, a well-known local lawyer who was busy serving a year's probation on charges that he asked a law client to obtain cocaine for him.

The client, also a police informant, went back to police, who wired him up and sent him back to Gifford with a drug substitute.

The 44-year-old father of three eventually copped a plea, admitted to being a heroin and cocaine addict and threw himself on the mercy of the court. One of his father's home boys cut the wayward son a break and the courthouse in-crowd all went back to la-la-land.

I called Gifford five months into his so-called probation, which included court-ordered drug testing.

Nope, said Gifford, Duffy hadn't tested him once.

"What about last week?" I asked.

"No comment," said the son of a judge.

The attorney general's office had received a tip that Gifford was saying "yes" to drugs and contacted Wilkes-Bare police who contacted probation officials.

Only then did somebody order Duffy to order Gifford to pee in a bottle.

The test came back hot for heroin and cocaine.

During the interview, Gifford denied almost everything except being named Gifford.

The day after the interview appeared in the paper, county damage control kicked into gear.

Even the Philly prosecutor acknowledged that probation officials had little choice but to move to revoke Gifford's probation.

So that's what they did.

The attorney general's office moved as well.

Agents there had opened an investigation into whether Gifford's family had influenced probation officials to grant Gifford the privilege of peeing without Duffy looking over his shoulder.

Even Dodie Cappellini, whose family name only helped her get a job in the very same county probation office, is accused of influence peddling in the affidavit.

So is the judge.

After "it" hit the fan, Dodie and Duffy sat in a sports bar worrying and whining and Dodie called her dad. The nice judge then talked to Duffy and consoled him.

That contact alone is improper enough to warrant censure from a judicial review board.

Judge Cappellini knows better than to talk to anyone who's involved in his son's case.

Who else did he talk to about the case?

The way things now look, enough Cappellinis could be subpoenaed in this case to start their own television sitcom.

Only there's very little that's funny about this matter.

Three's company but it's also a crowd.

And the courtroom might be very, very crowded when the Duffy case goes to trial.

If it goes to trial, that is.

Maybe Duffy will cooperate with authorities and cop a plea.

After all, Gifford did.

Steve Corbett's column appears Tuesday, Thursday and Sunday.

Probation officer vows innocence

■ *Eugene Duffy and his lawyer assume that the unidentified state charges are connected to the case of attorney Gifford R. Cappellini.*

By JERRY LYNOTT
Times Leader Staff Writer

WILKES-BARRE — Eugene Duffy proclaimed he would beat the charges — whatever they are — to be filed against him today in connection with a state investigation of the Luzerne County Adult Probation/Parole Office.

"When you've done nothing wrong, you have nothing to worry about in life," Duffy, a probation officer, said Wednesday.

Eugene Duffy

At home with the flu in West Hazleton, Duffy, 33, said he would surrender with his attorney, John Moses, about noon today at the office of District Justice Martin Kane in Wilkes-Barre. Duffy's illness pushed back the arrest by one day.

"It's just a shame this has to happen to me," Duffy said. "I've got a 10-year impeccable record ... I'm an upstanding citizen. I just think that this is a shame."

Duffy and Moses said they assumed the arrest is connected to the case of attorney Gifford R. Cappellini, who was under Duffy's supervision while on probation for attempting to buy cocaine from a client last year. Neither Duffy nor Moses said they knew the specific charges.

But Moses said, "This case will be vigorously defended."

Members of the state Department of the Attorney General's criminal investigation team in Scranton, who have filed the charges at Kane's office, could not be reached Wednesday for comment.

The attorney general's office opened an investigation of the probation office in February after The Times Leader reported Cappellini tested positive for heroin and cocaine in his first and only drug test five months into his one-year probation.

Under the terms of his probation imposed on Sept. 11, 1995, Cappellini, 43, of Dallas Township, was to receive counseling and undergo random drug testing. The probe focused on the

■ See DUFFY, Page 14A

Duffy placed on paid leave

■ *Probation officer faces criminal trial on charges of falsifying documents in case of Gifford R. Cappellini.*

By DAWN SHURMAITIS
Times Leader Staff Writer

WILKES-BARRE — One employee of the county probation office admitted falsifying documents. He's facing a criminal trial.

On Thursday, that employee — probation officer Eugene Duffy — learned he will be placed on paid administrative leave Monday from his $33,775-a-year job until his criminal case is resolved.

Another Luzerne County employee — Probation Assistant Chief James Marinello — wouldn't sit in a chair when ordered. For that, he says, he was suspended for five days without pay — costing him about $700.

Today, Marinello returns to work for the first time since the unpaid suspension.

Marinello said Thursday he was "totally, totally shocked" Duffy would continue to get a paycheck from the Luzerne County Adult Probation/Parole Department.

"He admitted he falsified documents. The taxpayer should be

■ See PROBATION, Page 16A

Probation

(Continued from Page 1A)

outraged," said Marinello, who retained attorney Ben Josielevski to look into his options regarding his own suspension.

Duffy had admitted making up dates for monthly supervision reports attorney Gifford R. Cappellini sent him as part of his probation for a drug charge, according to the attorney general's office.

Paperwork accompanying Duffy's arrest warrant quotes him telling investigators, "I panicked. I knew there was going to be an investigation. I made the sheet up and placed it in the (Cappellini's) file."

Marinello, a 22-year veteran of the probation department, said he had "no idea," why he was suspended. He said his boss, Chief Probation Officer Stephen Wolinsky Jr., called him into his office last week and asked him to sit down. When he refused, Wolinsky began screaming at him and then suspended him, Marinello said.

Wolinsky would not comment in detail on either employee. He would only say he decided on Duffy's paid leave after numerous discussions with department solicitor Joseph Carmody.

Duffy will continue to receive his salary until the criminal case is resolved, according to Wolinsky. John Moses, Duffy's attorney, said his client requested "administrative leave" in a letter delivered to the probation office Wednesday.

In the letter, Duffy assures Wolinsky and the entire office of his innocence, and draws attention to his 10-year tenure during which he has done an "outstanding job," according to Moses.

Duffy has been on paid vacation since his arrest April 25. The paid leave goes into effect Monday, according to a press release issued by the Luzerne County Adult Probation/Parole Department.

"The action is being taken primarily to insure the integrity of the office and also so as not to prejudice the rights of Mr. Duffy and the Commonwealth of Pennsylvania in the criminal proceedings," said a press release.

State agents charged Duffy, 33, of West Hazleton, with four misdemeanors stemming from allegations Duffy avoided drug testing the son of a county judge serving probation for trying to buy cocaine. A preliminary hearing on the charges is scheduled for May 28 before District Justice Martin Kane of Wilkes-Barre.

The allegations stem from Marinello who told state investigators Duffy avoided testing attorney Gifford R. Cappellini because he feared the power of the Cappellini family. Gifford Cappellini's sister, Dodie Cappellini, works alongside Duffy in the county probation department. His father is a senior judge.

Moses couldn't estimate the length of time involved until the charges are resolved.

The following article is kind of cutesy. There is actually an attempt here by Attorney Cappellini and his lawyer to say that Cappellini did everything that the Probation Office asked of him. Don't blame him if they failed to ask him to do anything. Blame the Probation Office. This is akin to throwing them under the bus.

Defense lawyer: Cappellini followed direction of county probation office

By TIM GULLA
Citizens' Voice Staff Writer

Attorney Gifford Cappellini, who allegedly failed a drug test while serving a one-year probation on drug-related charges, had nothing to do with alleged impropriety in the Luzerne County Adult Probation Office, according to his attorney.

Attorney Ferris Webby, co-counsel for Cappellini, said on Friday that his client has followed all the directions of the adult probation office and is removed from any alleged impropriety regarding the enforcement of his parole.

The state attorney general's office is conducting an investigation into the Adult Probation Office and possible criminal impropriety in its handling of Cappellini's probation at the request of the Luzerne County district attorney's office.

Attorney Cappellini and Attorney Joseph Sklarosky could not be reached for comment on Friday. Cappellini's telephone number is unlisted.

Pointing to the matter at hand for his client, the alleged failed drug test and Cappellini's alleged failure to complete a drug treatment program, Webby stated, "In a normal situation, we'd get a violation report (from the adult probation office)," if there was a parole violation.

In this situation, which Webby described as "not a normal situation," a parole violation report was sent directly to the prosecuting attorney. The prosecuting attorney, Michael Kershaw, responded by sending defense counsel a very "generalized" petition within 24 hours of the hearing.

"They say he violated but they

Gifford Cappellini

don't tell us how," Webby stated. "Tell us what the violations are. I want to see reports (on the drug test) and I want to talk to the people who say he didn't complete the program."

"We're not trying to delay anything or buy time," Webby added. "We're going to answer this petition and we're going to try to get more information."

Once again, Webby stressed that his client followed the directions given to him by the Adult Probation Office.

According to Kevin Harley, assistant press secretary for the state attorney general's office, "We have accepted a referral from the Luzerne County district attorney's office concerning possible improprieties in the Luzerne County Adult Probation Office."

But Harley was unable to state what kind of improprieties his office would be looking for.

Allegations surfaced in the Luzerne County Court House that Cappellini may have been shown preferential treatment because of his family and political connections within the courthouse. His father, Judge Gifford Cappellini, told the Citizens' Voice on Thursday that persons who would make such accusations are "sick people."

Attorney Cappellini's sister, Dotie Cappellini, who works in the adult probation office, could not be reached for comment.

Stephen Wolinsky, head of the adult probation office, was not in the office on Friday.

James Marinello of the adult probation Office, who sources have indicated is helping state investigators, said he was unable to comment on this situation Friday afternoon.

First Assistant District Attorney Daniel Pillets said on Friday, "We did, in fact, look initially into alleged impropriety. After initial interviews, we felt is was appropriate to refer the matter (to the state attorney general) for further investigation."

Pillets stressed that the DA's office acted "immediately" in notifying the state attorney general.

> "They say he violated but they don't tell us how. Tell us what the violations are. I want to see reports (on the drug test) and I want to talk to the people who say he didn't complete the program."
>
> **Ferris Webby**
> Cappellini lawyer

Cappellini petitions for parole

Lawyer, who pleaded guilty to drug charges, wants to avoid prison

Judge Michael Conahan has set a court hearing for May 2 at the courthouse on the petition of Attorney Gifford R. Cappellini for immediate parole and credit for time already served in connection with his drug case.

The court has issued a rule upon the attorney general to show cause why this petition should not be granted.

Cappellini, 44, of Kingston, formerly of Dallas Township, pleaded guilty Sept. 11, 1995, to one count each of criminal attempt to possess a controlled substance and criminal solicitation of a controlled substance.

He had been arrested in Wilkes-Barre March 29, 1995, by agents of the Attorney's General Bureau of Narcotics and the Wilkes-Barre Drug Task Force.

Judge Conahan placed the defendant on probation without verdict for one year. Special conditions included refrain from alcohol and drugs, continue drug and alcohol counseling, take random drug testing, and pay all court costs.

The court on March 4, 1996 revoked the defendant's probation without verdict because he had violated the probationary terms. The court then imposed a condition of total incarceration for 45 days to one year.

The defendant filed a motion for modification of sentence, but this was denied. He then filed an appeal with the state Superior Court. The latter, on March 18, 1997, affirmed the local court sentence. All appeal periods have expired.

The court has been notified that since March 4, 1996 Cappellini has complied with all monitoring of his personal liberties under risk of being sent to jail if he violated the terms of his bail. The defendant contends he is drug free.

It is noted in the petition filed through Attorney AL Flora Jr., that Cappellini has complied fully with the court ruling.

A favorable report regarding drug and alcohol testing of the defendant was issued March 30 by Ned Delaney, executive director of the Catholic Social Services.

Cappellini now wants the court to grant immediate parole and/or give him credit for 45 days of the one year in which he has been subjected to the restraints of his personal liberties.

Cappellini seeks immediate parole to prevent manifest injustice based upon a number of reasons, including that total incarceration will cause him to have his minor children placed in foster care.

Cappellini

Northampton County judge assigned to hear Duffy case

Senior Judge Richard D. Grifo of Northampton County has been assigned by the state Supreme Court to preside for a court hearing in the case of Eugene E. Duffy, Jr.

Meanwhile, a hearing scheduled for Sept. 3 at the courthouse has been postponed and the new date is Sept. 19 at 10 a.m. The postponement is due to the fact that Judge Grifo is not available to preside Sept. 3.

The hearing is to be conducted on a defense motion for dismissal of charges filed against Duffy by the state attorney general.

Duffy, a Hazleton resident, represented by Attorney John Moses, currently is on leave of absence from his duties in the Luzerne County Probation and Parole Department.

Duffy is accused of four misdemeanor charges. He is accused of providing preferential treatment to Attorney Gifford R. Cappellini in connection with the latter's court case for violation of the Drug Act. It is alleged Duffy falsified certain records of Cappellini in the Probation and Parole Department.

Cappellini currently is on bail pending his appeal from probation violation. His drug testing is now being supervised by Catholic Social Services.

Assistant Attorney General Robert O'Hara is prosecutor in the case against Duffy and is being assisted by special agents Barry Moran and Kevin Cogan.

Duffy is the son of Attorney Eugene Duffy, the County Prothonotary.

Cappellini is the son of Senior Judge Gifford S. Cappellini.

One would think that getting a judge assigned from out of the area would be a positive step in assuring fairness for everyone involved. In early 2010, I tried contacting Judge Richard D. Grifo as part of my research for this book. Unfortunately, the judge has passed away. I believe that if the judge had granted me an interview, it would have been one of the highlights of this book. Since he is not able to defend his actions, I will simply let the newspaper accounts do most of the talking. I strongly feel that Judge Grifo's insertion into this case is a shining example of just how far into the state the connections of the Luzerne County Network actually reach.

Judge Grifo was selected by the Supreme Court of Pennsylvania and not by a Luzerne County judge. Well, at least not directly. You would think that there would be a randomly established list of available judges who could be called upon to handle cases such as this. There is no such list. The Supreme Court hand picks the "drop in" judges as the Supreme Court sees fit with no accountability for their decisions. After all, if we can't trust the members of the Pennsylvania Supreme Court, who the heck can we trust? By the way, as of the day of this writing, the Chief Justice Ronald D. Castille of the Pennsylvania Supreme Court is is being looked at by the FBI in a matter concerning the construction of a 200 million dollar Family Court building in Philadelphia. You may remember the fact that I mentioned his name in the Preface of this book. A second Supreme Court Justice, Justice Joan Orie Melvin is also being looked at as both of her sisters have now been indicted and bound over for trial, accused of misusing government employees and tax payer monies to assist, among other allegations pending against the Justice, in her successful election to the Pennsylvania Supreme Court. To date neither Justice has charged with any wrongdoing.

So the stage is set. The Pennsylvania Attorney General's Office not only has the altered documents in hand, but they also have a full written confession from P.O. Duffy. Still, I had a very uneasy feeling. You see, P.O. Duffy's Defense Attorney, John Moses, has an incredible record, or should I say, an almost unbelievable record, for winning criminal cases that appear to be unwinnable. Combine that with the fact that P.O. Duffy is showing an unexplained amount of confidence and self righteousness. Well, low and behold, please read on.

Jurist rules Duffy conduct not criminal

By CAROL CRANE
Citizens' Voice Staff Writer

A Luzerne County adult probation officer who admitted to state agents that he placed a falsified document into an official probation file has been cleared of any criminal wrongdoing.

In a decision handed down Monday, Northampton County Senior Judge Richard Grifo found the conduct of Eugene Duffy Jr. may have been prompted by "ignorance or mistake," but it was not criminal.

"The court finds that the circumstances of this entire investigation and prosecution appear to be an excessive attempt to find somebody culpable for something," Grifo wrote in his decision.

Duffy was charged by the state Attorney General's Office with four misdemeanor counts in connection with a list of dates he put into the probation files of Attorney Gifford R. Cappellini. Grifo's decision overturns a ruling by District Justice Martin Kane who found that state investigators had presented enough evidence against Duffy to have the charges forwarded to county court.

In a statement released by his defense Attorney John Moses, Duffy thanked his lawyer as well as his many friends and co-workers who supported him since his arrest last April. "I am really happy that the court determined that I did not commit any crime. I will try to put this matter behind me as quickly as possible so I can get on with the rest of my life," he stated.

Prosecution comments on the judge's decision were brief.

An obviously elated Moses remarked, "This is a nice victory."

"The office of Attorney General is disappointed in the judge's ruling. The office felt it had the evidence to justify the charges that were filed," stated Jack Lewis, press secretary for outgoing Attorney General Tom Corbett Jr.

Lewis added Grifo's decision is being reviewed and a decision will be made over the next several days whether there will be an appeal.

Meanwhile, a state investigation into whether Cappellini received preferential treatment because of his political and family connections is continuing. Cappellini is the son of county Senior Judge Gifford S. Cappellini and brother of Dodie Cappellini, an adult probation officer. Duffy is the son of veteran county Prothonotary Eugene Duffy Sr.

Eugene Duffy Jr.
(V file photo)

Following Duffy's arrest last April, he was placed on fully paid administrative leave from his $33,700 a year job in the probation office. But that decision came under heavy fire from taxpayers who were irate that Duffy was still on the county payroll, but did not have to report to work.

On Nov. 22, former President Judge Patrick J. Toole Jr. handed down a policy to deal with court-related employees who are charged with criminal offenses. As a result, Duffy was dropped from the payroll at the beginning of December pending the outcome of the criminal charges against him.

According to Toole's policy, if a court-appointed employee is found not guilty, that employee shall be reinstated in his or her position and be fully compensated for any wages withheld during suspension. Moses said he plans to meet this morning with newly-elected President Judge Joseph Augello as well as Adult Probation Chief Michael Jorio to get the wheels in motion for his client to go back to work as soon as possible and to recoup the wages he lost while on eight weeks unpaid suspension.

Duffy had been charged with unsworn falsification to authorities, tampering with or fabricating physical evidence, tampering with public records or information, and obstruction administration of law. The charges stem from admissions that Duffy made to state agents that he placed the falsified document into Cappellini's probation file to "cover my ass," and to make it appear that he was doing his job properly.

In his 13-page opinion, Grifo concluded that investigators failed to establish a prima facie case for each of the four charges against

(See **DUFFY**, page 12)

Citizens' Voice, Wilkes-Barre, Pa. — Thursday, January 16, 1997

Duffy

from page 3

Duffy. He agreed with Moses' contention that the document Duffy put into Cappellini's probation file was not meant to be an official record, but merely a handwritten note to summarize dates of restitution payments.

"Duffy certainly had it within his capability to produce official forms to indicate facts that simply were not true. There is no evidence that this took place," Grifo opined.

"Although the court is not excusing the supervision of defendant Cappellini by Duffy, the court finds that the circumstances surrounding the contents of the Cappellini file, and more specifically, the hand written note prepared by Duffy, do not rise to the level of criminal activity as contemplated by the legislature when drafting these criminal statutes," Grifo concluded.

Cappellini had been on probation for a drug charge. As part of his legal disposition, he was to undergo random drug testing.

Duffy was Cappellini's probation officer. The flap over the handling of Cappellini's probation began when it was revealed that Cappellini was never ordered to submit to random drug testing as per the order of Judge Michael Conahan. When Duffy was ordered to get Cappellini to submit to a drug test, Cappellini tested positive for drugs.

Former Chief Probation Officer Steve Wolinsky testified at Duffy's preliminary hearing that Duffy did nothing wrong in handling Cappellini's case despite a court order for random drug testing. Wolinsky said it is the policy of the adult probation office to do drug testing on minimal risk offenders like Cappellini only when there is an allegation the parolee is using drugs.

Before stepping down as president judge, Toole demoted Wolinsky to assistant chief probation officer and named retired state trooper Michael Jordan to head up the embattled adult probation office.

After Kane ruled last May that there was sufficient evidence for the charges against Duffy to go to court, Moses filed to have the charges dismissed. Because of Duffy's association with the county court system, the state Supreme Court appointed Grifo to hear the motion to dismiss.

Special Agent Barry Moran is heading up the investigation into the adult probation office. He is being assisted by Agent Kevin Cogan.

Leading the state's prosecution against Duffy is Deputy Attorney General Bob O'Hara.

Duffy case thrown out

- *The suspended county worker was charged with mishandling records pertaining to the probation of a county judge's son.*

By RICK ROGERS
Times Leader Staff Writer

WILKES-BARRE — Calling the investigation and prosecution of Eugene Duffy Jr. an "excessive attempt to find somebody culpable for something," a judge dismissed all charges against the Luzerne County adult probation officer.

Senior Judge Richard D. Grifo's ruling delighted Duffy and dismayed the state attorney general's office, which had charged the 34-year-old West Hazleton man in April 1996.

The strong wording of the Northampton County judge's opinion left some in the attorney general's office bewildered.

"Either we were way off in bringing charges against Duffy or the judge was way off in his ruling," said a source in the attorney general's office. "According to the judge, the decision wasn't even close."

Following the decision, Duffy "feels great" and wants his job back as a $33,775-a-year adult probation and parole officer, a position he held for 10 years.

Duffy was charged April 25 with unsworn falsification to authorities, tampering with or fabricating evidence, tampering with public records of information and obstructing administrative law. The charges stemmed from his alleged mishandling of attorney Gifford R. Cappellini's probation.

A large portion of the prosecution's case dealt with a handwritten note that Duffy had placed in Cappellini's probation report. Duffy attempted, charges said, to use the note — a log of Duffy's dealings with Cappellini — to mislead state investigators into believing Cappellini was more closely monitored than he actually was.

In his 11-page opinion, Grifo repeatedly says that the state did not prove Duffy meant to mislead state investigators, who were looking into allegations that Cappellini — the son of a Luzerne County judge — received preferential treatment during his probation.

"Luzerne County President Judge Richard and Toole Jr. raised concerns about the supervision of this particular defendant," Grifo wrote, apparently referring to former President Judge Patrick Toole Jr.

Grifo decided, however, that "There is no evidence presented by the Commonwealth..."

■ See DUFFY, Page 16A

Eugene Duffy
Charges dismissed

Duffy

(Continued from Page 1A)

wealth that defendant Duffy intended to mislead a public servant by authoring this memo and placing it in the file ... Duffy simply placed a handwritten note into the official Cappellini file with the information he thought to be correct at the time the note was authored."

An elated John P. Moses, Duffy's defense attorney, said Grifo accepted his argument that there was no criminal conduct and no evidence to sustain any charge against his client.

"This was not a crime since day one. Clearly, Gene is vindicated," Moses said.

From his home in West Hazleton, Duffy issued a statement in which he thanked his friends and family for supporting him. He said he wants his probation job back.

"I plan, through my lawyer, to advise the local court and my employer of this decision and to begin whatever process is necessary to regain my employment at the Luzerne County Adult Probation Office," Duffy said.

Duffy was placed on administrative leave with pay on April 25, and the county paid his salary until late November. Under terms of a new personnel policy, Duffy is eligible to receive back pay.

Grifo's ruling might be appealed, said Jack Lewis, a spokesman for the attorney general's office. But a decision on that isn't likely until after incoming state Attorney General Mike Fisher is sworn in on Tuesday.

The state could either appeal Grifo's decision to the state Superior Court or possibly reinstate charges against Duffy, said the spokesman. However, Moses and District Justice Martin Kane of Wilkes-Barre said the only appeal option open to the state was appealing Grifo's decision to the state Superior Court.

Allegations that Duffy tried to alter Cappellini's probation records shook the courthouse because the investigation involved the sons of powerful Luzerne County Courthouse figures. Duffy is the son of county Prothonotary Eugene E. Duffy, and Cappellini's father is Gifford S. Cappellini a Luzerne County senior court judge.

Duffy supervised Cappellini's probation, but allegedly failed to randomly drug-test him as mandated by the court. An admitted drug abuser, Cappellini, 44, received probation after a March 1995 arrest for attempting to buy cocaine from a client.

At a preliminary hearing last May 28, Kane ruled the state had enough evidence to take the case against Duffy to trial. The case was then sent to the Luzerne County Court of Common Pleas to be listed for trial.

In July, Luzerne County Court of Common Pleas Judge Mark Ciavarella recused himself because of Duffy's ties to the county.

On Sept. 23, Moses appealed Kane's ruling.

Absolutely stunning! That is the best way to describe the conclusion reached by this out of town "Senior Judge." There were an awful lot of "I told you so" comments circulating the county in the days that followed.

After such an outlandish ruling is made, Luzerne County Judges usually attempt at this point to explain to the public that the complexities of the law are just too much for the general public to comprehend. But Judge Grifo didn't live or work in Luzerne County, so he just stayed away and said nothing. Everything he had to say, he delivered in his ruling.

I can now say Judge Cappellini was correct when he told P.O. Duffy that, "Everything is going to be all right." I believe a great deal more was said during that phone conversation between P.O. Duffy and Judge Cappellini but, we will never know.

What is equally important is the fact that the charges against P.O. Duffy were thrown out and the circumstances surrounding how the charges were dismissed. There was not a full blown trial followed by a "Not Guilty" verdict. That would have required many people to take the stand and either tell the truth or lie under oath. One of the most likely witnesses to have been put on the stand would have been Judge Cappellini's daughter, Parole Officer Dodie Cappellini.

Can you imagine the official record that would have been established should she be required to testify? Her conversations with P.O. Duffy concerning her brother possibly testing "hot," as well as anything her father, the judge, may have said would have been devastating to not only the Duffy case, but also to both her and her father's careers.

Then there was that exposed phone call to the judge from Pattie's Sports Bar where the judge assured P.O. Duffy that everything is going to be all right. The possibility of the judge being required to take the stand would have been very real. None of that could ever happen! It didn't matter about appearances, it simply couldn't happen and it didn't happen.

Instead of a formal hearing with all of its perils and pitfalls, how about a simple motion for "Habeas Corpus?" That accomplished everything desired, except for one item. P.O. Duffy was not adjudicated "Not Guilty." Instead, the charges were simply dropped.

P.O. Duffy, via his attorney, had all of the criminal charges against him dropped. No extensive record of wrong doing by any other players was established. Duffy was now poised to get his job back and retroactively receive his lost wages, benefits and regain his seniority. Guess what happens next?

The public was outraged. I know I was. According to the following front page story, almost two hundred Luzerne County residents contacted the Pennsylvania State Attorney General's Office in Scranton and Harrisburg to protest the decision and request an appeal. The A.G.'s Office claimed this outrage did not influence its decision for an appeal but, I beg to differ.

AG appeals Duffy decision

Son of county prothonotary was charged with falsifying records

By CAROL CRANE
Citizens' Voice Staff Writer

Just when he thought he was in the clear, Luzerne County Adult Probation Officer Eugene Duffy Jr. is back in hot water with the state attorney general's office.

On Tuesday, Attorney General Mike Fisher announced his office will appeal the decision rendered by a Northampton County judge to dismiss criminal charges filed against Duffy as the result of an ongoing investigation into the county adult probation office.

Duffy had been charged with four misdemeanor counts which included unsworn falsification to authorities, tampering with or fabricating physical evidence, tampering with public records or information, and obstructing administration of law.

Attorney John Moses, who is representing Duffy, said he was not surprised the state decided to appeal. "Certainly they have the right to take an appeal on this," Moses remarked, adding, "In this case, nothing would surprise me."

According to the affidavit of probable cause filed upon Duffy's arrest last April by state agents, Duffy admitted he placed a falsified record into the probation file of well-known defense Attorney Gifford Cappellini, son of Luzerne County Senior Judge Gifford Cappellini, and brother of county adult probation officer Dodie Cappellini.

Duffy told state agents that when he learned there was going to be an investigation into how Cappellini's probation was handled, he put the paper into Cappellini's official file to "cover his (Duffy's) ass," and to make it appear as if he (Duffy) were doing his job properly.

On May 29, District Justice Martin Kane ruled there was sufficient evidence to have the charges against Duffy held over for trial. However, Moses, through Moses, filed a petition for habeas corpus to have the charges dismissed.

Because of Duffy's close association with the county judicial system, Northampton County Senior Judge Michael Grifo was appointed by the state Supreme Court to hear the habeas corpus motion.

At the hearing before Grifo in Easton, Deputy Attorney General Robert O'Hara argued Duffy confessed to placing a document he knew was not accurate into Cappellini's official file.

However, Moses countered that the document was not meant to be an official record, nor was it written on any official record form. Rather, it was intended to be a summary to help Duffy remember the dates Cappellini checked in with the probation office and made restitution payments.

Judge Michael Conahan ruled that as part of the terms of his probation, Cappellini was to submit to random drug testing. However, Duffy did not order Cappellini to take a drug test until a confidential informant tipped police off that Cappellini was still using drugs.

The affidavit revealed that Dodie Cappellini allegedly predicted to Duffy that her brother would come up "hot" if tested for drugs. Based on the tip from the informant, Duffy was ordered to get Gifford Cappellini drug tested. When he did, Gifford Cappellini tested positive for drugs.

Former Chief Probation Officer Steve Wolinsky testified at Duffy's hearing that Duffy did nothing wrong in not having Cappellini tested until there was a complaint. Wolinsky said that was the usual procedure for low risk offenders such as Cappellini.

However, since the Cappellini controversy was brought to light, that policy has been changed. President Judge Joseph Augello has stated that if the court orders random drug testing by probation officers, then that is what will be done.

Duffy, is the son of Luzerne County Prothonotary Eugene Duffy Sr. When Judge Grifo dismissed the charges against the younger Duffy, almost 200 Luzerne County residents contacted the state attorney general's offices in Scranton and Harrisburg to protest the decision. The consensus of the calls was that Fisher should appeal Judge Grifo's decision.

Yesterday, Fisher's deputy press secretary, Kevin Harley, said the decision to appeal Judge Grifo's ruling was based on a review of the facts in the case, not the phone calls. "We believe the attorney general's office has enough evidence to justify the appeal. Based on that means charges against Mr. Duffy," Harley stated.

The appeal filed by Fisher is an "as of right" appeal to the state Superior Court. The attorney general's office explained that means no date has been set yet for any hearing. The notice of appeal was filed shortly after 2 p.m. in the Luzerne County Clerk of Courts office on Tuesday.

Duffy had been placed on fully paid administrative leave following his arrest. About seven weeks before Judge Grifo's decision was handed down, Duffy was cut from the county payroll.

Upon Judge Grifo's ruling, Duffy was reinstated as an adult probation officer and reimbursed for the pay he lost while on unpaid suspension.

Newly appointed Chief Probation Officer Michael Jordan confirmed that according to current court policy, an internal investigation was to be conducted to determine if Duffy was to face any job-related disciplinary measures. However, Jordan refused to reveal the results of the internal investigation or if Duffy was ever disciplined, claiming the information to be a confidential personnel matter.

Eugene Duffy

Rumors had been circulating for quite a while that someone from inside the courthouse was cooperating with the Pennsylvania State Attorney General's Office, but whom? As you already know, it turned out to be Assistant Chief Marinello. You also know that after Marinello discovered the attempted "cover-up" involving the Cappellini case, he had to make a choice. Take the matter to his boss or go over his boss's head. Marinello and his boss, Chief Probation Officer Wolinsky, did not see eye to eye on many issues. They had some history.

It seems back in 1990, Marinello was required to give a deposition in a Wrongful Death lawsuit (murder) that was brought against the county and his boss Chief Wolinsky. Because Marinello refused to perjure himself, the case ended up being settled out of court with a large payment by the county made to the plaintiffs. If Marinello had been a "team player" he would have been willing to cover up even something as serious as murder. The problem was that in order to be a team player, Marinello would have had to adjust his moral compass, you know, for the good of the team. The following article by Carol Crane provides a very clear picture of just how things were done in the Luzerne County Probation Office under the direction of Chief Wolinsky.

lawsuits with taxpayer funds

By Carol Crane
Citizens' Voice Staff Writer

The $90,000 out-of-court settlement paid to Adult Probation Assistant Chief Ann Marie Braskey is not the only settlement Luzerne County taxpayers have been saddled with in recent years.

Over the past decade, there have been at least two other lawsuits where the county's insurer has denied a claim prompted by a lawsuit and the money for the out-of-court settlement was paid out of the general fund.

One lawsuit stemmed from the murder of Kimberly Kruczek of Nanticoke by her boyfriend, Robert Halliday.

On the morning of June 4, 1987, Halliday ended the stormy relationship between him and Kruczek by shooting his girlfriend in the head and then turning the gun on himself.

The murder/suicide took place at the home of Kruczek's parents and left behind an 12-month-old baby girl.

According to a prior order issued by Judge Patrick J. Toole Jr., Halliday was prohibited from having any contact with Kim Kruczek.

After Kim was murdered, her mother, Patricia, filed a federal lawsuit against the Luzerne County Commissioners, the Adult Probation Office, then-Adult Probation Chief Stephen Wolinsky Jr., both in his personal capacity and that as a member of the adult probation office.

Federal court records now in storage at the National Archives and Records Administration in Philadelphia provide a chilling retrospect of the days leading up to Kim Kruczek's murder.

Three days before the tragic event, Richard and Patricia Kruczek pleaded with Luzerne County Assistant Adult Probation Chief James Marinello to have Halliday's probation revoked. Twice before Halliday killed Kruczek, Halliday had been sent back to prison for parole violations.

On June 1, 1987, Pat Kruczek called Marinello, complaining Halliday had continued to come by their home, squealing his car tires as he sped by shouting and

The Luzerne County Railroad

screaming for Kim. In his deposition, Marinello acknowledged that he believed Kim Kruczek was in fear of her life.

Marinello's deposition details that he promised Pat Kruczek, "I will lock [Halliday] up immediately."

Halliday had previously threatened the Kruczeks a number of times, according to court papers. Once, he even threatened to blow up their home.

Marinello had to leave for Philadelphia to attend a conference on the afternoon of June 1, according to his deposition, so he left instructions with another probation officer to carry out the task of getting Halliday into custody.

Meanwhile, Halliday's parents contacted Wolinsky, concerned that their son would be incarcerated once again. Depositions in the almost foot-high court case recounted the Hallidays complained Marinello had it out for their son.

When Wolinsky found out Kim Kruczek had been out on a few dates with Halliday despite the court order, he ordered all parties in for a meeting.

On June 3, 1987, the Hallidays and the Kruczeks, along with Kim Kruczek and Robert Halliday, met with Wolinsky. At the conclusion of the meeting, Wolinsky's deposition recalled he told both families to stay away from each other and that Robert was not to go near the Kruczek's home or Kim, or he would be remanded to prison.

Wolinsky then demanded that all those present in the room sign a document agreeing to the terms he had laid down.

Everyone did but Robert Halliday. According to depositions, Robert instead threw down the pen when it was handed to him and began to try and grab Kim Kruczek. When others physically restrained him, Halliday stormed out of the room.

He never signed the document. Wolinsky testified he told Halliday that even though he refused to sign the agreement, it still would be enforced.

Wolinsky said his perception of the situation was that the two families had been feuding for years and the Kruczeks had demanded Robert Halliday returned to prison because Kim had finally made up her mind that she did not want to see him any more.

On June 3, Marinello was still in Philadelphia at a conference, unaware his decision to have Robert Halliday returned to prison had been overruled.

Early on the morning of June 4, Robert Halliday charged into the Kruczek home and shot and killed the mother of his child. He then put the same gun to his own head.

During the deposition phase of the lawsuit, Wolinsky testified that Halliday's official probation file had mysteriously disappeared from his desk.

The file was never found.

On June 2, 1989, Pat Kruczek filed the three-count federal lawsuit accusing Wolinsky and his department of gross negligence; reckless, unlawful and wanton

> conduct; and the deprivation Kim Kruczek's liberty withou[t] due process.
>
> Court records show the cou[n]ty's errors and omissions ins[t] Maryland Casualty, retained Attorney Thomas Helbig to defend Wolinsky, his departm[ent] and the county.
>
> The lawsuit was resolved o[n] June 17, 1991 when an out-of-court settlement was paid to Kruczek.
>
> To this day, details of the s[et]tlement remain sealed on ord[er] of a federal judge, even thou[gh] the payment was made from county's coffers.
>
> However, records show the county, not the insurance co[mpa]ny, paid the settlement.
>
> At the time of Kim Krucze[k] murder, the county president judge was Robert Hourigan, Wolinsky's father-in-law.
>
> Wolinsky is still with the a[dult] probation department, but in capacity as one of three assi[stant] chief probation officers.
>
> The other two assistant ch[ief] probation officers are Marin[ello] and Braskey.
>
> Over the weekend, Wolins[ky] acknowledged the Kruczek l[aw]suit had been settled out of c[ourt] and that no internal departm[en]tal investigation was ever ordered.
>
> He also confirmed he was [nev]er disciplined in connection [with] the tragic events of June 4, 1[...]
>
> Court records show that w[hen] Wolinsky provided his deposi[tion] on Nov. 26, 1990, he claimed was unaware of any decision Marinello to have Halliday

Did you pick up in the prior article that the prior President Judge of the county was Wolinsky's Daddy-in-Law? Did you also notice that no disciplinary action was ever taken against Chief Wolinsky? I did………I sure did.

CHAPTER THIRTY-SEVEN

What to do about a Whistle Blower

With the exception of the initial arrest, everything else could have been controlled and dealt with, but it was not. In a number of minds, Assistant Chief Marinello was to blame for everything else. The question was at the time, what do we do about him?

A review of Marinello's personnel records showed that he was a good probation officer and a very good Assistant Chief. Twenty-two years on the job, the man had nary a blemish. Very good to excellent reviews of his decades of employment, even reviews from his less-than-enthusiastic Chief made it difficult to find fault. He even had commendations in his file.

But Marinello had to go. He had to be punished. The question was, how? The wheels of injustice spin a little faster than the wheels of justice in the Luzerne County Courthouse. It must have taken some real "Brainiacks" to come up with this scenario.

As I wrote earlier in this book, I appeared two times in front of President Judge Toole for one hearing. He ruled 100% in my favor. I should really like this guy and praise his character. That is not going to happen.

At a much later date, U.S. Senator Worford of Pennsylvania nominated Judge Patrick Toole to President Clinton for a judgeship on the Federal Bench. Toole was considered a shoe-in for the lifelong appointment. I was contacted by the FBI and subsequently interviewed concerning Judge Toole's nomination. My interview was candid, to the point, and very, very critical of Judge Toole. I gave the FBI example after example of how Judge Toole ran the Luzerne County Courthouse. I also actively participated in a statewide effort to oppose his nomination. His nomination was withdrawn from consideration.

As President Judge of the County, Judge Toole had complete control and power over the Parole Office, except for the positions of Assistant Chief and Chief of the department. Appointment to either of these two positions required the court En Banc (or in full) to vote on the candidates. All other appointments to the Luzerne County Probation office flowed directly through Judge Toole's office. Don't ask me why (I think I know), but that is the way it was set up in Luzerne County.

Let us go back in history for just a moment. We need to set the stage for future festivities. In 1982, Marinello had a brief, four time rendezvous affair with a female Luzerne County Probation Officer by the name of Ann Marie Braskey. A review of published reports indicates that it was a mutual relationship by consenting adults of equal rank. Shortly after the affair began, P.O. Marinello was promoted to the rank of Assistant Chief. At that point in time the relationship between Marinello and the female P.O. was mutually terminated, as he was now her boss. To my knowledge, these facts have never been disputed by either party.

Now fast forward twelve years. Out of the blue, P.O. Braskey is promoted from Probation Officer to Assistant Chief, even though that position is already held by Marinello (Why?). In other words, there were now two Assistant Chiefs of the Luzerne County Probation Office where historically and officially, only one Assistant Chief has ever existed (Why?). The appointment was made by President Judge Patrick Toole, over the telephone (Why?). The "required" procedure of having the vote "En Banc" was not followed and to my knowledge no other sitting Luzerne County judge had the stones to question Toole about the appointment (Why?).

Judge Patrick Toole is also the father of Luzerne County Common Pleas Judge Michael Toole who, as of this writing, is awaiting sentencing after pleading guilty to Federal charges of "Theft of Honest Services" and "Tax Evasion" while on the bench.

As I wrote this chapter, I was totally naive as to where the story would lead me. As a matter of fact, I thought for the most part I already knew the story. I thought I was simply refining my knowledge of the details. But I was wrong...... very wrong. After I finished this section of the book, I sat back from my computer, took a deep breath, and asked myself that one word question.......Why? As you can see, I went back and inserted the one word question. As you read on, ask yourself the same question.

According to Marinello, he questioned the appointment of P.O. Braskey to Assistant Chief, right from the start. Neither he nor his boss, Chief Wolinsky, had received a Court Order authorizing the appointment. As I have already pointed out, the slot for a second Assistant Chief of the Luzerne County Probation Office didn't even exist. A few weeks into it, Marinello and Wolinsky not only received a Court Order, but also an explanation.

President Judge Patrick Toole wrote in his order that he did not create nor vacate a position. Judge Toole stated he merely changed the job title of an existing position, even though it was a higher rank at a higher salary. That's some fine Luzerne County logic if I ever heard any. Go ahead, ask yourself that question and see if you can answer it yet.

According to Marinello, for about four months things ran smoothly, but every once in a while tempers would flair. Problems would occur when Chief Wolinsky left the office and the two Assistant Chiefs were in charge. After one such "blow up," Braskey went directly to President Judge Toole and complained about Marinello. The President Judge at that point removed Marinello's seniority, thus making Marinello and Braskey equal in authority even though Marinello had over ten years more experience. The question is, why? The Probation Office was then divided into his and hers sections. Marinello took half of the P.O.s and Braskey took the other half when the chief was gone.

Marinello never alluded to anything inappropriate going on between Braskey and the judge. When I pushed him on the subject he simply stated if something were going on between the two of them, he was not privy to it. He did tell me that on countless occasions, Assistant Chief Braskey would get a phone call, don her makeup, and announce to the department that she was going to see the "Big Guy." Marinello also found it curious that he could not recall a single instance that Braskey would return from such a meeting and announce anything that was discussed or decided while she met with the judge. I even pushed Marinello to speculate as to "why" the President Judge had taken such an interest and gone the extra mile for Officer Braskey? He told me he couldn't even begin to speculate. If Marinello knew, he sure wasn't going to tell me. I thought to myself, "After all these years the fear is still there." I think he knows.

It turns out that Braskey did more than complain to the President Judge. She filed an EEOC complaint, but not against Marinello, against Chief Wolinsky, Personnel Director Jack Mulroy, and County Personnel Director Gene Klein. Her EEOC complaint basically stated that none of them had taken action against Marinello even though she had made numerous complaints to them. Her specific complaint was that Marinello, while attending a wedding reception, admitted to other Probation Officers that he had had an affair with Braskey some twelve years prior. She claimed that sort of information weakened her authority and created stress in the workplace.

Fair enough. Was it true? Yes, by her own admission, it was. Was it mutual? Again, yes it was. Did it rise to the level of an EEOC Complaint? You be the judge…..

After some wrangling back and forth, all parties agreed that everything would go away if Marinello attended a sexual harassment seminar and agreed not to talk about their prior relationship going forward. Everything was done in a closed door meeting. No harm, no foul. Everyone walked away. Done deal! At this point it seemed the focus was to force gentlemanly behavior on Marinello and to also solidify Braskey's authority. Documents were prepared by county attorneys outlining the agreement. A thousand dollar payment to Braskey was included as part of the settlement by which she waived ALL rights by her to sue anyone for any reason going forward from anything arising out of these specific allegations. I have copies of these documents.

The Monday following the agreement, agents from the Attorney General's Office announced their presence in the Probation Office and immediately cornered P.O. Duffy. Marinello was called off of the road by his chief who was on vacation that week. He was ordered to the Personnel Director's Office to meet with the chief. Also present at the meeting was Braskey. Upon walking into the office Marinello was ordered to "SIT!" by his Chief. After telling his chief he preferred to stand, Marinello was suspended on the spot for a week without pay. The good old "Luzerne County Railroad was a-chugging-along."

Officially, a suspension without pay is reserved for only the most egregious offenses, or in this case, if your boss REALLY hates what you did no matter how right it was. Marinello immediately asked for a hearing on the suspension. The hearing didn't happen, at least not for a while. Actually, it took about two hundred and forty days before the hearing was held. Keep in mind that this hearing is "REQUIRED" to take place "BEFORE" an employee can actually be suspended.

The point to all of this is simple. This is just a great example of how these people operate. The "OLD WEST" followed rules better than this group. Judge Toole was hearing murder cases as well as multi-million dollar civil proceedings yet he was unable or unwilling to follow very simple, yet important, procedures when it came to his own house.

I can't help but saying that he really looked like the big bully on the playground who wasn't getting his own way. What is truly telling and "VERY" scary here is the fact that all of the bad things happened to Marinello because he DID THE RIGHT THING, NOT THE WRONG THING! It seems to me that if Marinello had simply kept his mouth shut, he would probably have retired as the Chief of the department with a nice fat pension. Where was Judge Toole's outrage over the Cappellini cover up???? WHERE?

I believe that all of Judge Tool's outrage was place squarely on Assistant Chief Marinello's shoulders because he "blew the whistle."

Marinello asks for suspension hearing

Judge hasn't given answer to deputy probation chief

By CAROL CRANE
Citizens' Voice Staff Writer

The attorney representing Luzerne County Adult Probation Assistant Chief James Marinello fired off a second letter Wednesday which requests a hearing before the court en banc to air his client's five-day suspension.

Attorney Ben Josielevski of Scranton issued a first request for a hearing for Marinello on May 17. Yesterday, he reported he has never received a reply to that request.

President Judge Patrick J. Toole Jr. acknowledged Wednesday that he has not yet responded to Josielevski's request. "I don't do things in the newspaper as Mr. Marinello's lawyer does," stated the president judge who has been on sick leave. "I'll respond to him when I am able and he can make it public if he likes."

Toole characterized Josielevski's comments to the press as "unprofessional."

Marinello has filed a complaint against his boss, probation chief Steve Wolinsky, for allegedly attempting to intimidate him as a state witness in the case against fellow probation officer, Eugene Duffy Jr.. The state attorney general's office is conducting an investigation into allegations that Attorney Gifford Cappellini received preferential treatment while he was on probation for drug charges. Duffy is Cappellini's probation officer.

Sources said state agents visited the probation office again yesterday. The attorney general's office has declined to comment on the probe except to say that it is continuing.

Marinello was suspended by Wolinsky for five days without pay for alleged "unprofessional conduct, attitude, mannerisms and demeanor" after he refused to sit when Wolinsky commanded him to.

In the second request for a hearing for Marinello, Josielevski pointed to Section V of the Adult Probation/Parole Department's policy and procedures chapter on personnel. That section states, "Department heads may suspend employees in their department for periods longer than three days or initiate dismissal procedures only by preparing and serving written charges on the employee. The employee will have 10 days to answer said charges after which a hearing will be scheduled by the court."

Marinello was suspended on May 9. However, a letter outlining the reasons behind the disciplinary action was not presented to him at the time of his suspension. Wolinsky did not draft a copy of the charges against Marinello until May 16. Prior to the May 9 suspension, Marinello had never received any reprimands or other disciplinary action in the 22 years he has been with the department. Marinello through Josielevski responded within the 10-day time frame as outlined in the department policy by denying the charges.

According to the department's policy and procedures, disciplinary actions include oral reprimands, written reprimands, and suspension of up to three days. The policy also states, "Department heads may suspend employees for periods longer than three days or initiate dismissal proceedings only by preparing and serving written charges on the employee."

The policy also states that if after a hearing, the court en banc does not uphold the charges, the employee shall be given full pay for the time he was suspended.

Duffy was arrested after confessing to state agents that he placed false information in Cappellini's probation file. Last month, Duffy was placed on "administrative leave" with full pay pending the outcome of the criminal charges against him.

Marinello had already been feeling the heat. Fellow parole officers shunned him. Some started to whistle when he walked by their desks. According to Marinello, two fellow officers even simulated running him over in the parking lot with a county car. I had a sense about Marinello that even though he had a few short comings (don't we all), he was an honest and honorable man. He knew that he was going to take some heat for doing the right thing, but that didn't stop him. As the heat turned up, so did Marinello.

Marinello had been staying late to copy records of expense reports that he claimed had been falsified by subordinate probation officers. Marinello claimed that officers who were under the direct control of Assistant Chief Braskey were filling out mileage vouchers for trips that they never made. He also claimed that she knowingly signed off on the expense reports and approved them. He started making copies of the vouchers and copies of the office log in and log out sheets. He told me that he had dozens of verified fraudulent mileage requests which he turned over to the state investigators.

After Marinello's suspension without pay was over, he continuously requested a hearing on the matter. A local talk radio show host had picked up on the suspension through the newspapers and provided a daily count of the number of days that Marinello's request for a hearing was ignored. Around day two hundred and forty, all hell broke loose. Marinello got a phone call from a very irate President Judge Toole. Apparently, the judge was not a talk radio fan so it took him a while to hear about the daily radio count. He didn't find it amusing, nor should he.

"You want a hearing, Buster, you got one. Monday morning, bright and early," screamed the judge at the other end of the phone.

Marinello then told me that he had to call the judge back and ask for another day for the hearing because his attorney was at trial in Lackawanna County that Monday. Toole didn't want to hear it. According to Marinello, President Judge Toole called the President Judge of Lackawanna County and had that court proceeding changed in Lackawanna County so as to accommodate Marinello's date with destiny. Talk about inappropriate behavior! Keep in mind that this was the President Judge of the county, the boss judge of all the judges.

The hearing that Marinello asked for was actually a simple matter. The court controlled the Probation Office. Judge Toole was the President Judge of the county court, thus Marinello's boss. The President Judge would normally have the Personnel Director present at such a hearing, as well as the person's direct supervisor, in this case, Chief Wolinsky, and if serious enough, a county attorney. The charges would be read and copies of prior warnings and evidence would be presented. The employee would then have a chance to defend him or herself. That didn't happen.

CHAPTER THIRTY-EIGHT

Judge Toole's Kangaroo Court

The way Marinello described it, none of the required elements for an employee disciplinary hearing happened. This hearing was held in open court and not in the Judge's Chambers as would normally be the case. Judge Toole donned his robe and grabbed his gavel. Marinello told me the atmosphere just reeked of intimidation and bullying. There was even a stenographer present. Marinello stated that the President Judge started reading accusations from the bench off of a hand written note pad which were outrageous. When questioned as to who made these claims, the judge refused to supply the names of the accusers. When asked as to the nature of the evidence of the claims, nothing was offered. Toole then stated from the bench that he believed that Marinello was guilty of sexual harassment. Marinello found this extremely troubling as the confidential EEOC suit in which he was not even named had been settled. A storm was a brewing and Marinello's Express Train was heading right into it.

Toole announced that he would make his final decision in due course and court was dismissed. As of 2010, Judge Toole has rendered no such decision. This "hearing" was held on November 25, 1996.

I thought to myself, although Marinello's story was very compelling, and it sure sounded like a classic "Kangaroo Court" to me, I would not include this information in my book because I did not have anything to back it up. I have not forgotten that Judge Patrick Toole is still a very powerful man..........with a temper.

Well, as you can see, I did include details of this hearing my book. It is a rare instance indeed when any attorney files a sworn affidavit against the President Judge of any county. It is even rarer when he does so in a Federal Lawsuit. Take a look.

IN THE UNITED STATES DISTRICT COURT
FOR THE MIDDLE DISTRICT OF PENNSYLVANIA

JAMES MARINELLO, JR.

        Plaintiff,   :   CIVIL ACTION-LAW

        Vs.   :   JURY TRIAL DEMANDED

MICHAEL JORDAN, individually
and as Chief Probation   :   JUDGE CAPUTO
Officer of the Luzerne
County Adult Probation and
Parole Department;
JOHN P. MULROY, Individually
and as the Court Personnel
Coordinator for the Luzerne
County Court of Common Pleas;
STEPHEN WOLINSKY, JR.,
Individually and as the
Assistant Chief Probation
Officer for Luzerne County
Adult Probation Parole
Department;
ANN MARIE BRASKEY,
Individually and as the
Assistant Chief of Luzerne
County Adult Probation
Parole Department;
THE LUZERNE COUNTY ADULT
PROBATION PAROLE DEPARTMENT
and
THE COURT OF COMMON PLEAS
OF LUZERNE COUNTY,

        Defendants.   :   No. 3:CV-99-1193

AFFIDAVIT OF BEN JOSIELEVSKI

Ben J, being duly sworn, deposes and says:

1. I, Ben Josielevski am an Attorney in the Scranton area and have been asked to provide information concerning Jim Marinello's suspension hearing which occurred on

November 25, 1996.

2. I represented James Marinello for a five day suspension without pay he received May 1996.

3. Mr. Marinello received this suspension for refusing to sit on command.

4. It was Mr. Marinello's contention that he was essentially being treated like a dog, being ordered to "sit" on command and when he objected to this ill treatment, he was given a five day suspension without pay for insubordination.

5. A timely Notice was sent requesting a hearing on this matter.

6. We waited for months and Mr. Marinello was not given a hearing.

7. Apparently The Fred Williams radio program found out about Mr. Marinello's suspension and the fact that he had not been given a hearing.

8. Mr. Williams began his program stating how many days it has been and that Jim Marinello still had not been given a hearing.

9. Mr. Williams apparently did this as a parody on the Iranian Hostage Crisis.

10. On November 25, 1996 a "hearing" was finally held.

11. This hearing was held with little or no notice, and failed in my estimate any reasonable test of "due process".

12. Judge Toole spent the first fifteen minutes excoriating me for giving information to Fred Williams regarding the Marinello matter.

13. When I explained that I never spoken to Fred Williams about this or any other matter, Judge Toole accused me of going to someone that worked for Williams' program or having someone do this for me. I viewed this as an allegation that I was attempting to deceive the Court.

14. I ccouldn't believe that he was making such allegations and that such was done in open court.

15. My feeling is that Judge Toole did not believe my representations to the Court regarding Fred Williams and that this set the tone for the hearing.

16. I was furious at these groundless allegations, but at all times Mr. Marinello and I maintained a professional and courteous manner during the hearing.

17. It should be noted that I did speak to Mr. Williams when he telephoned me several weeks after the hearing. Our conversation concerned the hearing itself, and the allegations concerning Ms. Braskey as well as Mr. Marinello's excellent record and accomplishments.

18. Part of the hearing was held in open court and part in Judge Toole's chambers.

19. Not all of the hearing was transcribed.

20. At some point during the proceeding, Judge Toole discussed whether or not the request for the hearing followed proper procedure.

21. The rule at that time was that a request for a hearing was to be done by notice not by filing a formal Complaint or petition and I pointed this out to the Judge, reading the text of the rule.

22. Judge Toole indicated that he read the rule to require a formal Petition or Notice and noted that I had not filed such a formal document.

23. I finally stated that I followed the rule and that if the Court wanted a more formal filing, it he should have changed the rule to so require one.

24. I do vaguely recall that the Judge mentioned Ann Marie Braskey's name during the hearing.

25. I recall that the hearing ended with the Judge essentially stating that he would rule on this but refusing to set any timeline or date by which he would file his ruling.

26. To this day and to my knowledge, Judge Toole never made a ruling, at least I have never been served with such a ruling.

27. I was familiar with the fact that Mr. Marinello had been contacted to cooperate with the Attorney General's Office and that he later provided additional information and co-operated.

28. It was my position at the hearing and afterwards that this suspension was at least partly related to the fact that Mr. Marinello was cooperating with the Attorney General's Office, and the Braskey matter, and had little or nothing to with the alleged incident of insubordination.

29. Mr. Marinello alleged that he saw things that were questionable in the Probation Office and that as a law enforcement officer he was obligated to report these matters.

30. Mr. Marinello refused to keep silent when he saw conduct that he believed to be illegal.

31. Mr. Marinello, to my knowledge, has always been both forthright and vocal when he believes he is in the right on a matter.

32. I have read each paragraph and sign my name below attesting to the truthfulness and accuracy of this Affidavit.

_____
Ben Josielevski

Sworn to and subscribed before me this 26th day of July, 2001.

_____
Notary Public

NOTARIAL SEAL
CHRISTINE M. SPANGLER, Notary Public
Abington Twp., Lackawanna County
My Commission Expires Sept. 29, 2003

I would like to make a prediction at this point in time: I will predict that Attorney Josielevski will never, ever, ever win a court case in front of Judge Toole no matter what the evidence presented is. That's just my guess.

A funny thing happened right after P.O. Duffy was arrested and had his talk from Pattie's Sports Bar with the ever concerned "Family Friend," Judge Cappellini. P.O. Braskey filed a brand new suit in Federal Court alleging sexual harassment. Even though it was Marinello's actions that were the subject of the suit, he was locked out of the loop. I thought, how clever. Sue the pocketbook but not the pocket. By law, you cannot insert or defend yourself in a suit that you are not a party to. Clever, clever, clever.

After two or three months, Marinello discovered that a county attorney filed answers to the complaint without ever talking to him. Marinello claims that the answers were written in such a form as to imply that the attorney was getting the information directly from Marinello, in the first person, if you will. Marinello was never subpoenaed for a deposition or document production. Marinello claims that he was kept in the dark and only after complaining to the Federal Judge that the case was assigned to was he invited to any of the proceedings. When Marinello tried to sit in on the depositions of others in the case, he was not allowed to.

Under the law, he was not a litigant in this case. All of the depositions were about him and his activities and yet he was not only barred from the depositions, but was also never allowed to respond to any of the claims. I am not, nor will ever, be a lawyer, but wouldn't it make sense to have the person listen to the allegations and testimony of the people who you will confront in court in order to put on an efficient defense? It just makes sense and you don't have to be a lawyer to see the logic in that. Additionally, wouldn't the attorneys for Braskey love to get Marinello to either admit to certain allegations or lie under oath?

Well, during this love fest one of the attorneys from the county's insurance carrier (Titan Insurance Company) noticed something. Something was shining out brilliantly amongst all of the fodder. None of the individuals named in the suit were county employees. Everyone named was a state employee who worked at the county courthouse. The county has no liability or exposure in regards to state employees. The county attorneys should have been thrilled. Instead they were left wringing their hands and wondering......now what?

The insurance attorney filed the proper motion and just like magic, the county was free and clear of any financial liability. According to Marinello, Luzerne County was officially dropped from the case within a very short period of time by the Federal Judge.

Game over!

Not so fast. The Luzerne County Railroad has not reached its final destination.

Mr. Marinello found it incredulous that Braskey made the claim in Federal Court that because of the sexual harassment orchestrated against her by him she could not do her job and suffered immensely. Mr. Marinello, in-fact, documented that during this exact time frame Braskey's career skyrocketed. She got a promotion, huge raise, new car, prepared the budget, conducted seminars, and was voted the Luzerne County representative to the Pennsylvania State Parole and Probation Association. Marinello's legitimate question to me was, "If any of this is true, then where the hell is the harm?" I thought that was a very good question.

Please read the following documents carefully. You would almost think that Marinello and Attorney Dougherty were adversaries. In-fact, Attorney Dougherty was hired by the county to represent Marinello. Maybe I'm reading this wrong but why wouldn't this attorney allow Marinello to read the depositions and respond directly to the attorney BEFORE a decision was made to settle or not? I have a pretty good idea why............do you?

Marinello declines to release depositions

Sex-harass data staying under wraps for now

By Carol Crane
Citizens' Voice Staff Writer

Embattled Luzerne County assistant probation chief James Marinello said Monday he has his reasons why he will not give his permission for public release of 14 depositions taken in connection with sexual harassment charges against him.

Braskey

And one of those reasons is that he gave the state Attorney General's office documentation that he alleged could have led to the arrest of Ann Marie Braskey, the woman who filed the sexual harassment lawsuit.

Further, Marinello argued, he also gave state agents information that could lead to the arrest of another of Braskey's co-workers.

Last month, county commissioners gave their approval to pay Braskey $90,000 in return her withdrawal of a federal lawsuit against the county based on claims that Marinello created a hostile work environment by repeatedly making statements about their past sexual relationship. The statements, Braskey claimed, were meant to undermine her authority as an assistant chief of adult probation.

Attorney Patrick Dougherty, who was retained by the county to defend Marinello, advised the county that, based on statements contained in the depositions, it would be advantageous to settle with Braskey out of court as opposed to allowing her claim seeking $300,000 to go before a jury.

Dougherty said since Marinello was his client, he could not release the depositions without breaking the Rules of Professional Conduct that govern attorneys. Dougherty said only if Marinello agreed to the release of the depositions, would they be made public.

In his letter declining to give his permission to release of the documents, Marinello listed 11 reasons for his decision.

Dougherty referred requests for copies of Marinello's letter to Marinello.

The day before the commissioners approved the payment to Braskey, Marinello was suspended without pay for 30 days pending the outcome of an internal investigation.

Chief Probation Officer Michael Jordan has stated that since it is a personnel matter, he is not free to provide any details.

But yesterday, in an exclusive interview with The Citizens' Voice, Marinello said he believes the suspension is just a prelude to his firing. "I don't think I am going to get my job back," he predicted. "When I got suspended, they told me to turn in my badge and gave me two boxes to clean out my desk, so it doesn't look too optimistic to me."

Marinello said he has never seen the depositions. "I have never been given the opportunity to defend myself against any of the allegations," he said, adding that he would have preferred that Braskey's lawsuit went before a jury instead of being settled.

In his response to Dougherty, Marinello alleged, "All but one of the persons deposed are close friends of Ms. Braskey. The majority were under her direct supervision at the time of the depositions."

Marinello also pointed out in his letter that one of the persons deposed was arrested by the state Attorney General as a direct result of his cooperation with state agents.

In 1996, probation officer Eugene Duffy Jr. was arrested and charged with four misdemeanor counts that still have not been adjudicated because of appeals.

At the present time, Duffy is awaiting formal court arraignment.

Marinello said he believes statements were taken only from persons who could provide testimony favorable to Braskey's case.

For instance, some years ago, Braskey allegedly made a derogatory statement about Marinello in the presence of another probation officer. However, Marinello alleged that when the probation officer was deposed recently, he was never asked about the statement. Had the officer been asked, he would have testified it never happened, thus impugning Braskey's veracity.

"For me to allow the depositions of Ms. Braskey's close friends and subordinates to be published without me being able to face my accusers and giving my side would amount to me being tried in the newspaper without a defense," Marinello's letter stated.

"To publish unproven facts by people who may have a reason to be untruthful may irreversibly damage my reputation and I feel the public should know their motives," the letter added.

A copy of Marinello's letter declining public release of the depositions was sent to state Attorney General Mike Fisher.

Dougherty said he advised the county to settle out of court because Braskey was seeking $300,00 and there would be no way to predict how a jury would react to her lawsuit.

Moreover, Dougherty underscored, the county's case, had it gone to court, would have been considerably weakened because at the time Braskey is alleging the sexual harassment took place, the county did not have a firm sexual harassment policy in place.

Titan Insurance allegedly denied to defend Braskey's claim, saying the county's policy contained no provisions for coverage of judicial system such as probation officers.

Since any payment to Braskey would have to come out of the county coffers, Dougherty said he advised the payment of $90,000 instead of gambling that a jury would rule in Braskey's favor for $300,000.

As part of the settlement, Braskey has signed a statement agreeing not to comment.

On October 20, 1998, Marinello was escorted by his chief to the new President Judge's Chambers. He was advised that he was suspended for 30 days without pay while an internal investigation was conducted into the Braskey matter. His chief ordered him to turn in his badge and to clean out his desk. This was prior to the internal investigation beginning.

The next day, October 21, 1998, the Luzerne County Commissioners voted to pay Braskey $90,000.00 to settle her suit. With legal fees, the amount was over $100,000. Since the county's insurance company successfully had the county removed from the litigation, it refused to pay anything towards the settlement. Guess where the money came from to pay the settlement? If you guessed directly from the taxpayers of Luzerne County you would be correct. The county had been dismissed from the suit, but still paid a substantial settlement.

Why not? It wasn't their money, besides the LCRR was still chugging along and hadn't reached its final destination....just yet.

The Luzerne County Railroad

County pays off, silently

10-22-98

■ *Details sketchy in $90,000 award in sexual harassment lawsuit.*

By DAVID J. RALIS
Times Leader Staff Writer

WILKES-BARRE — Luzerne County officials Wednesday wouldn't say why they agreed to pay $90,000 to silence a manager who sued for sexual harassment.

They also wouldn't say why James Marinello, whom Ann Marie Braskey accused of harassment, suddenly was suspended without pay four years after she first made the allegations.

And the public might never get answers. The lawyers and officials familiar with the case either are legally barred from talking, or have refused to do so publicly.

Depositions from a dozen witnesses who testified in the case are locked in the private office of Patrick Dougherty of Kingston, a county-hired attorney, rather than in a public court file. He said he would consider media requests to release them, but made no guarantees.

The same attorney also had Braskey, assistant chief of the county Adult Probation Office, sign a confidentiality agreement as part of the settlement. It would force her to give back the money if she speaks publicly about the case.

The confidentiality agreement does not bar other officials from talking. But the commissioners unanimously agreed Wednesday to pay Braskey the cash without any debate.

Mary Kamp, a member of the Coalition of Luzerne County Taxpayers, asked county commissioners why the case wasn't taken to court.

Commissioners Frank Crossin and Tom Makowski said they relied on the advice of Dougherty, whom they hired to defend the county in its first sexual harassment lawsuit.

Dougherty later said Braskey had sought $300,000 — the maximum compensation allowed by federal law.

Marinello told me that he immediately asked to use his two weeks of accumulated vacation time during his suspension so he could continue to pay his personal bills. He pointed out that P.O. Duffy had been allowed to do this after he was arrested by the Attorney General's Office. His request was denied.

Mr. Marinello claims he was kept so much in the dark that he could predict what was coming. Prior to the out-of-court settlement, Marinello approached the county attorneys and told them to their faces that they were not representing the county to "win this case." He told them that they were going to lose the case intentionally and then use the loss as a reason to fire him. They assured him in their very lawyerly way that his fears were totally unfounded. He also went public with his fears. The following is actually the front page headline of the daily paper.

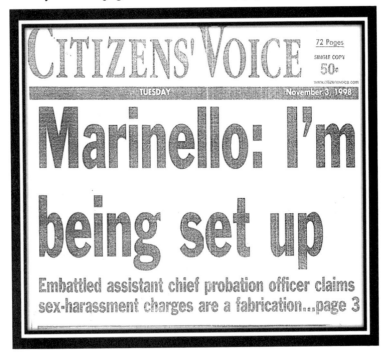

Marinello's suspension was extended on two more occasions for a total of two months and a week. His Chief then recommended that he be fired. Marinello requested a hearing which was held in front of the New President Judge.

Judge Joseph Augello had taken over the reigns from Judge Patrick Toole as the new President Judge of the county. I happened to have liked like Judge Augello, after all, he was the judge that earlier issued the stay of my proceedings. That took guts to go against a fellow Luzerne County Judge. Since this hearing was a closed "personnel" matter, I have no way to independently verify what you are about to read, but Marinello assured me that if push comes to shove and anyone takes issue with his recollection of the proceeding, or anything else for that matter, he will gladly take a polygraph test as long it is administered by an out of state, certified operator.

Marinello claims that the charges he was brought up on were, being accused of gossip, telling secrets and spreading rumors over the past twenty-four years.

Specifically, he called another Probation Officer "fatso" years prior. He gossiped about two female county employees having inappropriate sexual relationships with judges. He was accused of throwing "playful" punches with fellow co-workers. He talked about his relationship with Braskey. He was disrespectful to his Chief. Keep in mind that Judge Augello did not have a single written warning about any of the above activities in his possession for review. That is because there were none in Marinello's extensive employment jacket.

Why the next point was allowed into this hearing is truly a mystery to me. He was accused of pressuring a co worker who lived next door to his chief to take pictures of their chief siphoning gasoline from his county car and putting it into his own personal vehicle. At this point I stopped the interview and told Marinello that I simply did not believe his last statement and that I would not include the unfound accusation of theft from the county by the Chief of the Probation Office in my book. I felt that even if it was true, I didn't believe that there was any way that they would include it as a reason to fire him. I started to question everything that Marinello had already told me.

Instead of being offended, Marinello calmly asked me to look for a document dated January 14, 2003 that was included in a packet he had given me prior to this particular interview. I simply couldn't believe what I was reading. This article is out of sequence from a timing point of view but wait till you read it!

I want to formally apologize to Mr. Marinello right here and right now for doubting his honesty and integrity.

Official admits to allegations

By TERRIE MORGAN-BESECKER
tmorgan@leader.net

SCRANTON — The county's former chief of probation admitted Monday that he committed some of the acts self-proclaimed whistle-blower James Marinello has alleged, including altering the file of a parole violator who had killed his girlfriend and himself.

Stephen Wolinsky, now a supervisor in the Luzerne County Adult Probation Department, also admitted he once siphoned gasoline from a county vehicle for personal use, and that he performed unauthorized background checks on juveniles for a supermarket on county time.

Called as a hostile witness by Marinello's attorney, Peter Loftus, Wolinsky acknowledged he twice tried to have Marinello fired, once in 1987 and again in 1996. But he insisted his actions were not related to Marinello's allegations against him.

Wolinsky's admissions came during the fourth day of Marinello's wrongful discharge trial against the department before Judge Richard Caputo in the U.S. District Court for the Middle District of Pennsylvania. Wolinsky is also a defendant along with department employees Ann Marie Braskey and Michael Jordan, and Jack Mulroy, deputy court administrator.

It's unclear if any disciplinary action was ever taken against Wolinsky for the incidents. He was ousted as chief in December 1996 by then-President Judge Patrick Toole, but no official reason was ever given.

Marinello claims he was fired as assistant chief in 1999 because he aided the state Office of Attorney General in its 1996 investigation of wrongdoing within the department. The department maintains he was fired for sexually harassing Braskey and for creating a hostile working environment for other employees.

Questioned by Loftus, Wolinsky admitted he and another department employee, Matt Kelly, "whited out" part of the file of Richard Halliday, a probation department client who killed his girlfriend, Kim Kruczek, and himself in 1987.

See WOLINSKY, Page 8A

Former chief of probation acknowledges in wrongful discharge trial he did some things charged by self-described whistle-blower.

WOLINSKY

1-14-05

Continued from Page 1A

Marinello reported Wolinsky to the Attorney General's Office and also testified for Kruczek's family in a civil suit they filed after learning the department failed to act on Marinello's order to jail Halliday the day before he killed Kruczek.

Wolinsky testified he believes he committed a crime when he and Kelly changed a date in the Halliday file as the Kruczek civil case prepared to go to trial. He insisted they did so only to correct inaccurate information.

"At the time I didn't know it was illegal," Wolinsky said. "If I had it to do all over again, I would do a sworn affidavit (changing the date) instead of the stupid mistake of whiting it out."

A similar action led to charges of tampering with a public record against probation department employee Eugene Duffy, who was accused of falsifying the record of his client, attorney Gifford R. Cappellini. Duffy was acquitted of the charges. Wolinsky was never charged in the Halliday incident.

Wolinsky admitted he was "not happy" Marinello had made public a list of 15 allegations against Wolinsky that he circulated. But Wolinsky insisted he did not seek to fire Marinello in retaliation, but because Marinello was undermining Wolinsky's authority and threatening him.

"If Jim had a problem with something I did, I expected he would come to me. I don't know why he threatened to ... I think he said to me, 'Everyone has skeletons in their closet.' I took that as a threat he planned to expose what I'd done in the past."

Wolinsky admitted he also tried to have Marinello fired in 1996 after the state Attorney General's Office began investigating allegations that Duffy, the son of the then prothonotary, had failed to drug test Cappellini, the son of a county judge.

Marinello maintains his cooperation with the attorney general in the Duffy case was a major factor behind his firing. But Wolinsky again insisted he was not seeking to retaliate against Marinello.

"He was harassing numerous members of my department, accusing them of wrongdoing. I didn't think his actions were appropriate. I felt, once again, I couldn't work with Jim Marinello and I asked for his termination."

Regarding the gasoline theft, Wolinsky said his car was empty and he siphoned about one gallon of gas from a county car that was parked in front of it.

He admitted he at first denied the allegation when questioned in 1998 by Jordan, who took over as chief of probation. But he maintained he did not intentionally lie.

"I didn't remember it. It was so insignificant," he said. "I never thought that it would be such a big issue."

As for the juvenile background checks, Wolinsky said he stopped doing the checks in 1990, when he was advised by Toole that they were "improper."

Questioned by John Gonzales, attorney for the defense, Wolinsky said he was continuing a practice that had been done by his predecessor in the office and did not believe he was doing anything wrong. He also noted that Marinello helped him do the checks and never complained to him that the action was illegal.

Loftus is expected to wrap up his case today or tomorrow.

The probation department will then present testimony.

The case is expected to last until at least Friday.

I was dumbstruck.

So, here we have this "Official Employment Hearing" taking place in front of Judge Augello. According to Marinello, not a single written warning for any infraction existed in Marinello's twenty-two year old personnel file. The county paid over $100,000. in taxpayer money for an out of court settlement that is, at the very least, "suspect." What does Judge Augello do?

Marinello terminated from probation post

Saturday, January 9, 1999

By Carol Crane
Citizens' Voice Staff Writer

The Luzerne County adult probation official who blew the whistle on some of his fellow probation officers was fired Friday.

Assistant Chief Probation Officer James Marinello was terminated yesterday by President Judge Joseph Augello based on the recommendation of Chief Adult Probation Officer Michael Jordan, according to numerous courthouse sources.

Marinello was suspended without pay last October just one day before the county commissioners approved a $90,000 out-of-court settlement to Assistant Adult Probation Chief Ann Marie Braskey who had filed a federal lawsuit claiming she had been sexually harassed by Marinello but county officials did nothing about it.

Contacted at his Pittston home yesterday, Marinello would neither confirm nor deny his dismissal. "On the advice of my attorney, I cannot comment," he stated.

Augello and Jordan have previously stated that it is their policy not to comment on matters involving personnel.

Chief Clerk/Administrator Eugene Klein said Friday that the personnel office had not yet been advised of any action regarding Marinello.

In November, Marinello sent a five-page letter to the state Attorney General's office, alleging that his two suspension from his county job were in retaliation for his cooperation with state agents in an ongoing probe into the adult probation office.

Information provided to state agents by Marinello resulted in several of his co-workers coming under scrutiny and the arrest of probation officer Eugene Duffy Jr.

However, Duffy and many of those same co-workers were among the more than one dozen people contacted to give depositions in connection with Braskey's claim.

The state Attorney General's office has consistently declined to comment on the probation office investigation which began after a confidential informant told police that Attorney Gifford Cappellini was not being tested for drugs as per the terms of his probation.

Duffy was Cappellini's probation officer.

While the state remains tight-lipped about the probe, sources have indicated that federal intervention is possible.

County taxpayers ended having to foot the $90,000 bill to settle with Braskey because the county's liability carrier said her lawsuit was not covered under the terms of its insurance policy.

Marinello had said he would have preferred the case go to trial as opposed to being settled out of court. He was not named as a defendant in Braskey's lawsuit. Marinello has denied harassing Braskey, saying, "All I did was tell a secret she did not want told."

Over the past decade, taxpayers have had to shoulder the burden for other lawsuits that the county's insurers refused to cover.

In 1989, Pat Kruczek filed a three-count federal lawsuit accusing former Chief Probation Officer Steve Wolinsky with gross negligence.

The lawsuit stemmed from the 1987 murder of Kim Kruczek by Robert Halliday. After shooting his girlfriend Kim in the head, Halliday turned the gun on himself.

Federal court records archived in Philadelphia detail that Marinello ordered Halliday's probation revoked and that he be remanded to prison for repeatedly threatening Kim and the Kruczek family.

However, after a meeting with the Kruczek and Halliday families, Wolinsky agreed to allow Robert Halliday to remain free even though he refused to sign an agreement saying the families would keep their distance from each other.

The day after that meeting, Halliday burst into the Kruczek's

> Nanticoke home, killed Kim, and then turned the gun on himself.
>
> Court records recount that Wolinsky said he believed the Kruczeks had requested Robert Halliday locked up because Kim had wanted to terminate their relationship.
>
> Wolinsky confirmed last month that he was never reprimanded or disciplined because of the Kruczek lawsuit which was eventually settled out of court.
>
> Wolinsky now works as an assistant chief probation officer. He was demoted after Duffy's arrest.
>
> Duffy is the son of a former county prothonotary. Wolinsky is the son-in-law of a former county president judge and Cappellini is the son of a retired county judge.
>
> Marinello has worked in the adult probation office for the past 24 years. Other than the two suspensions without pay, he has never been reprimanded for his performance.

I strongly feel that what we have here is pure and it is simple. This, in my opinion, is "In Your Face" corruption. Luzerne County has perfected this style of corruption. It is actually an art form here. It simply doesn't matter how it looks. The most important issue is that the train gets to its final destination. If someone looks silly along the way, if someone looks goofy along the way, if someone commits a crime or two along the way.............so be it. As long as the powers that be get what they want.

Every time I look at the title of the following article, I think the author was having a little fun with the order of the words, but that's just me.

— MIKE McGLYNN

The Cabbage Patch

A pig in a poke

As Holmes once remarked, the world is awash in armchair reasoners, which today we call Monday morning quarterbacks or second-guessers.

The point is that it's easy enough to sit here and criticize the way in which the Luzerne County Adult Probation is run, but it's not quite so easy to recommend the tonic that will reinvigorate the office as a completely functional, above-politics instrument of law enforcement. That is a quest of almost cosmic proportions. In all candor, what it probably would take to achieve such an end is a top-to-bottom overhaul — and that's not likely to occur anytime soon, or, anytime not so soon.

As is the case with any situation in which proper procedure routinely is flouted in favor of protecting the politically connected and rewarding the fixers at the expense of those who follow the rules of the game, a large part of the problem is public apathy. For every 50 people who write letters to the editor and blow their tanks on the local radio talk shows, you're lucky to find one person who will make a legitimate effort to effect needed change.

The media are largely at fault, as well, for failing to focus on the mess in the probation office. Oh, they print the daily line, but when was the last time you saw any of the three local television news channels ask the tough questions which should be asked at a time when the taxpayers have been stuck with a $104,000 sexual harassment tab? The attorney respresentating the county has recommended that the settlement be made — although no one has seen specific, detailed documentation supporting the charges — and if the case is settled as has been recommended, no one ever will see it. This is a case of a political appointee suing her employer, the county, with the overt approval, even encouragement, of those who hired and promoted her, without any public review of the matter, and the county bosses sorrowfully telling us that they're over a barrel because the evidence is so overwhelming.

> The county taxpayers are the ones who are being sexually harassed.

What bloody evidence, for crying out loud?

We're being asked — no, ordered — to buy a pig in a poke, at the bargain price of $104,000, $14,000 of which will go to line the pockets of the attorney who has been representing the county. What makes this whole Keystone Kops scenario viable, aside from media indifference and the traditional tendency of Luzerne County people to moan and groan but vote for the same people who make these messes anyway, is the convenient capacity of charges of sexual harassment to set off bells and whistles.

Despite the failure of the county to divulge any documentation to provide a basis for doling out $104,000, some components of Ann Marie Braskey's sex harassment case against fellow assistant chief of adult probation James Marinello have trickled out. According to the usual sources, Marinello, who once dated Braskey, blurted out at a wedding that his relationship with her was intimate and repeated this line at various times in the probation office itself. Such behavior may not be worthy of what once was called a "gentleman," but if it's legitimate sexual harassment, there are a lot of people who should be coughing up $104,000 for their offhand remarks.

Using an accusation of sexual harassment has the effect of diverting attention from the real issue — that Marinello is on the hook because he blew the whistle on illicit activity in the probation office. Because the law offers protection to such "whistleblowers," the only option available in the war on Marinello was to find a mechanism with which to discredit him personally and professionally.

Another problem is institutional:

The county apparatus is a two-headed animal — the commissioners and the courts. The commissioners are in charge of managing the county's finances, but they rarely can resist the demands of the courts for money. And, because courts have virtual autonomy — judges only answer to voters in 10-year "retention" elections — there's not a lot the commissioners can do at their end when presented with an outlandish $104,000 bill like this one.

Of course, we all might feel better if they were to ask the lawyer for Braskey to show us the documentation which supports this generous settlement.

Mike McGlynn is The Citizens' Voice political writer.

I especially like the following document. It is the "Official Notice of Determination" as issued by the Pennsylvania "Unemployment Compensation Board." Let's really look at this document and what it really says about this entire termination of Marinello.

According to the county, Marinello was fired not just for cause, but for "HUGE" cause. His supposed actions cost the county taxpayers OVER $100,000.

Marinello filed a simple claim for Unemployment Compensation. His overwhelming task at hand was to "PROVE" at a formal hearing that his termination by Luzerne County was unjustified. The county fights his claim and sends its best and brightest to defend the county's actions. With something as simple and straight forward as an UC hearing, the county loses and loses in spectacular fashion.

Whoever W.J. Howley is……….This Bud's for you! Mr. Howley saw right through the BS. If the county could not pass the test of this hearing, how was it going to do in Federal Court against a Whistle Blowers lawsuit?

But wait…………….is that a train whistle I hear?

NOTICE OF DETERMINATION

k0G:OMMONWEALTH OF PENNSYLVANIA
DEPARTMENT OF LABOR AND INDUSTRY
BUREAU OF UC BENEFITS AND ALLOWANCES

TYPE CLAIM - UC

SOCIAL SECURITY NUMBER

CLAIMANT   James C Marinello Jr.
            Pittston   Pa. 18640

AB DATE - January 10, 1999

MAILED ON - January 26, 1999

EMPLOYER   Luzerne County Adult Probation Department
           Luzerne County Courthouse
           Wilkes Barre   Pa. 18711

FINDINGS OF FACT

1. The claimant was last employed on October 20, 1998.
2. The claimant's job title was assistant chief parole officer.
3. He was discharged for: creating a hostile work environment for a female co-worker due to his conduct.
4. The employer provided firsthand information regarding the incident which caused the separation.
5. The claimant denied the employer's allegations.
6. The claimant's statement was more credible than the employer's information.

DISCUSSION

In situations where the claimant is discharged, the burden of proof is on the employer to establish that the claimant's actions which caused the separation constituted willful misconduct. Once this is established, the burden shifts to the claimant to show good cause for his actions. In this case, the claimant denied the employer's allegations regarding the incident which caused the separation. Although the employer provided firsthand information regarding the incident, the claimant's statement was more credible than the employer's information. As such, the employer has not sustained its burden of proof and benefits must be allowed.

DETERMINATION

The claimant is eligible for benefits under Section 402(e) of the Pennsylvania Unemployment Compensation Law beginning with waiting week ending January 16, 1999. In addition, the following compensable week(s) are eligible: 01-23-99

UI Representative _____

The last day to appeal this determination is February 10, 1999.
(See Reverse for Appeal Instructions)

MIKE McGLYNN

The Cabbage Patch

Tell the public why

On Friday, the powers that be at the courthouse fired James Marinello (although no one has officially confirmed that report), the whistleblower who exposed alleged special treatment in the county Adult Probation Office.

Why?

That's not intended to be a sarcastic or disingenuous question. We all know why, as a practical political matter, Marinello was canned. He was not a team player. He did not approve of the coddling of certain probation office customers because they were politically connected and he caused the county considerable embarrassment and trouble. No one should be surprised. You could see his dismissal coming a mile way, like an automobile which has just moved over the horizon and into your line of vision.

But, there's another "why" for which no satisfactory answer, in fact no answer whatsoever, has been provided.

Why was Marinello fired, in the sense of "for what transgressions?"

Naturally, to the extent to which they have been saying anything, county officials who are in this mess up to their elbows have maintained the position that they cannot comment on personnel matters.

Where was Bill Clinton's head when they hauled him before Ken Starr's grand jury and asked if he'd been tripping the light fantastic with Monica Lewinsky?

> It's high time that the nature of James Marinello's crimes is made public.

He should have replied, "Monicas Lewinsky was a White House intern at the time in question and I can't comment on personnel matters."

That would have thrown a monkey wrench into the works.

Maybe that's why we don't empanel grand juries in Luzerne County. We don't need 'em. We handle these matters strictly in-house.

In a controversial case which already has cost the taxpayers a nice piece of change and may yet cost more when the lawsuits we all assume Marinello will file, one for wrongful termination and another for the violation of his civil rights under federal law, come to fruition. Instead of cleaning this matter up, ending it and moving on, the county powers continue to heap more radioactive waste on the pile. The state attorney general's office continues to probe the antics in the probation office, with rumors of federal interest and involvement now making the circuit. It's difficult to imagine what defense the county will employ if Marinello brings suit, unless, of course, a story has been scripted, distributed and memorized by all in whose interests it has been to bring Marinello down. That's a dangerous game, because if even one player makes a mistake or a slip of the tongue on the stand, the whole house of cards comes down.

Maybe the county already has set money aside to settle Marinello's potential lawsuits, thereby killing two birds with one stone — the whistleblower is out of the office and his voice will not be heard in court. Such a brazen handling of the matter should have severe repercussions at the polls, but in a county which really has only one political party, people have no realistic outlet for venting their anger.

The citizens of Luzerne County have a moral right to a full accounting of the facts of this high-profile, public case. There should be no question of hiding behind the mother's apron strings of keeping mum on personnel matters. That ban does not extend to the practice of firing a public employee who, by all indications, has maintained a spotless record in order to protect the butts of a handful of political legacies who quite obviously, whatever Marinello himself did or did not do, have been involved in acts of misfeasance at the very least.

Even if that stricture did apply to the Marinello episode in the probation office, the public's right to know must take precedence here.

The public should have a play-by-play account of everything that has happened in that office which has led to so extreme a disposition as termination, particularly when that termination looks so very much like nothing more than an act of cheap, cynical and defiant political reprisal — and nothing more.

By the way, did they arrest Dodie Cappellini yet?

Mike McGlynn is The Citizens' Voice political writer.

4A The Times Leader, Wilkes-Barre, Pa, Friday, July 9, 1999

Self-proclaimed whistle-blower sues county probation department

▪ *James Marinello claims he was fired after years of being mistreated for reporting wrongdoing.*

By TERRIE MORGAN-BESECKER
Times Leader Staff Writer

SCRANTON — He has claimed for years he was harassed for reporting corruption in Luzerne County's Adult Probation Department. Now James Marinello wants the department and several co-workers to pay.

Marinello, a self-avowed whistle-blower who was fired this year, on Wednesday filed a scathing six-count federal lawsuit claiming he endured years of intimidation and retaliation for reporting alleged wrongdoing of politically connected department employees.

Falsifying expense vouchers, siphoning gasoline from a county car for personal use and giving preferential treatment to certain parolees are among the illegal acts Marinello claims he uncovered during his 24 years with the department.

His reports of that suspected wrongdoing to the offices of the Luzerne County district attorney and state attorney general led to his ouster from his $45,500-a-year job in January, he claims.

The lawsuit, filed in U.S. District Court in Scranton, names as defendants Adult Probation Chief Michael Jordan, Deputy Court Administrator John Mulroy and assistant chief probation officers Stephen Wolinsky Jr. and Ann Marie Braskey. The Adult Probation Department and Luzerne County Court of Common Pleas also are named as defendants.

The suit turns the tables on Braskey, who last year was awarded $90,000 in a settlement of a sexual harassment suit she filed against Marinello and the Probation Department.

According to Marinello's suit:

Marinello admits he had sex with Braskey four times in 1982, but it was Wolinsky who did not like Braskey and made sexist remarks about her. Other agents told Braskey of Wolinsky's alleged remarks, but Braskey named only

Marinello as a defendant in her harassment suit.

Marinello's suit claims Jordan, Mulroy, Wolinsky and Braskey "kept a book" on Marinello and engaged in a "systematic pattern of conduct" designed to intimidate him into resigning. When the plan failed, the four held clandestine meetings to discuss allegations they would manufacture to get him fired.

County and court officials took no action to halt the harassment. Instead, officials "praised and encouraged" employees to continue the conduct.

Marinello, of Butler Street, Pittston, says his right to free speech and several other constitutional rights were violated. He further claims his reputation has been destroyed and his ability to find other work irreparably harmed.

The suit seeks more than $80,000 in compensatory and punitive damages for each of six counts, including wrongful discharge and violations of the state Whistle Blowers law.

Contacted Thursday, Jordan and Mulroy said they could not comment on pending litigation. Wolinsky and Braskey did not return phone messages left at the Probation Department. County spokesman Jim Torbik said county commissioners would have no comment on the case.

Marinello was the key figure in the attorney general's investigation of former probation officer Eugene Duffy Jr.'s supervision of attorney Gifford R. Cappellini. Cappellini, the son of Luzerne County Court of Common Pleas Senior Judge Gifford S. Cappellini, was on probation for a drug conviction, but was never randomly tested for drugs.

Marinello claims he was harassed and subjected to an "extremely hostile work environment" for cooperating with investigators in the Duffy case.

That harassment included a five-day suspension in May 1996 for insubordination after he refused to sit when ordered during a meeting with Wolinsky. The suspension came days after Marinello filed a complaint with the state, alleging Wolinsky intimidated him for his cooperation in the Duffy case.

The suit says Marinello also was targeted for telling investigators probation officers were falsifying expense vouchers — allegations he says are supported by physical evidence he turned over.

Kevin Harley, spokesman for the Attorney General's Office, said Thursday the investigation into Marinello's allegations is continuing.

Marinello was fired by President Judge Joseph Augello in January after a hearing at which Jordan accused him of "gossip, telling secrets and rumors over the past 24 years."

The suit claims Jordan's allegations included that Marinello once called a co-worker "fatso," that he gossiped about two female employees having inappropriate relationships with judges, that he playfully threw punches at a co-worker, that he talked about sexual contact with Braskey and that he allegedly bragged about lying under oath.

Jordan also accused Marinello of asking an agent who lived next door to Wolinsky to photograph him siphoning gas from a county vehicle and putting into his personal car, the suit says.

The suit says Jordan admitte he wanted Marinello fired for hi "behavior," and not because Jordan had a problem with Marinello's job performance. Marinell successfully argued for unen ployment compensation benefit despite the county's opposition.

It was unclear Thursday wh will defend the county and er ployees against the lawsuit.

The Probation Department part of the state court syste therefore employees are eligit for a state-appointed attorne said Art Heinz of the Administr tive Office of Pennsylvar Courts. Heinz said it is too ea to determine if the state will involved.

Chief Clerk/Administra Gene Klein said commissione will meet soon with county Soli tor James Blaum and Augello discuss the appointment of cou sel.

So, Marinello was fired from his job and decided to file a Federal "Whistleblower" lawsuit of his own. The powers that be decided that instead of settling this case "out of court" they would fight to the death. They probably could have offered Marinello his job back and half of what they settled the Braskey case for and he probably would have taken it.

Marinello told me that the first four days of testimony went extremely well. They had put his old boss, former Chief Wolinsky on the stand as a hostile witness. They got everything they wanted out of him and then some. His testimony was so outrageous that the following article has been reproduced again for your viewing pleasure.

Marinello's federal suit moves forward; depositions next

By Kevin Donlin
Citizens' Voice Staff Writer

The majority of a civil rights lawsuit filed against members of the Luzerne County Probation Department by a former department employee has been cleared to proceed following a ruling last month by a federal judge.

James Marinello, a former deputy chief adult probation, was fired Jan. 8, 1999 after 24 years in the department. According to court records, Marinello of perpetrating gossip, telling secrets and rumors over the past two years. In July 1999, Marinello filed a federal lawsuit against Luzerne County court, Jordan, court personnel coordinator John P. Mulroy, and assistant probation department supervisors Steven Wolinsky Jr. and Ann Marie Braskey. Luzerne County court has been named as a defendant.

United States District Judge A. Richard Caputo issued an order on May 24 allowing the more serious counts to proceed. In his order, Caputo denied the defense motion to dismiss counts involving the violation of First Amendment rights, the intentional infliction of emotional distress, whistleblowing and wrongful discharge.

Caputo also dismissed several counts of the lawsuit, including Fourth, Fifth and 14th amendment violations.

Under the Third Circuit Court of Appeals, the plaintiff must show the activity in question was protected by free speech statutes and that the protected activity was a substantial and motivating factor in the alleged retaliatory action.

Caputo said he could not dismiss the complaints because he could not find "as a matter of law, that the plaintiff's activity was not protected and was not a substantial motivating factor in... the decision to terminate his employment."

Marinello's lawsuit essentially claims he was fired for blowing the whistle on the alleged improper conduct of some of his "politically connected" co-workers. At least one arrest resulted after the office of the state Attorney General began looking into the matter.

According to the original lawsuit, the alleged retaliation began after a lawsuit was filed against Wolinsky in connection with the death of Kim Kruczek, who was killed in 1987 by her boyfriend, Robert Halliday. Marinello ordered Halliday, who had been on probation, arrested after Kruczek complained her former boyfriend had been stalking her. Wolinsky overruled Marinello's order following a meeting with the Halliday and Kruczek families.

The next day, however, Halliday burst into the Kruczek's home and shot his former girlfriend in the head, then turned the gun on himself.

An out-of-court settlement was reached in response to a lawsuit filed by the Kruczek family. But Wolinsky, who is the son of the late President Judge Robert Hourigan, was never suspended or investigated by the county.

The original lawsuit also claims Wolinsky made sexist remarks about his assistant, Braskey. A second lawsuit claiming sexual harassment was filed by Braskey for unauthorized background checks on juveniles for Weis Markets.

The defendants in the case have been advised by their attorneys not to discuss any aspect of the case.

See SUIT, page 11

Federal judge denies defense claims to toss Marinello suit

from Page 3

Braskey received a $90,000 out-of-court settlement from the county after he provided state agents with information regarding alleged illegal activities by Cappellini and then Marinello was suspended.

Another parole officer, Eugene Duffy, the son of the Luzerne County Prothonotary Eugene Duffy Sr., has since filed a federal lawsuit claiming Marinello admits he had consensual sex with Braskey four times in 1982, when both worked as probation officers. A part of the Braskey lawsuit charged sexual harassment because Marinello told a co-worker about the relationship.

Marinello also alleged he was suspended for five days without pay a few days after he wrote up parole officer Dodi Cappellini, the daughter of Senior Judge Gifford S. Cappellini, for insubordination.

The reason provided to Marinello for his suspension was that he had refused to sit when ordered to do so by Wolinsky.

Marinello also contends the work environment became difficult after he provided state agents with information regarding alleged illegal activities by Cappellini and Duffy. Marinello and Duffy were the only one arrested and he later beat the charges.

The lawsuit also states that among the accusations provided by Jordan to justify Marinello's firing were that he had called another probation officer "fatsky," and that he had bragged several years prior, that Marinello gossiped about female employees having "inappropriate relationships" with judges, that he played fully threw punches at a co-worker, that he talked about his relationship with Braskey, that he was disrespectful towards Wolinsky, and that he had bragged about lying under oath.

Official admits to allegations

Former chief of probation acknowledges in James Marinello's wrongful discharge trial he did some things charged by self-described whistle-blower.

By TERRIE MORGAN-BESECKER
tmorgan@leader.net

SCRANTON — The county's former chief of probation admitted Monday that he committed some of the acts self-proclaimed whistleblower James Marinello has alleged, including altering the file of a parole violator who had killed his girlfriend and himself.

Stephen Wolinsky, now a supervisor in the Luzerne County Adult Probation Department, also admitted he once siphoned gasoline from a county vehicle for personal use, and that he performed unauthorized background checks on juveniles for a supermarket on county time.

Called as a hostile witness by Marinello's attorney, Peter Loftus, Wolinsky acknowledged he twice tried to have Marinello fired, once in 1987 and again in 1996. But he insisted his actions were not related to Marinello's allegations against him.

Wolinsky's admissions came during the fourth day of Marinello's wrongful discharge trial against the department before Judge Richard Caputo in the U.S. District Court for the Middle District of Pennsylvania. Wolinsky is also a defendant along with department employees Ann Marie Braskey and Michael Jordan, and Jack Mulroy, deputy court administrator.

It's unclear if any disciplinary action was ever taken against Wolinsky for the incidents. He was ousted as chief in December 1996 by then-President Judge Patrick Toole, but no official reason was ever given.

Marinello claims he was fired as assistant chief in 1999 because he aided the state Office of Attorney General in its 1996 investigation of wrongdoing within the department. The department maintains he was fired for sexually harassing Braskey and for creating a hostile working environment for other employees.

Questioned by Loftus, Wolinsky admitted he and another department employee, Matt Kelly, "whited out" part of the file of Richard Halliday, a probation department client who killed his girlfriend, Kim Kruczek, and himself in 1987.

See WOLINSKY, Page 8A.

WOLINSKY

1-14-05

Continued from Page 1A

Marinello reported Wolinsky to the Attorney General's Office and also testified for Kruczek's family in a civil suit they filed after learning the department failed to act on Marinello's order to jail Halliday the day before he killed Kruczek.

Wolinsky testified he believes he committed a crime when he and Kelly changed a date in the Halliday file as the Kruczek civil case prepared to go to trial. He insisted they did so only to correct inaccurate information.

"At the time I didn't know it was illegal," Wolinsky said. "If I had it to do all over again, I would do a sworn affidavit (changing the date) instead of the stupid mistake of whiting it out."

A similar action led to charges of tampering with a public record against probation department employee Eugene Duffy, who was accused of falsifying the record of his client, attorney Gifford R. Cappellini. Duffy was acquitted of the charges. Wolinsky was never charged in the Halliday incident.

Wolinsky admitted he was "not happy" Marinello had made public a list of 15 allegations against Wolinsky that he circulated. But Wolinsky insisted he did not seek to fire Marinello in retaliation, but because Marinello was undermining Wolinsky's authority and threatening him.

"If Jim had a problem with something I did, I expected he would come to me. I don't know why he threatened to ... I think he said to me, 'Everyone has skeletons in their closet.' I took that as a threat he planned to expose what I'd done in the past."

Wolinsky admitted he also tried to have Marinello fired in 1996 after the state Attorney General's Office began investigating allegations that Duffy, the son of the then prothonotary, had failed to drug test Cappellini, the son of a county judge.

Marinello maintains his cooperation with the attorney general in the Duffy case was a major factor behind his firing. But Wolinsky again insisted he was not seeking to retaliate against Marinello.

"He was harassing numerous members of my department, accusing them of wrongdoing. I didn't think his actions were appropriate. I felt, once again, I couldn't work with Jim Marinello and I asked for his termination."

Regarding the gasoline theft, Wolinsky said his car was empty and he siphoned about one gallon of gas from a county car that was parked in front of it.

He admitted he at first denied the allegation when questioned in 1998 by Jordan, who took over as chief of probation. But he maintained he did not intentionally lie.

"I didn't remember it. It was so insignificant," he said. "I never thought that it would be such a big issue."

As for the juvenile background checks, Wolinsky said he stopped doing the checks in 1990, when he was advised by Toole that they were "improper."

Questioned by John Gonzales, attorney for the defense, Wolinsky said he was continuing a practice that had been done by his predecessor in the office and did not believe he was doing anything wrong. He also noted that Marinello helped him do the checks and never complained to him that the action was illegal.

Loftus is expected to wrap up his case today or tomorrow.

The probation department will then present testimony.

The case is expected to last until at least Friday.

Talk about serving up a huge portion of "crow" on a silver platter. This was Marinello's boss, not some kid fresh out of Probation Officer School.

"I didn't remember that I siphoned gasoline out of my county car. I only did it once, and it was only a gallon. I didn't know it would be such a big deal."

It begs the obvious question: How does one block in one's county car with a personal vehicle that is "out of gas?" If he pushed it there then maybe he should have pushed it back out of the way. Oh, wait, I know. He parked it there and it ran out after he put it in park. There must be more to this story because I know that there is no way this man would get on a witness stand in Federal Court, take the oath, and then lie (I'm Kidding). Don't forget he is a Law Enforcement Officer or better yet, an Officer of the Court. and has been for decades. I just wish I knew the rest of the story. Did I mention the fact that he is the Son-in-law of a former "President Judge Hourigan" of Luzerne County? Maybe that is the rest of the story.

Can you imagine being on that jury after Wolinsky was done on the stand? Marinello confessed to me that he started seeing dollar signs. So far, things could not have gone any better. But wait, is that a train whistle I hear? I hear a chugging sound and, yes, it is a whistle. Sounds like the good old, Luzerne County Railroad's "Express Train to Hell". I am sure of it.

What exactly does a Federal Judge do when such an impression has been left on a jury? Let's keep in mind that this is just the first witness. Holy smokes, the stage has been set for one hell of a "Train Wreck".

Marinello lawsuit bounced by judge

A court order states the former probation worker didn't produce enough evidence backing up his wrongful discharge claim.

By TERRIE MORGAN-BESECKER
tmorgan@leader.net

SCRANTON — James Marinello's blistering three-year court battle against the Luzerne County Adult Probation Department ended Tuesday with as much controversy as it began as a federal judge dismissed the case before it went to the jury.

Attorneys for the Probation Department did not present a single witness, convincing U.S. District Judge Richard Caputo that Marinello failed to meet his burden of proof after five days of testimony.

Caputo ruled Marinello failed to produce any evidence that the department employees he sued had the authority to terminate him. Without that, the case could not proceed, he said.

The decision ended a contentious trial that left the reputations of players on both sides bruised as allegations of sexual harassment, petty rivalries and retribution for exposing wrongdoing of the politically connected played out in open court.

Deputy Court Administrator Jack Mulroy pumped his fist in triumph as his co-defendants, Ann Marie Braskey, Stephen Wolinsky and Michael Jordan, exchanged hugs after Caputo announced his decision in the U.S. District Court

As I stated earlier, I am not an attorney, but don't you think that the county attorneys would have come up with this defense years prior to the case going to trial? Pretty simple, Marinello. Your chief can't fire you. The county Human Resource Director can't fire you. Only the President Judge can fire you and he has complete and total immunity. He is immune from civil prosecution even if he commits a crime while on the bench and, by the way, you didn't sue him. Just think of the tens of thousands of dollars the county attorneys could have saved the taxpayers of Luzerne County in just their fees alone if they would have pointed this out when the suit was originally filed. No, no, no. That is not how the game is played.

I asked Marinello if his attorney offered to give him his money back since apparently this case was lost due to such an egregious oversight on the attorney's part? He did not, nor do I believe there was an oversight. Marinello sued his boss who recommended his firing to the President Judge as well as his former boss who literally set the stage. He also sued the Court Personnel Coordinator. Seems like the right cast of characters to me.

Judge Caputo made only half a point as far as I am concerned. He stated in his opinion that Marinello did not meet his burden of proof that the people he sued had any authority to terminate his employment. Judge Caputo, is that the very best you could do? Marinello certainly did show that all of the people he sued worked in concert with each other to convince the President Judge of the county to fire him. They most certainly "caused" him to be fired and they most certainly were in a position of power over Marinello. Caputo, you split a hair that you had no business splitting and not only did your ruling speak for itself, but it also reeks.

The name Caputo kind of rang a bell with me, so I did some digging. And what to my wondrous eyes should appear but………………..a Luzerne County connection. Not just a little connection either.

A. Richard Caputo (born 1938) is a United States federal judge.

[edit] **Biography**

Born in Port Chester, New York, Caputo received an A.B. from Brown University in 1960 and an LL.B. from the University of Pennsylvania Law School in 1963. He was in private practice in Wilkes-Barre, Pennsylvania from 1963 to 1964, and in the U.S. Air Force JAG Corps from 1964 to 1967. He was an assistant public defender in Luzerne County, Pennsylvania in 1968, returning to private practice in Kingston, Pennsylvania from 1968 to 1997.

On July 31, 1997, Caputo was nominated by President Bill Clinton to a seat on the United States District Court for the Middle District of Pennsylvania vacated by Richard P. Conaboy. Caputo was confirmed by the United States Senate on November 9, 1997, and received his commission on November 12, 1997. (courtesy of Wikipedia)

So, I ask this simple question: Can't a resident of Luzerne County go anywhere for a fair trial or at least something that looks like a fair trial?

Marinello was now out of money and more importantly, had absolutely no faith in the court system. I don't blame him. Just as I had done, he simply picked himself up and moved on. It sure seems to me that justice for Marinello should be out there somewhere. There I go again with that Disney guy. There will be no justice for him. I fear that the only justice Marinello will receive is the acknowledgement between these pages that he has been wronged and wronged in a big way. Small consolation.

As I mentioned earlier, I sought out Mr. Marinello, he did not look for me. I knew his case was outrageous but until I actually wrote about it I didn't know just how outrageous it was.

Everyone else mentioned in this portion of the book has gone on to live "happily ever after" and, yes, most have been promoted and gotten substantial pay raises.

Judge Toole has since retired and as of this writing is not only collecting his full pension but is also serving as a Senior Judge for Luzerne County at somewhere around five hundred dollars per day on top of his pension. With the arrest of three sitting judges, including his son, he has been very busy indeed.................. filling in.

I want to take a moment to thank Mr. Marinello for sharing his story with me. The pain that it rekindled cannot be described by me in the words of these pages, but Jamie Marinello can know in his heart that I personally know its cut.

Riding the Luzerne County Railroad is akin to being in combat with someone from your hometown, but never knowing you were in the same company or regiment together. It is like fighting in the same epic battle but from two different ridge tops. You were both there and fought as hard as you could though your vantage point was different. The anger, the frustration, the total wrongness of the proceedings are all the same. The power these people have been given without any accountability for their actions is staggering. If anything, they are totally protected by law no matter what they do. They are free to sue you in civil court, but you are barred from suing them because they are judges and are protected by law. The Mafia could only hope for such protection in their endeavors.

CHAPTER THIRTY-NINE

The Dynamic Duo and Michael Leftchak

The Dynamic Duo Tag Team of Judge Cappellini and Attorney Arthur Piccone have become legendary in Luzerne County, if not the state of Pennsylvania. Their brand of "justice" and "impartiality" are terrific examples of "in your face, what are you going to do about it?" I feel it screams of injustice as I have never seen or ever hope to see again.

I am not going to spend as much time with this case as I did with the last case but it, too, serves as a shining example to further my personal prejudice against the team.

Once again we have the Tag Team of Cappellini/Piccone at work. Bear with me here. I promise it will be worth your time. This case unto itself makes for pretty boring reading and in the end the good guys do win. However, the dynamics that surround this case will shock you right out of your seat. I promise.

Judge Cappellini heard this case for his former law partner, Piccone. Three years prior, this exact same case had been tried and decided by another county judge and should not have been reheard. The prior ruling simply should have been enforced. Of course, Cappellini ruled opposite of the prior judge and found in favor of his self admitted "best friend," Piccone. The plaintiffs appealed and won their appeal, thus reversing Cappellini. As I told you earlier, less than 5% of all cases that are appealed are reversed. The reversal by the Pennsylvania State Superior Court was made because the court ruled that Judge Cappellini's decision was "legally insufficient." The other legal term I have heard used is "no basis in law."

The plaintiffs not only questioned the Cappellini/Piccone connection, but they also question their original attorney. Forty property owners banded together and funded this fight. None of the forty were wealthy by anyone's standards. That fact alone is pretty incredible. Turns out that their original attorney's father and Judge Cappellini were law partners together way back when Cappellini was a mere mortal. They fired their attorney and hired a new one for their appeal. The attorney that they had fired had the nerve to defend Judge Cappellini's ruling as fair and just after he lost the case and took his fees.

Now, let's get to the fun part. Why would a judge hear such a case? Why would he even care? Why would Piccone take on such a ridiculously small case, after all, he was the President of the Pennsylvania Bar Association as well as a Senior Partner at the region's largest law firm?

For some possible answers I will focus on one of the three Defendants in this case,. Michael G. Lefchak. According to official court documents, Mr. Lefchak stole well over one million dollars in cash from the United Credit Bureau Services Inc. where he was employed as Executive Director. How much more than a million is not known by me. The original arrest affidavit of Probable Cause, dated 1/6/92, states approximately 1.3 million dollars. I am sure that prosecutors were restricted as to how far back they could go by the Statute of Limitations when they finally arrested him. There is reason to believe that the thefts go back prior to the above court proceedings. You can be the judge as to whether or not this is relevant.

COMMONWEALTH OF PENNSYLVANIA
PENNSYLVANIA STATE POLICE

COMMONWEALTH OF PENNSYLVANIA
　　　　VS.
　Michael G. Lefchak

DOCKET NUMBER:

CLN:

AFFIDAVIT OF PROBABLE CAUSE

Tpr. Jeffrey T. BACKENSTOSS, of the Pennsylvania State Police, having been duly sworn (or Affirmed) before me, according to law, deposes and says that there is probable cause based on the following facts and circumstances:

1. On or about 08/13/90, the Pennsylvania State Police, White Collar Crime Unit-East received a complaint from the United Credit Bureau Services Inc., identifying a large sum of monies having been stolen from them. Based on this complaint an investigation into the allegations was commenced. Through the course of the investigation Michael LEFCHAK, Executive Director, United Credit Bureau Services Inc., was identified as the central figure involved with the theft of approximately $1.3 million dollars in funds from the United Credit Bureau Services Inc..

2. An audit was commissioned by the United Credit Bureau Services Inc., Board of Directors, on or about 08/09/90 of the United Credit Bureau Services Inc. account. This audit was conducted by the accounting firm of PARENTE, RANDOLPH, ORLANDO, CAREY & associates. This audit revealed that $614,770.77 was diverted from the United Credit Bureau Services Inc. to the Scranton Credit Bureau, from 01/20/84 through and including 07/20/90.

3. On 05/04/92, your Affiant met with Michael LEFCHAK. During this meeting LEFCHAK diagramed and explained how the monies were diverted from United Credit Bureau Services Inc. to the Scranton Credit Bureau and then converted for personal use by LEFCHAK and Stanley GILBERT. Michael LEFCHAK stated that he would send a United Credit Bureau Services check to the Scranton Credit Bureau were it would be posted to a fictitious account. Stanley GILBERT would then issue a Scranton Credit Bureau check payable to one of LEFCHAK's personal credit card accounts as identified by LEFCHAK. GILBERT would issue the check(s) minus ten (10) percent, which he retained for his personal use. Additionally, LEFCHAK stated that he was a partner with Stanley GILBERT in the collection division of the Scranton Credit Bureau, and that GILBERT was the sole proprietor of Scranton Credit Bureau. Due to this partnership LEFCHAK stated that he purchased and/or supplied funds from the United Credit Services Inc. to the Scranton Credit Bureau to acquire up to date equipment to keep them competitive with the other credit bureaus. LEFCHAK also identified that when the United Credit Bureau Services bought of sold credit reports the would charge or pay @ $1.00 per report. However, the Scranton Credit Bureau being smaller in size would only have to pay @ $ .50 fifty cents for a credit report from another credit bureau. Because of the price difference, LEFCHAK stated that he would sell credit reports through the United Credit Bureau Services Inc. accounts and buy the needed reports through the Scranton Credit Bureau's accounts. The profit that was realized through this system was then split fifty-fifty (50-50) with Stanley GILBERT, for personal use.

Tpr. Jeffrey T. BACKENSTOSS
Pa. State Police, White Collar Crim

Larry Hohol

    Renita Fennick, a great journalist and staff writer for the Wilkes-Barre based Citizens' Voice Newspaper, authored the following investigative report. Special note should be given to the fact that this case had already been heard and ruled on just three years earlier by Luzerne County Judge Bernard Brominski.

Cappellini ruling was found 'legally insufficient'

■ **Pittston Twp. property owners feel judge's friendship with an attorney worked against them.**

By RENITA FENNICK
Citizens' Voice Staff Writer

    The state Superior Court ruled that a decision of Judge Gifford S. Cappellini was "legally insufficient." The Cappellini decision favored the position of his longtime friend, Attorney Arthur Piccone, and examination of the case again focuses attention on the question of the friendship's influence on judicial rulings in Luzerne County.
    Several Pittston Township property owners involved in a land dispute several years ago told the Citizens' Voice they feel they were disadvantaged in the courtroom because of the Cappellini-Piccone connection.

    The case, which centered around a right-of-way dispute, was resolved on the appellate level when the state Superior Court overturned Cappellini's decision against the 40 plaintiffs on the grounds it was "legally insufficient."
    One of the plaintiffs, who requested anonymity, said, "So many things with that case just didn't sound right. There you had all of these people telling a judge that they use the alley and the judge tells them, 'No, you abandoned it.'"
    The local jurist's ruling against the 40 property owners allowed Michael G. and Josephine Lefchak and Salvatore and Doris Sperrazza to maintain the fences they had built six feet onto the alleyway. One of the defendants, Lefchak,

was placed on 10 years probation last Jan. 29 by Cappellini in an unrelated criminal case.

Former executive director of the United Credit Bureau Services, Inc., Lefchak pleaded guilty last June to 13 counts of theft and one count of criminal conspiracy stemming from the misuse of over $1 million in credit bureau funds. According to the affidavit issued at the time of his arrest, Lefchak was identified as the central figure in the scam.

After the Superior Court reversed Cappellini's ruling, the Lefchaks and Sperrazzas, who were represented by Piccone, were ordered to remove the fences.

Piccone took the case to the state Supreme Court which denied a petition to hear the case, allowing the ruling in favor of the property owners to stand.

So here we have a guy that is stealing huge amounts of cash involved in a simple land dispute. He didn't like the outcome of the first trial, so he simply ignores it. Forty surrounding land owners, (I like to call them taxpayers or citizens), take him to court again. This time Mr. Lefchak has lots and lots of cash. He hires one of the finest attorneys in all of Pennsylvania.

After he does so and by the luck of the draw, he gets Judge Gifford Cappellini as his judge. I know you will find this hard to believe, but Piccone wins the case. Did I mention that I have never found a single instance where Attorney Piccone ever lost a case when it was heard in front of Judge Cappellini? I think I mention that, but I am not sure. The Superior Court finds the ruling "legally insufficient" and reverses Judge Cappellini. The Supreme Court then refuses to hear Piccone's appeal. Done deal! Leftchak is required to remove his illegal fence.

Now fast forward a couple of years. Mr. Lefchak is arrested and one of the most spectacular coincidences in judicial history occurs. Once again Attorney Piccone is called upon to represent Mr. Lefchak. The criminal case is by the sheer luck-of-the-draw assigned to Judge Gifford Cappellini. I am not kidding you. I told you it would be worth the wait. Get ready to spring from your chair but not yet.

Mr. Lefchak pleads guilty to four criminal counts in front of Judge Cappellini. The only thing that was missing here was the use of a firearm. Once again Judge Cappellini acknowledges in open court that he has a direct conflict of interest. He tells the world that he is personal friends with Mr. Leftchak but assures everyone, including Mr. Millionaire, I mean Mr. Leftchak, that he will not allow this friendship to influence his duties on the bench.

Friday, November 13, 1992 — 6

Ex-credit bureau chief pleads guilty to theft charges

Michael G. Lefchak returned to Luzerne County criminal court Thursday afternoon to enter guilty pleas to additional charges stemming from an investigation into the misuse of nearly $1 million in transactions between the United Credit Bureau Services Inc., Wilkes-Barre, and the Scranton Credit Bureau Services.

At least one other person in the case has pleaded guilty.

Lefchak, 51, of 158 Flag St., Pittston, appeared before Judge Gifford Cappellini Thursday afternoon and pleaded guilty to criminal conspiracy and theft by deception.

It was noted before the court in the plea bargain agreement that the defendant would cooperate with officials in the continuing investigation and also will offer court testimony.

It was also stated the defendant will make full restitution following a special court hearing.

Judge Cappellini stated sentencing will be scheduled and the defendant is continued in $50,000 bail on his own recognizance.

Lefchak previously pleaded to three counts of theft by unlawful taking and one count of criminal conspiracy.

He was scheduled to be sentenced Nov. 18 on those charges. This sentencing has been continued.

Lefchak will probably be sentenced in January.

Meanwhile, Annette Paula Gromelski, 28, of 243 New St., Duryea, was scheduled to be sentenced today on her guilty plea entered Sept. 8 to a charge of criminal conspiracy to commit theft. This sentencing has been continued until Dec. 4.

Stanley Gilbert of Clarks Summit and Scranton waived arraignment in Luzerne County criminal court on Nov. 6 on charges of criminal conspiracy and theft by deception in the same case.

An audit of the funds of the two credit bureaus revealed that in one incident, $614,000 had been diverted from the UCS to the SCB in the period between January, 1984, and July, 1990.

It was also stated that another $250,681.27 was diverted.

Also accused in the case is Lorie M. Lefchak Hoeffner, 25, of Lockville Road, Harding, daughter of Michael Lefchak.

Michael Lefchak served as former executive director of the United Credit Bureau Services Inc. He was suspended from his duties on Aug. 14, 1990.

Appearing in court for the guilty pleas of Michael Lefchak Thursday were Assistant District Attorney Daniel Pillets, Luzerne County Det. Gary Capitano, and State Police White Collar Crime Investigator Jeffrey Backensloss.

Lefchak was represented by Attorney Harvey Sernovitz.

CHAPTER FORTY

Unreported Cash

Mr. Lefchak had acquired a huge amount of unreported cash, unreported cash, unreported cash. That term kept swirling around in my head. I thought to myself that the IRS was going to have a field day with this guy. I looked and I looked and I looked, but not a single word about the IRS could be found anywhere. I was sure that the IRS would want to go after any assets that Mr. Lefchak had acquired with his ill gotten "TAXFREE" booty.

There is an old saying where I grew up (yes, Luzerne County). It goes: "Every once in a while, even a blind dog finds a bone." I would love to say that it was due to my incredible investigative skills that I uncovered the following newspaper article. It was simply days of reviewing microfilm at the Osterhout Library in downtown Wilkes-Barre and dumb luck that I found the following.

Ex-IRS official gets year in jail for taking gratuity

SCRANTON — A former Wilkes-Barre Internal Revenue Service official was sentenced to one year in jail and fined $10,000 after pleading guilty in Federal Court to one count of unlawful receipt of a gratuity by a public official.

Robert D. Zoka, 60, of Lathrop Drive, Kingston, was accused of accepting $1,000 in exchange for helping an unidentified person file a false income tax return. The U.S. attorney said the felony took place between May 1991 and March 1993.

Zoka, a retired group manager of the IRS examination division in Wilkes-Barre, must surrender himself to jail on Sept. 18.

I sure hope you picked up on it, too. The word "gratuity" is used in place of bribe. A further examination of the record shows that the IRS Agent in question was a senior management official with the IRS and did more than help with someone's income tax return. In his supervisory position he had the authority to sign off on investigations and make them go away. Such is the culture of Luzerne County. Does this IRS agent have any connection with this story? I simply don't know, but, once again it is one hell of a coincidence.

Now for the big question. Do all of these incredible coincidences come together and connect? I am missing but one connection of the dots. That connection would be cash changing hands. I have absolutely no proof of that. However, that being said, Cappellini would have to do something pretty outrageous if the circumstantial evidence is to amount to anything besides mere coincidence. One thing that can be said about Judge Gifford Cappellini is that he will never disappoint anyone, when it comes to being outrageous.

First off, Judge Gifford Cappellini by his own admissions should have voluntarily "Recused" himself from this case and the land dispute case that he had heard prior. Why? Is it because of the Attorney Piccone Connection? Well, sure that is a good reason. Add to that, the fact that Judge Cappellini has admitted in open court that he is personal friends with Michael Lefchak, as I mentioned earlier!

You would think at this point I would tell you that you should now spring from your seat as I promised. Almost but NOT YET! Judge Cappellini sentenced Lefchak to: Take a guess.

How does, no jail time, ten years probation, and seventy five dollars per month in restitution sound for outrageous? Nowhere, but nowhere does the term unpaid, back taxes come up. Boy, I better have the back up on this one!

8A The Times Leader, Wilkes-Barre, PA, Wednesday, September 15, 1993

ED[

The Times Leader
A Capital Cities/ABC, Inc. Newspaper

DALE DUNCAN
President and Publisher

ALLISON WALZER
Vice President and Editor

CLIFF SCHECHTMAN
Managing Editor

BILL GRIFFITH
Associate Editor

TOM DENNIS
Editorial Page Editor

PAMELA C. TURFA
City Editor

Those named above are members of The Times Leader's editorial board.

Steal big, spend big, walk away (almost) free

If you're lucky enough to:
A. have friends;
B. own a suit, a clean criminal record, and the habit of being on time;
and C. spend money like a drunken government contractor — then have at it, friends. Stuff cash, anybody's cash, into your pockets, and away you go. Half a million ought to cover it.

Probation and "restitution" (ha-ha) are literally small prices to pay.

Or so goes the lesson in the Luzerne County Courthouse, apparently. For that's the gist of the explanations why Michael Lefchak, who stole more than $600,000, got 10 years' probation and a penny-ante restitution as punishment, while Alfred D. Hull, who stole $109, got 10 to 20 months in the slammer.

Lefchak, courthouse noteworthies noted, "deserved" the mild sentence. He entered a plea bargain, had a clean record, cooperated with authorities — and had the good sense to spend every dime of his stealings, according to Tuesday's Times Leader. [The spendthrift trait apparently helped keep Lefchak out of jail, the story reported. The better to pay his creditors, you know.]

[We hate to think of his sentence had he been a saver.]

Oh, and one more thing: A prominent lawyer spoke up for him.

Hull had no such advantages. He was a petty crook with a bad attitude and broken watch.

But he did steal 1/6000th of the amount of money that Lefchak did, remember. Is the petty thief's character somehow 6,000 times darker than the white-collar man's? Does a prior record and a lack of friends multiply a $109 misdeed by 6,000, so that it exceeds in seriousness the theft of half a million?

We don't know. We do know this: Michael Lefchak got $600,000 worth of enjoyment out of his criminality. He spent every sou.

That's more material "fun" than many people buy in a lifetime. And Lefchak is paying for it by — well, to a jaundiced eye, he hardly seems to be paying for it at all.

The lesson is clear. If you're going to steal, steal big, then spend it all. Maybe on a lawyer and a suit: In Luzerne County, the right tie-s seem to count for an awful lot.

I am not kidding. Seventy-five dollars per month in restitution for over a million dollars stolen. The best part is that Lefchak doesn't always make his payments on time. By court order, his restitution is supposed to be reviewed every six months by the probation office and increased accordingly. Since 1993, it has never been increased.

I can't make a direct connection, but the fact that a Supervisor for the Luzerne County Adult Probation Office told me his brother bought Mr. Lefchak's house before Lefchak moved to Philadelphia may or may not have a bearing on the review. Nice house and he got a good deal. I wonder if Mr. Lefchak made any money on the sale of his house? If he did, he sure didn't pay any extra towards his restitution. I know this for a fact because I have all of his payment records.

If I can get you back into your seat keep in mind the following facts: Mr. Lefchak did not have a weak moment and stuff a few dollars in his pocket. He set up a fake company to bill his employer for services not rendered. He set up ghost employees, and recruited family members to help cash stolen checks. This happened over a period of years.

What was the motivation for Judge Cappellini's extreme leniency? I personally would not call what judge Cappellini doled out as a lenient sentence. It is far beyond lenient. I, personally, am offended by this sentence and so were a whole lot of fellow residents of Luzerne County. This sentence screams of more "in your face, what are you going to do about it?" politics as usual in Luzerne County. This was not punishment at all as it most certainly did not match the crime committed. So, what happened to all that money? I never found any information about how he spent it or hid it. I kind of remember something about Leftchak saying he gambled it away, but I am not sure. Better yet, what a great way to explain away his not being able to repay the money. "I lost it at the tables" while he buried it in the back yard. Boy, am I tainted, or what?

CHAPTER FORTY-ONE

Corruption and the County

---

*I*f you are from Luzerne County or have lived here for a long period of time, there isn't much that would surprise you as far as public officials who have gone bad. Most of the officials that have gone bad here were really bad right from the start. I believe they were bad before they ran for office. Being a "GOOD" public official in Luzerne County was judged by what you actually accomplished for the people while you were raping and pillaging the public coffers. It was expected and accepted. It was a reality of life in this county.

One of the most notorious figures in Luzerne County history was Congressman Daniel J. Flood. He was affectionately known as "Dapper Dan." He always sported a handle bar mustache and I remember on occasion a top hat, cane, and cloak. He reminded me of "Mr. Peanut" with a huge mustache. After spending decades in Washington, he became almost a "Godlike" figure both here in the county and in D.C. He was extremely accessible by any resident of the county, who had money. People of power in the county would not hesitate to call him in Washington and have him leave the "House Floor" to take their call. I saw it with my own eyes. At first, the sense of power that this instilled in the local "power" community struck me as a very good thing. The idea that he was so accessible to his constituents was what the democratic process was all about, or so I thought. I witnessed a family friend, with a very Italian last name, make such a call while I stood there and listened. I was 18 years old at the time.

Dapper Dan was the fellow who named our airport, The Wilkes-Barre/Scranton International Airport. He controlled the

Federal money so he got to put Wilkes-Barre in front of Scranton even though Wilkes-Barre was smaller and second alphabetically to Scranton. Scranton has never forgotten that.

It turns out that Congressman Flood had become the Chairman of the House Appropriations Committee, thus making him one of the most powerful men in Washington. The access to him was there because he was stuffing his pockets with cash. He became so blatant and outrageous that even by Washington standards, he had to go. The FBI set up a sting and caught him stuffing over $4,000.00 into his pockets while promising Federal Aid to Hahnemann Hospital in Philadelphia. Flood's top Aid, Stephen B. Elko went on to be convicted of bribery charges and testified under oath that the Congressman had received well over $100,000 in various bribes that he was personally aware of.

Did the congressman go to jail? Was he held accountable for all of the other hundreds or probably thousands of bribes he had taken over the years? No, he was censured by the United States Congress for bribery and forced to retire in 1981. No jail, just a pension. A parade was held in his honor and the Wilkes-Barre area School District named an elementary school after him. I am glad that my children did not go to that school. It still bears his name. I think about all of the outstanding residents of the county who should have their name on that school and it makes my blood boil.

As a child in Luzerne County, I witnessed a family friend who was running for town council in Luzerne Borough lay a brand new $20 bill on our kitchen table as a "thank you" for a vote already promised by my mother. The council position paid $30 per month at the time. I got a badly needed pair of shoes out of the deal.

When I was sixteen years old (1972), Luzerne County, as well as most of the state, was hit by Tropical Storm Agnes. The flooding in the Wyoming Valley was epic. A neighbor of ours got the contract to clean out the Biscontini Warehouse Complex on Division St. in Kingston after the flood waters had receded. He used heavy equipment to smash and load thousands of cases of hard liquor that were stored in this warehouse under contract from the Pennsylvania State Liquor Control Board. The bottom two or three cases in every stack were contaminated by flood water while the top few cases where not touched. All were to be destroyed. The State Police who were assigned to guard the liquor during its destruction filled every vehicle they had with cases of the good stuff. I saw marked, unmarked, as well as undercover vehicles loaded with illegally obtained liquor, so much so, that the trunks of marked State Police cars had to be tied shut with string that I supplied to the troopers. I also saw the same troopers handcuff, slap and then threatened to arrest one of the equipment operators after he tried to take one bottle home with him after his shift was over. He got the slap because he mentioned the fact that the troopers were stealing the booze by the car load, so why couldn't he take just one bottle?

As a Police Officer in Luzerne County I saw an automobile towing company pay police officers $10 in cash for every vehicle towed by order of the officer. My chief showed up at my doorstep one morning with a pocket full of cash after the towing company became nervous because I never stopped by to collect my "thank you for the business" stipend. To the horror of my Chief, I declined the money. I saw the fear in his eyes as I argued with him about how wrong it was.

I contacted the State Attorney General's Office while I was a Police Officer and supplied copies of over one hundred (moving traffic) citations which I had personally issued that simply disappeared from the local District Magistrate's Office. Yes, the District Magistrate had fixed each and every one of them.

I also gave the Attorney General's Investigators detailed information concerning a serious DUI case that I was prosecuting only to have it "fixed" by the Luzerne County District Attorney at the time. This District Attorney eventually went onto become "President Judge" of Luzerne County, and no, it wasn't Toole. I met with the AGs investigators many times during the investigation. At our last meeting, the senior investigator simply told me to buy and carry a larger caliber "off duty weapon." I laughed out loud when he advised me to do so. He sternly told me that he wasn't kidding. That meeting and that advice was the conclusion of the formal investigation. I never heard from him again, but the district judge became a big supporter of the Pennsylvania State Attorney General in his quest for reelection.

I was fired by my mayor from my fulltime, Civil Service Police Officer position because I refused to fix tickets for him. Ironically, Attorney Arthur Piccone was the attorney for the borough at the time. Little did I know that we would someday become a sworn, lifelong, adversary. Piccone actually convinced the mayor that firing me for such a reason would result in a huge monetary award against both the Mayor and the town should my lawsuit go to trial.

I got my job back, along with my back pay, seniority, and pension funding. Shortly thereafter, I threw in the towel and quit the department. Everyone was glad to see me go, including me. I didn't fit. I wasn't one of the good old boys. As proud as I was with being a police officer, being an officer in a small Luzerne County town didn't come close to any episode of "Cops" that I had ever seen on TV.

In the late eighties Luzerne County President Judge Dalesandro began going through an ugly divorce. His wife of many, many years began telling stories in public about the secret room in the basement of their home that was full of cash and machine guns. With the help of fellow Luzerne County judges, Judge Dalessandro helped his soon-to-be ex-wife get the mental help she needed in a mental institution. I knew one of the Attorneys who represented her at the time. He told me flat out that she was no different from anyone else that he knew and that he believed her about the money and guns. After years of institutionalization, she finally broke. She was released from the facility, became a bag lady and eventually died on the streets of Wilkes-Barre. By the way she was telling the truth. The FBI eventually raided Luzerne County President Judge Dalesandro's home. They found the secret room, the money, and the machine guns. He spent about a year in Federal Prison.

Somebody told Dalesandro that his arrest and search warrants were coming. The day before everything went down, he resigned from his position as President Judge of Luzerne County. Since he was not charged with a crime or found guilty of a crime while he was in office, he was able to collect his full pension when he got out of Federal Prison. Oh, by the way he was also re-admitted to the Bar. To this day, he is still collecting his pension and his ex-wife is still dead. I have a close family relative who simply adores this man. As she puts it, there are two sides to every story.

CHAPTER FORTY-TWO

*L*uzerne County: This is the Scary Part

---

*A*ll of the stories that you have read in this book were the result of what duly elected judges did out in the open. Tens of thousands of citizens of Luzerne County were watching their every move. Not only didn't these judges care who was watching, they became very angry when someone, anyone, questioned their actions or questioned their integrity. People were screaming bloody murder when they did the things that they did. I know. I was one of those people. The scary part is what have these judges been doing behind our backs? We are just starting to find out since the "Kids for Cash" scandal has broken wide open.

I personally went so far as to testify before a State House Judiciary Panel in Harrisburg on May 16th, 1994. I gave them an earful. I personally leveled allegations of widespread corruption in the Luzerne County Court System and gave them specific examples of exactly what I was talking about.

It was all I could do to keep the members of the panel awake and breathing during my testimony. I was outraged by their lack of sincerity and I told them so. Unless they are newly elected officials, there isn't a soul in Harrisburg that doesn't know of the many problems in Luzerne County and the similar problems in the 66 other Pennsylvania counties, yet they do nothing. The Feds have to come in and clean up the pig sty.

Citizens' Voice, Wilkes-Barre, Pa.   Thursday, May 19, 1994 — 3

2 critics of county judicial system meet with FBI

Pair meets with agents who are conducting background check on Judge Toole

By CAROL CRANE
Citizens' Voice Staff Writer

Two local residents have been asked to meet with the FBI this morning in connection with a routine background check on Luzerne County Judge Patrick J. Toole Jr. Carolee Medico of Laflin and Larry Hohol of Dallas confirmed they have been requested by Agent Kevin Donovan to give statements to the FBI as part of the background check.

The FBI could not be reached for comment. Judge Toole declined to comment specifically on the background is taking ex-

cept to say, "I would assume the FBI will contact anyone they think is appropriate."

Last May, U.S. Sen. Harris Wofford recommended Toole to President Bill Clinton for a nomination to the federal bench. Last week, federal agents visited the Luzerne County Courthouse and spoke to several officials including District Attorney Peter Paul Olszewski. Sources said the background check is a prime indication that Toole's nomination is moving forward.

On Monday, Mrs. Medico and Hohol testified before a state House Judiciary panel in Har-

risburg where both leveled allegations of wide-spread corruption in the Luzerne County court system.

Mrs. Medico recently filed criminal charges against Luzerne County judges Toole, Chester Muroski, Hugh Mundy, in addition to court stenographer Maxine Williams, attorneys Sandor Yelen and Larry McDonald; and her ex-husband, Charles Medico, a well-known local businessman. In her complaint, Mrs. Medico is alleging obstruction of the administration of the law and tampering with public records and information. She filed the complaint with Wilkes-Barre District Justice Mar-

tin Kane who forwarded it to Luzerne County District Attorney Peter Paul Olszewski. Mrs. Medico Wednesday said she received notice from the DA's office this week that the charges were sent to the office of state Attorney General Ernest Preate Jr. who has assigned a special prosecutor from the Pittsburgh DA's office to investigate the allegations.

Mrs. Medico has been embroiled in a bitter divorce with her ex-husband for 11 years. She has charged the local courts with repeatedly violating the Pennsylvania Rules of Civil Procedure in that court orders in her case were

not honored and were eventually removed from her file, that testimony was omitted when notes of a
(See CRITICS, page 9)

Critics
from page 8

master's hearing were transcribed and that she has received three different transcripts of a 1989 settlement hearing. Despite the transcripts being different from each other, the court has approved all three as "true and correct."

Hohol is alleging his civil rights were violated by the county court in the course of his attempt to maintain his business.

More money has been "STOLEN" in Luzerne County with a briefcase and gavel than ever with a gun. This is a harsh reality here is "Coal Cracker" country. I heard that statement as a kid growing up. Little did I know just how true a statement it was or how directly it would affect my family and the hundreds of families of my future employees. Do I feel things have been stolen from me? You bet I do and I want my stuff back.

I had a judge and his best friend "TAKE AWAY" everything, monetarily, that I had ever hoped or dreamed of having in my life. I worked extremely hard and made the sacrifices I needed to make in order to achieve my goals and I accomplished my goals while all the while, playing by the rules. I wasn't a drug dealer or a loan shark. I didn't run an illegal gambling ring or deal in stolen merchandise. I was a legitimate, honest, hard working, productive, taxpaying, citizen of Luzerne County. I came from a family of good, hardworking, honest people and I am mad. Damn mad. Am I going to get back what has been taken away from me? Never, but at the very least, my adversaries are going to know they have been in one "Hell of a Fight".

Please keep this in mind as I wind down this book. If someone falls on your property or you go through a divorce and end up in court, you may be affected by this corruption. If you are ever in an automobile accident, your fault or not, you could be affected by this corruption. If you pay property taxes in Luzerne County, Pennsylvania you ARE affected by this corruption.

CHAPTER FORTY-THREE

The Dynamics of Being a Judge
(It's no Joke)

Question: What do you get when you cross a lawyer with a Politician? Answer: A judge.

I wish the above question and answer was a joke. Unfortunately it is not. Here are some harsh realities of those who judge us. Power and egos are the name of the game. As much as we all would like to believe that once a judge is elected or selected to his or her lofty perch they miraculously stop being politicians. It is simply not true. If anything, politics become a sometimes overwhelming constraint to the selected elite that we call judges. How so, you may ask?

First and foremost is the money. Most judges that are elected have campaign debt that must be retired. Try to get someone to contribute to a campaign after you have already been elected to a ten year term with little chance of ever being thrown out of office. Tough to do! It is not unusual for judges to pay many multiples of their annual salary in campaign advertising in order to become elected. Many ask why?

There is no single answer to that question but "Power and Vanity" play huge factors in why lawyers want to become judges. Keep in mind that the best and the brightest attorneys are making the big bucks representing Corporate America and wouldn't remotely consider the pay cut necessary to become a judge, regardless of the perks. My statement is not intended to slight all judges, mind you. I happen to know a few really good ones, but I can honestly say I am talking about a good majority.

As you already know, I am not a big fan of Attorney Piccone so it will come as no surprise that I wrote the following "Letter to the Editor" that was published in the Citizens' Voice on September 22, 1997.

'I can't wait to read report'

Editor:

I almost choked to death on my breakfast bagel when I read your editorial "The price is wrong." But after reading that our now famous local attorney Arthur Piccone has been appointed to a panel to analyze why politicians (judges) pay multiples of their future salary to become judge, I thought to myself, who better?

Who better can explain this phenomenon than the former president of the Luzerne County Bar Association? Who better than the former president of the Pennsylvania Bar Association? Who better than a former Supreme Court want-to-be himself?

I strongly feel that Attorney Piccone is the most qualified fox to guard the hen house of anyone I know. Here is your chance, Attorney Piccone. Show us your stuff, and make a difference. I can't wait to read your report.

Larry Hohol

It is extremely important we all understand that just because a wrong doing has been exposed, it does not mean it will be corrected. Mere exposure does not automatically translate into action. Someone needs to file a complaint or a law enforcement entity must be given its marching orders by...................you guessed it, a politician. All we can do is all we can do. As individuals, we don't have a snowballs chance in hell of making a difference.

The only way this book or I, will make a difference is if enough people read it, understand it and then band together and say, "Enough is enough". I have no desire to be the conduit for such an undertaking. There are plenty of angry citizens available to lead that charge. Besides, I will be busy writing my next book and exposing the world to a view of what the worst is that Luzerne County has to offer.

Unfortunately, after all of the screaming and shouting that I have done over the years as well as countless others, things have only gotten worse in Luzerne County.

I filed a complaint with the Judicial Conduct Board. I filed a complaint with the Pennsylvania Attorney General's Office. I tried to file a complaint with the FBI.

Someone needs to convene a Grand Jury and do a thorough investigation of the Pennsylvania Judicial Conduct Board and go as far back in time as the law will allow. The Supreme Court of Pennsylvania that oversees the JCB presently has two of its own members under investigation. The Pennsylvania Attorney General that I filed my complaint with (Ernie Preate) was removed from office and went to Federal Prison for a year on Corruption charges.

Your Voice

No sympathy for Ernie

Editor:

It angers me to read and watch all the sympathetic stories about our freshly fallen Attorney General, Ernie Preate. "What a nice man," "A real god guy". I am having a hard time explaining to my children why a man who is going to jail for committing a felony while in office is being spoken about so highly.

I vividly remember Attorney General Preate publicly lashing out at the Pennsylvania Crime Commission and demanding it be abolished as they attempted to investigate him. I remember our citizens and legislators agreeing with our impeccable crime fighter, and abolishing it, while all the time he was as guilty as sin itself.

Apparently I have not learned my lesson that one should not criticize a corrupt politician no matter what. When he rises from the ashes, will he seek me out for being a critic? Who cares? We should be holding Ernie Preate's conviction up high and shaking it in front of every politicians while viciously demanding "Who's next?" Who is next?

Larry Hohol
Hunlock Creek

CHAPTER FORTY-FOUR

What Have We Learned?

Well, one thing I have learned, for sure, is that a whole lot of bad things can happen in full view of the public but the train can still continue on down the tracks. When all is said and done, these things are still wrong. They can happen in plain sight with howling protests and regardless of the public outcry, still get to their final destination. I call this "In Your Face Corruption". It is not only the arrogance by which these travesties occur but the "Confidence" of the perpetrators that alarms me most.

When elected officials have absolutely no fear of any type of accountability, tyranny will reign supreme. This is a fact that history has bared out over the centuries. It is an unfortunate fact of life here in Luzerne County.

When I was a young man, growing up in the early seventies, the culture of the day was to not trust "The Government" or anyone over 30. I NEVER subscribed to any of that nonsense. I volunteered for military service during a war and became part of "The Government" as a police officer. Now that I am in my mid 50's I can tell you that the "Culture of the Day" had half of the motto right on the money.

As you have read through this book, I am sure you noticed the amount of detail I provided via copies of court documents and newspaper articles. There are also a few letters. I had to do some real soul searching when it came to including the letters to and from the Pennsylvania Judicial Conduct Board.

My sharing the contents of these letters with anyone is a direct violation of a Judicial Conduct Board gag order. I had decided to include these letters BEFORE this gag order was declared unconstitutional by the United States 3rd Circuit Court of Appeals in July of 2010. Do yourself a favor and Google the name "Gene Stilp". He single handedly took on the JCB and won. We need more heroes like Mr. Stilp.

While you are on the computer please Google "Attorney Robert Surrick." Attorney Surrick served on the Judicial Conduct Board as an unpaid member of that board. He was appointed by then Governor Dick Thornburg. Attorney Surrick voted to remove a Supreme Court Justice from the bench for alleged misconduct as did two other non-judge members of the Judicial Conduct Board. ALL of the remaining members of the board were sitting Pennsylvania Judges and voted "NO" to the Supreme Court Justice's removal. The Judge in question stayed on the Supreme Court but Attorney Surrick eventually had his law license suspended for five years via charges by the same Supreme Court Justice in question for divulging information about the inappropriate behavior of the Judicial Conduct Board to the public regarding this action. He wrote a book about it titled, "Lawyers, Judges and Journalists...The Corrupt and The Corruptors". I highly recommend reading it.

By the way, the same Supreme Court Justice, Rolf Larsen became the first Pennsylvania Supreme Court Justice to ever be impeached and removed from office at a later date (1994). Imagine that!

CHAPTER FORTY-FIVE

"Kids for Cash"

Well, since I packed up what little personal belongings I owned and moved to Florida in 1999 things in The Luzerne County Courthouse have gotten worse..........MUCH,.MUCH WORSE!

The arrest of Judge Conahan and Judge Ciavarella, at the Luzerne County Courthouse by the FBI in 2009, was the catalyst that prompted me to write this book. What these two judges are accused of doing is so despicable that your first reaction will probably be, "This could never happen in modern day America, no possible way". Well it did, and hundreds of good honest people knew most of what they were doing and did and said "NOTHING" to stop them. The few brave souls that did speak up were promptly placed aboard an "Express Excursion" of our mythical, but ever so real train to hell.

As this book goes to press and begins its journey to your doorstep, I will have already begun writing about the next sequence of events in Luzerne County that seems to have started around the time I vacated the county. In my research of this book, I have even found documents in my case that were adjudicated and signed by at least one of the "Kids for Cash" Judges. Everything in Luzerne County seems connected and related somehow.

CHAPTER FORTY-SIX

I Am a Reluctant Author

The citizens of Luzerne County, or Pennsylvania for that matter should not have to depend on the FBI to come in a clean up all of its messes. The State Attorney General and the County District Attorney should handle the bulk of these matters. They don't and they will not until it is demanded. The other problem is that these two offices are as "Politically" charged as any judgeship.

I am a reluctant author. I would much rather be writing a series of books on how you could become successful in business. Instead, I have written in great detail a horror story of sorts, describing how I rode a mythical train into obscurity. If only I had been left to my own devices, I would venture to say I would have become one of the largest employers in current day Luzerne County. I already had a track record of achievement that anyone would be proud of. Instead, my former headquarters building now lies vacant and yes, all of my former employees have lost their jobs, even the ones who perjured themselves for their new employer and testified against me.

I often think about how I knew from a very young age that I was put on this earth to be a builder, a creator, a person who solved problems and tried not to create any. I have estimated that over 500 people have worked directly for me in my lifetime. I have done over 50 million dollars in business throughout the United States as well as nine other countries and no, Korea is still not one of them. I am however hopeful that maybe someone from Korea will buy a copy of this book.

Yes, I am a reluctant author. I know, first hand, the severity of the allegations that I am making. I also know the personal jeopardy these extraordinary allegations put me in but above all, I am a patriot.

My Uncle Joe did not volunteer for the 101st Airborne in order to die for his country. I am sure his intent was to help a few patriotic enemy soldiers do that instead. He was however, willing to risk everything that was sacred to him, including his life. He did so because he had the courage, conviction, and the belief in his country and our way of life. He could have stayed far away from enemy lines and been a bread baker like he was assigned to be when he was drafted. Instead, he left the warmth and security of the mess kitchen and went through "Airborne" training not because he had to, but because he needed to.

Our country is being seriously tested today on many fronts. All of these fronts are important to our future. Not one person amongst us should try to impact all of these challenges but all of us should have an impact on some of them. We are failing miserably when it comes to our Judiciary and most certainly our political representation. We should never allow attorney/politicians who have become a judge, demand of us that we blindly trust them. They are to be held accountable and they are to be kept under a microscope at all times. They, of all professions, need to be held to the highest of all standards and unfortunately, not trusted, but scrutinized on a daily basis. Folks, we simply have it backwards.

We have a great military consisting of 100% volunteers that are fighting our wars for us on foreign soil. While they are protecting us from our enemies, we should be taking care of the home front. I can't imagine one of our soldiers coming home from war and possibly being exposed to a judicial system that is so corrupted that he or she would be treated better and fairer in a court of a foreign land.

This book will not change anything. This book and I as an individual are totally powerless against this form of corruption. So are you. I talked about "hope" in the Preface of this book. If you remember I told you I had "hope" but that I didn't know what I was hoping for. Completing this book has now allowed me to answer my own question. My hope is that enough good people read this book, ban together with other good people, and make a meaningful difference. It is also my hope that *you* do it as soon as humanly possible.

Is that a "Train Whistle" I hear?

Unfortunately this is
NOT THE END

To be continued……………….

For the latest updates and information about my next book or to read my blog about judicial corruption, please visit:

www.LarryHohol.com

About the Author

Larry Hohol

Born 1956, Luzerne County, Pennsylvania
Wyoming Valley West High School 1974, Kingston, Pennsylvania
United States Air Force (Strategic Air Command)
109th Field Artillery (Combat Medic)
Emergency Medical Technician (8 Years)
Pennsylvania State Police Academy for Municipal Officers
Police Officer: Luzerne, Pennsylvania

Founder/Owner:

Pensee Medical Corp.
Penox Technologies Inc.
Penox Leasing, later known as Leasecor Inc.
Cryco Cryogenics Inc.
Hohol Marine Products
Accurate Fence Solutions

Awards:

Wilkes-Barre Chamber of Commerce "Businessman of the Year"
Governor's New Product Award 1st Place (Engineering) State of PA.
U.S. Patent # 4,909,545 Cryogenic Coupling
U.S. Patent # 4,783,969 Cryogenic High Flow, Heat Exchange Manifold

U.S. Patent # 4,747,172 Medical Device Transporter (Emergency)
The previous list of patents were also awarded in nine other countries, Korea was NOT one of the countries.

Special Achievements or Positions:

Represented President Reagan on an official trade mission to Taiwan

Provided direct consultation to His Majesty Juan Carlos, King of Spain regarding "Durable Medical Equipment", deployment and reimbursement programs into private homes throughout the country of Spain

Attended: Harvard University's by invitation only Young Presidents Organization Program.

Personal:

Married to the former Alice Clem from upstate New York
Two daughters:
Michele, Austin, TX
Sarah, Kingston, PA

Memberships:

Present and Former:
Wilkes-Barre Chamber of Commerce
Florida Marine Contractors Association
Volusia Manufacturers Association
DeLand Chamber of Commerce
Benevolent Protective Order of the Elks
Young Presidents Organization, YPO
Secretary of the Back Mountain Police Association

Personal Milestones:

Self made millionaire by the age 27
Self made multi-millionaire by the age 28
Employed over 500 full-time employees, conducted over $50 Million in business based in Luzerne County

ACKNOWLEDGEMENTS

- I would like to start off by thanking the Citizens' Voice and Times Leader newspapers both of Wilkes-Barre, Pennsylvania. Your reporting of events over the years has been second to none. Both papers have proven time and time again that they are willing to take on the tough, investigative stories to get to the truth, sometimes at great risk. I also want to thank both papers for their permission to re-print the many articles that have been included in this book.
- My family has always been there to support me. Dad, I could always count on you, no matter what. My two incredible brothers David and Danny, as well as their fantastic wives Denice and Kathy were always there. Corey, Rachael, and Erin, Uncle Larry loves you.
- To most of my former employees, thank you! Without your great work ethic, my ride to the top NEVER could have happened.
- Thank you to all of my friends in Pennsylvania. It still amazes me how many of you remained by my side when I was down and out.
- I also want to thank the good, honest, hard working residents of Luzerne County. It is too bad we have all been exposed and affected by the graft and corruption but maybe, just maybe, brighter days are ahead.
- My daughters Michele, and Sarah, you have no idea of the joy and happiness you have brought into my life. You were my grounding rod when the storm of corruption passed through my life. You never knew this but, the toughest single day of my life was when I walked into your bedrooms and you and your stuff was gone. I simply fell to the floor and could not stand back up for hours. We have weathered the storm together and we are stronger for it. The world could not produce a prouder father.
- My editing and design team was fantastic. Janie Owens, Cyrus Cox, and Craig Surrick. Thank you for your talent and dedication.

- Finally, to my loving wife Alice, without your total support of me and this book, it never would have happened. After you read the details about the man you married, you became my biggest fan and cheerleader. You worked around our kitchen full of newspaper articles and computer hardware. You understood the 3am tapping of the keyboard in the next room. Your love is not only amazing, it is contagious. I am the luckiest man on the face of the earth for having YOU as my wife and soul mate. Thank you for being you and thank you for loving me.